Governor Edward Coles
and the Vote to Forbid Slavery
in Illinois, 1823–1824

Governor Edward Coles and the Vote to Forbid Slavery in Illinois, 1823–1824

DAVID RESS

McFarland & Company, Inc., Publishers
Jefferson, North Carolina, and London

LIBRARY OF CONGRESS CATALOGUING-IN-PUBLICATION DATA

Ress, David.
    Governor Edward Coles and the vote to forbid slavery in Illinois, 1823–1824 / David Ress.
        p.   cm.
    Includes bibliographical references and index.

    ISBN-13: 978-0-7864-2639-3
    (softcover : 50# alkaline paper) ∞

    1. Coles, Edward, 1786–1868. 2. Governors—Illinois—Biography.
    3. Slavery—Political aspects—Illinois—History—19th century.
    4. Illinois—Politics and government—To 1865. 5. Illinois—Race relations—Political aspects—History—19th century. I. Title.
    F545.C695R475   2006
    977.3'03092—dc22   2006024943

British Library cataloguing data are available

©2006 David Ress. All rights reserved

No part of this book may be reproduced or transmitted in any form or by any means, electronic or mechanical, including photocopying or recording, or by any information storage and retrieval system, without permission in writing from the publisher.

On the cover ©2006 Photospin; Illinois State Seal ©2006 clipart.com

Manufactured in the United States of America

McFarland & Company, Inc., Publishers
    Box 611, Jefferson, North Carolina 28640
        www.mcfarlandpub.com

Acknowledgments

It would be nearly impossible to write about Coles without consulting the work of Elihu Washburne, the one-time Senator from Illinois, crony of President Ulysses S. Grant and minister to France, to say nothing of the dedicated effort by the great early 20th-century scholar of Illinois history, Clarence W. Alvord. The more current work of Suzanne Cooper Guasco, in her dissertation "Confronting Democracy: Edward Coles and the Cultivation of Authority in the Young Nation," and Kurt E. Leichtle's dissertation "Edward Coles: An Agrarian on the Frontier" were valuable. James Simeone's *Democracy and Slavery in Frontier Illinois: The Bottomland Republic* offered an interesting view.

Staff at the libraries of the Historical Society of Pennsylvania and Princeton University were particularly helpful; my thanks go as well to the Abraham Lincoln Presidential Library, Chicago Historical Society, Library of Congress, Northern Illinois University Library and Winterthur Museum and Country Estate for their help and for permission to use the illustrations in this book. The New York Public Library, the Library of Virginia and the Richmond Public Library were also of much help. Karl Kageff, at Southern Illinois University, and his associates provided useful feedback and helped me focus some of the analytical effort here.

The support of my colleagues and friends Chip Jones and Michael Martz at the *Richmond Times-Dispatch*, as well as Kevin Shinkle, at the *Star-Ledger* of Newark, N.J., was a tremendous help. I am especially grateful for the maps, and the enthusiasm for this project, from *Times-Dispatch* graphic artist John Ailor.

Mostly, though, I wish to thank my wife, Karen, and sons Morgan and Jared for their patience and encouragement as I explored what I think we all felt was a neglected but important part of the history we share with those who are about to read this book.

David Ress

Table of Contents

Acknowledgments — v
Preface: Argument for a forgotten man — 1

Chapter 1: Jubilee — 9
Chapter 2: Youth — 22
Chapter 3: The White House — 37
Chapter 4: To the West — 49
Chapter 5: A new home, a new challenge — 75
Chapter 6: The coup — 101
Chapter 7: To the people — 119
Chapter 8: Hard road to victory — 139
Chapter 9: A kind of rejection — 156

Notes — 177
Bibliography — 191
Index — 197

Preface: Argument for a forgotten man

In the steamy summer of 1824, the people of the new state of Illinois gathered at their county courthouses, at tiny backwoods "groceries," at log-cabin taverns in gloomy forest clearings, at churchyards in their brand-new hamlets, to take up a ballot and declare whether they thought their home should become a slave state. It was the first, maybe the only real, referendum on slavery held in the United States. And it was a near thing.

Barely big enough to be a state, Illinois was at that time very much of the South. It had seen only the very beginnings of the flood of land-hungry Yankees and New Yorkers who would, in the decades to come, shape its institutions and its politics; its people were, for the most part, Southerners, mainly from the backcountry of Virginia and the Carolinas and the new states of Kentucky and Tennessee. The attitudes and politics they carried west were the attitudes and politics of the South—complex, conflicting and fragmented as they were at that point—though the trickling of Northerners and (mainly English and German) immigrants coming into the state was already leavening the mix, working a transformation. As Illinoisans trekked to the polls on those hot August days—and sometimes, trek it was, for polls could be scores of miles away in that barely settled frontier—they must have sensed the import of the votes they were about to cast, they understood they were about to say what kind of state they wished to live in, what kind of livelihoods they wished to earn, what kind of neighbors they wished to have, what kind of values, moral and political, they wished to declare. They may well have sensed a thrill of rebellion, for almost all the state's professional politicians, loudly declaring their populist roots and love of democracy, had pushed for slavery. Only one, an awkward, aspiring would-be aristocrat from Virginia, who had just squeaked by to be elected the state's second governor, opposed them. This book is the story of how his conscience led him to reject the economic system that had enriched his family, by freeing his slaves, and about how that decision led him, inexorably, inevitably, to find the courage to challenge the most powerful and influential men of his new home—appealing, successfully, to his fellow citizens' love of liberty. His challenge brought the referendum. His courage won the vote.

Edward Coles would hold just one elected office in his life: he was the second governor of the state of Illinois. But he won, as well, when he told the people of that state that they should vote against calling a convention to rewrite the state constitution to allow slavery. In the end, he found both fire and focus in pursuing a more important cause than his own advancement. He buckled down for a hard fight in a rough-and-tumble frontier society where it is hard to see, sometimes, how a man with his background and his style of politics could ever have accomplished anything: the improbable Edward Coles, as he has been labeled.[1] He seems to have been satisfied—reluctantly satisfied, perhaps—with having fought slavery and with having won that fight, prouder of that than he could ever have been had he seen his share of the political triumphs his opponents later won. If so, that would have been an attitude towards political life more spoken of than actually evidenced in our history.

He had to fight his battle because of a misapprehension. Coles came to Illinois to free his slaves. He had—it is easy enough to do—misread the Northwest Ordinance, the federal law that governed settlement in the territories to the north of the Ohio River, as straightforwardedly banning slavery there. That was, in any event, the intention of many, if not all, the legislators who in a flush of post–Revolutionary War enthusiasm made their stand for the liberty of all. There was, however, the fine print. So, officially Free Soil, Illinois was nevertheless home to hundreds of black slaves, many owned outright, in direct and blatant violation of its laws, others a class of property (held by the first, French-speaking settlers of the region) especially exempted by both national law and the state constitution. Most slaves, though, were considered "servants" who worked under indentures that Illinois law said were to be voluntary and of a limited term but that almost never were. Enforcement of the laws supposedly governing indentures was so lax that some settlers, including some of the state's political leaders, simply brought their slaves from Southern states, continuing to own them and to use them as if they had not crossed the Ohio River. Coles called for an end to all human bondage in his inaugural speech, sparking a furious reaction from almost all of the state's political establishment, eager to follow where the contemporaneous Missouri Compromise had shown them they could go: first, to shrug off a fading ideology of human rights; and second, to win great wealth speculating in lands that were newly attractive to slave-holders from the old South. For as the great planters' children headed west to reseed in virgin ground the large-scale, slave-dependent plantation system that had so badly wasted the soil of the Tidewater, the idea of liberty for all was becoming less and less convenient, easier to ignore, whether in Congress or in the taverns and inns where Illinois' political leaders gathered to plot their new state's future. Coles' successful campaign in 1823 and 1824, when Illinoisans rejected a proposal for a new constitutional convention aimed at formally allowing slavery, started the state on a long, slow road to freeing slaves and ending the indenture system.

Coles' struggle against slavery won him few political friends at the time, and surprisingly little honor in the years that followed. To consider his story is, in part, to ask why that might be. Something in him, the awkward manner that so many remarked on? Maybe a diffidence that led him, like an aristocrat from another time, to await the public's call, instead of seeking it? Perhaps something in us still, a resentment of being told the moral path we ought to follow instead of finding it ourselves, or simply our distaste for wealth and privilege? The youngest son of one of the richest men in Virginia, private secretary to President James Madison, a correspondent of Thomas Jefferson's, a diplomat who helped one president rally a fractious Congress through a war the country nearly lost and who helped another fend off confrontation with the Tsar of Russia, Coles could have become, perhaps should have been, a nationally important political figure. He never would. A certain lack of energy, of concentration, in pursing that goal may have been a issue. He "appeared to have the opportunities to do extraordinary things and to champion great causes," and yet "through human frailty missed most of the opportunities," in one historian's view.[2]

In 1847, former Illinois governor Thomas Ford introduced his *History of Illinois* saying he would write "about small events and little men" because "there was nothing else in the history of Illinois to write about."[3] Ford, admirable as his still-classic history is, had, like most who have sought to tell the story of the state, missed one point, however: the anti-slavery campaign Coles led was one of the first in the United States, and the very first to mobilize relatively large numbers of citizens to break with their leaders and oppose slavery. When Vermont banned slavery in 1777, when Ohio did so in 1802, they were the acts of constitutional conventions; it was Pennsylvania's legislature that banned slavery in 1780; in Massachusetts, emancipation came with the 1783 decisions in "Quock Walker" cases (notably *Commonwealth v. Jennison*) when juries held that though the 1780 state Constitution did not specifically ban slavery, its declaration that "all men are born free and equal" had that effect. Not until the national election of 1860 would there be anything like a direct referendum on slavery, if indeed even in that vote. (Dueling pro- and anti-slavery "referenda" in Kansas in the late 1850s appear to be as much in the nature of petition drives as open calls to the people to express their will; Wisconsin voters approved granting blacks the right to vote in an 1849 referendum). It may be a kind of Illinoisan modesty that tends to focus on the campaign of 1823 and 1824 as merely a precursor to the national partisan battles to come, a view that then is inclined to paint Coles as a rather small man himself: a snobby, 19th-century version of a limousine liberal or an ineffectual would-be Jeffersonian worrying as much about finding a wife as liberating slaves. It seems oddly limiting, somehow, to reduce Illinois' slavery crisis to a contest, as one scholar does, of "the White Folks" over "the Big Folks," and then to suggest the "White Folks" (the southern men and women who had settled Illinois) managed a kind of ahead-of-its-days victory of identity politics over "Big Folk" elitists led by Coles.[4] Odd because, in point of fact, it was Coles and his allies who won when Illinois voted in 1824. It seems peculiar, too, to hail the anti-slavery campaign as a struggle in which a democratic assault on privilege triumphed, while casting the leader of the campaign as the epitome of the elitism that Illinoisans so resented. It may, perhaps, more to the point to consider, as other scholars have, how a self-described Jeffersonian wrestled to reconcile his belief in the plain words of Mr. Jefferson's Declaration of Independence with the reality of the slave-owning society he saw around him, including at Monticello, just up the road from Coles' childhood home.* But this, like the 1823–24 campaign,

---

*Counting on the forbearance of readers, there will be just a couple of footnotes with this story, intended for those with a particular interest in the varying views of Coles and early Illinois. For them, then: James Simeone's Democracy and Slavery in Frontier Illinois: The Bottomland Republic (DeKalb: Northern Illinois University Press, 2000) paints Coles and the "milk-and-cider Arminian" (as opposed to "whole-hog Calvinist") preachers and anti-slavery men who allied themselves with him as leading an anti-democratic movement that was seen by resentful "White Folks" as an attempt by "Big Folks" to maintain their control over Illinois. What he sees in the 1823–1824 campaign is a reaction to Coles and his ilk by the White Folks that marks a shift towards a more democratic political culture in Illinois, putting the new state at the cutting edge of the Jacksonian transformation. Kurt Leichtle's "Edward Coles: An Agrarian on the Frontier" (Ph.D. diss., University of Illinois–Chicago Circle, 1982) sees Coles as a man who missed an opportunity for greatness, because of a propensity to delay and to dither in taking political action and a strong concern for his own comfort and ease; Coles' failure, to Leichtle, seems largely to consist of his inability to win elective office after his term as governor. Suzanne C. Guasco's "Confronting Democracy: Edward Coles and the Cultivation of Authority in the Young Nation" (Ph.D. diss., College of William and Mary, 2004) casts Coles as an aristocrat struggling to find a political role in a democratic society, but argues that Coles was neither as ineffectual in Illinois nor as irrelevant to the nation's later struggles over slavery and its understanding of what popular democracy really means as other historians suggest, pointing out his active role in trying to convince the nation's leaders that a program of gradual emancipation and restricting the expansion of slavery to the west would both preserve the Union and allow for slavery to wither away.

doesn't seem to be a struggle for a small man to undertake, and it is unfair to look back from the certainty of modern moral standards to say the time it took Coles to resolve it is a sign of a flaw in character or will.[5]

To defy, as Coles did, the advice of the Sage of Monticello himself, to face the anguished opposition of a close-knit family to his plan to free his slaves and to move west would not seem to bespeak a frailty of spirit, or desire for ease or the fear of isolation on the frontier. It would take nearly a decade for Coles to finally take the steps he knew he had to take, to bring his slaves west, and free them. He was one of only a handful of men to do that. Why did he take so long? Why did so few do as he did? Reflecting on both might tell us as much about the times as the man—but the way the man ultimately resolved the conflict between belief and advice, conviction and family, might have meaning even now. A small man? A big one?

If we focus on what Coles did, in both his personal and political life in Illinois, do we see the snob? The hypocrite? The man who won just one elected office? If we do, and if the questions we choose to ask of Coles are limited to the politics of his time or the smaller dramas of the place where he staged the main act of his own life's theatre, we may well then see only that "curious mixture of sunlight and shadow—of success and failure, with the failures seeming to clearly outweigh the successes."[6] This book takes a different view.

Perhaps it will not be the most original, though. It is true, as Illinois historian Theodore C. Pease would note, reflecting on the state's centennial, that Coles "made no political advantage" from the triumph of the anti-slavery cause (just as Pease deprecated Coles' opponents' loud and hypocritical proclamations that it was they who stood for true "republicanism"). The men who knew Coles, like Governor Ford, the people who heard the stories that men who saw what Coles had done, like U.S. Senator Elihu Washburne, saw him as a man who had made a great thing happen. But time passes, and in a way Coles was a man who was not of his time. A skirmish, important as it is, in the nation's long war with itself over slavery, becomes obscure as the decades pass. The echoes of the battle faded, its victor claimed no other victories. He never led another movement, despite his ambitions. He would not lend his name to a trend historians would later label, or found a party, or win another office. For many that failure may be enough to judge his contribution. But perhaps, as in so many things, Ford can lend a sense of some perspective here: "calling to mind the prominent actors in the scenes of that day, the fierce struggles and quarrels amongst them, the loves and hatred, the hopes, fears successes and disappointments" and reflecting that "one cannot but be struck with the utter nothingness of mere contests for office."[7] It may well be that the real Coles and his significance in American history is to be found in the words of the people who fought both alongside and against him, as well as in his own writings. In the same way, the voices of the people of Illinois of 1824 should make clear that many, if not most, of the so-called "White Folk" migrants to Illinois from the South detested slavery and that it was the real "Big Folks," the state's political elite, acting in their own self-interest, who sought to impose slavery. In their blunt speech, in Coles' words, formal and stilted as they sometimes are, we may catch glimpses of something quite modern. When Coles tells us that all men and women, black and white, have an equal right to peace and prosperity in our country, he is telling us that at least some Americans, from the country's earliest days, had a clear and liberal understanding of what the human rights promised in our founding documents really meant.

Perhaps, too, in Illinois of the early 1820s, there is another flash-forward to our own times to be seen, for the manipulation of populist sentiment and the mouthing of "just-folks" rhetoric for the cause of privilege is not a new thing in the United States. In Illinois, in 1824, however, Coles called the Big Folks to account. It was Coles who made slavery an issue, it was Coles who fought to keep the Big Folks from imposing slavery, and it was Coles and his allies who won the day. And if Coles was not alone in his opposition to slavery, he was, as his somewhat younger contemporary Joseph Gillespie would say, "the most unrelenting foe to Slavery I ever knew. His time, money, everything belonging to him, was expended in the cause so dear to his heart."[8]

A cause claimed him, but people did, as well. And would for decades to come. On a quiet evening, former slaves Robert and Kate Crawford would dictate to a letter-writer, remembering how they had started their lives' journeys with Coles, a path that took Robert to the pulpit of his own church and their family to the center of a close-knit community of freedmen and a rich farm on the Illinois prairie. "We recollect at your fathers death that severall of the poor oppressed that was choosing their masters," they told the scribe. "But God choosed for us—that we walks around our farm and look at the blessing of God—that we say in the language of the [Psalmist] and say Lord Great things for us wherewith we are glad." The Crawfords looked at the freedom they had found and the prosperity that came with it, modest and heavily qualified though we would find it today, and told Coles, simply and from the heart: "We believe that God have made [you] the means of doing us this great good."[9] Perhaps that could stand as as good a verdict as any on Coles and his career.

As Americans, it may be that we are uncomfortable with the idea that freedom can be a gift. And yet it is, really. When men like Coles or like the thousands of Illinoisans who stood up on those baking August days in 1824 to say they opposed slavery wrestle with conscience, struggle against power, to declare for freedom, their acts become a gift to us—just as our acts today contain the possibility that we, too, can give that prize to those who follow.

CHAPTER 1

Jubilee

So eager is he to lead his people west (his people because he owns them) that Edward Coles, ex-secretary to a President, once Envoy Extraordinary to the Tsar of all the Russias, former master of eight hundred acres of plush Blue Ridge farmland, has on this bright spring morning taken up the long oars of the flatboat himself and is rowing his slaves down the river. Most of them lie below, coughing and sick. The rest, uncertain and clumsy, for they have never before ridden on a boat of any kind, stumble across the flatboat's gently bobbing deck, too awkward to help him much. Still, the rowing is pleasant enough. The mild, mid-April morning could not be more perfect. There is barely a breeze, the blue sky is cloudless. The hills to either side, Ohio to his right, westernmost Virginia to his left, are washed with the fresh, pale green of spring's first buds. It is 1819, on the peaceful Ohio River, and Coles is about to do something that few other Americans had ever done, or would ever do.[1]

So sure is he of the course he plans to follow, one he has been planning for more than a decade now, that he has sacked the river pilot, a drunk, whom he had hired just three days before.[2] Though he has no experience with boats to speak of, save as a passenger, he is unshakably confident that he can guide his lumbering, box-like craft past snag and sandbar, lashed firmly though it is to a second scow, which no one rows. He really should know better. This is his fourth trip down the Ohio.[3] He has seen its hazards, he has seen, if not himself actually suffered, the hardships and dangers of life in this new and empty western country, a huge and wild land that indifferently breaks the toughest newcomer. And Coles, a tall and thin 34-year-old, brown hair already receding from a high forehead, is far from tough. Never a robust man, in recent years mysterious ailments have kept him abed or close to home for months at a time.[4] Healthier now, as excited and bright-spirited as he has ever been, he beams with the enthusiasm that has so long charmed his friends, and convinced them of a great promise in this young man—although not even the closest of those friends, nor his protective older brothers and doting sisters, would ever call him a practical man. Four years earlier, he had trotted out in horse and carriage, a trusted older slave riding by his side on a fine saddle horse, to explore the dark forests and desolate sloughs of southern Indiana and Illinois, as nonchalantly as if he were parading down Philadelphia's Market Street to one of the grand ballrooms where he had loved to dance and to flirt with the daughters of the new nation's new grandees.[5] Now, though, as he pauses for breath there on the rough wood planking of the flatboat's stern, his dark gray eyes watching the passing shore, he seems oblivious to the difficulties and dangers that he faces, rowing nearly two dozen people into the unknown west, the newly-purchased pilot book in his pocket his only guide.[6]

The river here slices the barely settled land in two, Free Soil and slave, north and south. Coles and his slaves drift, uprooted, between the two. Although it is hard for them to see here, as they float by the bottomlands on the Ohio shore or the mostly empty forests of what would someday be West Virginia, the valley is slowly flattening out. The distance from shore to shore is growing.

Slavery is one reason. The grand idea that Coles' father, a colonel in Virginia's Revolutionary militia,[7] and his friend Thomas Jefferson had grandly, gravely called "The Rights of Man" had rallied a people to make for themselves a new nation, and in the first flush of victory, many had seen in that ideal of human rights the possibility that slavery might soon disappear. In 1787, the year after Edward Coles' birth, the new Congress enacted the Northwest Ordinance, a constitution for the new west that predated the nation's own final version, a basic law that banned slavery throughout the territory north of the Ohio River (though carefully preserving the rights of a handful of French settlers in the mostly empty land to continue holding some several dozen slaves).[8] Elsewhere, a few aging Revolutionary veterans, George Washington among them, would promise in their wills to free their slaves. More, of course, said they would, if only they could, for farms needed tending, harvests must proceed, debts must be repaid and slaves, though people, were assets, too. In 1790, a handful of men in Virginia's capital, Richmond, formed an anti-slavery society. But impulse to liberate was tentative, uncertain. It soon started fading. By 1789, the authors of the new national Constitution, wrangling in Philadelphia and desperate to hold the former colonies together, had bid for the support of wealthy slave-holders from the Lower South by agreeing that, for purposes of counting population and apportioning votes in the national legislature, a slave could be counted as three-fifths of a man. With equal votes for small states in the Senate, and extra votes for Southern states in the House of Representatives, the founders forged their more perfect union.[9]

The bargain, once struck, bothered very few. Some were not sure the men, women and children who labored in their fields were quite the same sort of humans as they were. Some could see no way around the words in their law books that said that slaves were property, whose owners' rights and wealth would be unfairly damaged were freedom granted. Most felt the question was simply too remote from their daily concerns to matter.[10]

Still, in the earliest years of the new republic, the dissonance sounded by what Americans understood to be American ideals—the inalienable right to liberty that Jefferson's Declaration proclaimed—and the American fact of slavery, including the scores of slaves Jefferson

Edward Coles (courtesy Abraham Lincoln Presidential Library).

himself owned, was beginning to trouble a handful of citizens. A few months before Coles and his slaves started their journey west, one of these men, an eccentric congressman from upstate New York named James Tallmadge, had been moved to stand in the House Chamber and shock his fellow legislators by objecting to the bid for statehood by the Territory of Missouri because its proposed constitution allowed slavery. In the furor that erupted, some Americans began to see that the very future of their country could be at stake, to see that their union and their ideals could collide in blood and battle and bitterness echoing down for generations to come.[11] They would fight intensely for that future. And as he pauses to catch his breath on the stern of his flatboat, Coles is about to step into the middle of one of the very first skirmishes in this most central of American sagas.

The step is this: On that spring day, on the Ohio River, drifting between Free Soil and slave lands, Coles puts down his oar and calls his bondsmen and their families to gather by him on the flatboat's wooden deck. There are 17 in all; two families, a newly married couple, a young man and his teenage sister. Five are adults, the rest are children. With

Coles, his friend, a Mr. Green, and all their household goods, they have filled two 50-foot-long flatboats, rough-built floating boxes, each about the size of a truck trailer and lashed firmly together. They had left Rockfish, the 782-acre farm Coles had inherited in Nelson County, Virginia, where Rockfish Creek carved out its pretty little valley though the soapstone and granite of the Blue Ridge Mountains, more than a fortnight before, on April 1. None of them, except for Ralph Crawford, who is now 46 or 47 years old, has been this way before. None, except for Crawford, has ever been away from the Blue Ridge before—mountain men Coles will affectionately call them, in a letter to his mother a few days from now. Crawford is the slave who had accompanied Coles on his first exploration of Illinois in 1815, riding attendance on that saddle horse while his owner happily, blithely drove his fine buggy west; a short man, and a guarded one, Crawford is keeping his thoughts to himself this April morning. He is the one who has led the others north, across the Potomac River, across Mason's and Dixon's Line, over the last ridges of the Allegheny Mountains to the Monongahela River, at Brownsville, Pennsylvania, about a day's ride south of Pittsburgh. Coles had let them travel ahead, only catching up with the caravan the day before they reached the Pennsylvania river town. The idea of the slave Crawford leading the other slaves west had caused "much merriment" to Coles' Virginia friends, he would write afterwards, with a not untypical little edge of sarcasm: "I am happy to be able to add, he falsified all their expectations, and conducted the part with as much judgment and economy as any one, even of the glorious Saxon race, could have done."[12]

Coles has not told the slaves what he was planning. All they know for certain as they stand there on the flatboat's deck is that this man who has owned them for 11 years, but who had spent virtually all that time away from Virginia, this man whose father had owned some of them before, and who had owned their parents, is taking them down a route more and more Virginians are following, over the mountains to Pittsburgh and the Ohio River, the easy route to the new cotton country along the Mississippi River. They know this is the route that leads to the booming new slave markets in Louisville and New Orleans that supply the newly-cleared cotton country of the lower South. Yet no one flees.[13]

Perhaps they are afraid. Perhaps they merely hope. Coles has made no secret of his feelings, no secret of the fact that he detests slavery. He will not whip his slaves, and, shortly after his father died and he left the family's main plantation to take up his duties as secretary to President Madison, he forbade the overseer his father had hired from using the lash, noting later that "I fed, clothed, and treated my negroes with all the kindness and attention in my power and introduced several ameliorating alternations in their treatment, among others forbid any grown person being whipped." He had argued long and loud with his brothers and his mother over what to do with his slaves.[14] Just four years before setting off for the west, he had written Thomas Jefferson, urging the former president and the friend of his late father to lead an abolition movement in Virginia: "The fear of appearing presumptuous distresses me," Coles wrote the Sage of Monticello, "I will not enter on the right which man has to enslave his brother man, nor upon the moral and political effects of slavery on individuals or on society; because these things are better understood by you than by me." Instead, he would continue in the letter, he wished "to entreat and beseech you" to come up with and put in place "some plan for the gradual emancipation of slavery"—a duty, "as I conceive, that devolves particularly on you ... from the principles you have professed." Jefferson's temporizing reply was that "the love of justice and the love of country plead equally the cause of these people, and it is a mortal reproach to us that they should have pleaded it so long in vain." But, the ex-president tiredly continued, "[T]his, my dear Sir, is like bidding old Priam to buckle the armor of Hector" and urges him to stay home and work for gradual change. Like so many of the great man's pronouncements, it would become well known over the course of the emerging debate over slavery. Less known, naturally enough, was Coles' sharply-worded reply that while "I feel very sensibly the force of your remarks on the impropriety of yielding to my repugnancies in abandoning my property in slaves and my native State," he felt he had no choice, and that as a young and uninfluential man he had not "supposed myself capable of being instrumental in bringing about a liberation." Nor did Coles believe "that I could by my example ameliorate the condition of these oppressed people." It was no wonder, the younger man wrote, that most of his fellow Virginians might be indifferent to the plight of slaves and disinclined to change "where a mere principle of right has to contend against the weighty influence of habit and interest." Virginians needed, he wrote, a reminder of what they really had fought for in the Revolution, of what the words of the Bill of Rights really meant: "I looked to you, my dear Sir, as the first of our aged worthies to awaken our fellow citizens," Coles wrote. "Your time of life I had not considered as an obstacle to the undertaking."[15]

The slaves, of course, knew nothing of these letters. While some of Coles' slaves had known him all his life, and the rest for all of theirs, he had spent hardly any time in the rough little frame house at Rockfish, preferring, even when he was in Virginia, to stay with his mother at the family's main plantation a few miles away on Green Mountain. They may have known he told his farm manager not to whip them, that he had asked his brother John not to lend Ralph to his mother for fear that she would work him too hard.[16] His slaves could not be sure they knew his heart. They might well have known that plenty of Virginians agonized in public over slaves—and kept slaves nevertheless. They likely knew, too, that slumping tobacco prices had lead many more Virginians, no matter what they said they felt about slave-holding, to sell out and move west, as they were doing now. Their fate, they knew, they had to know, was entirely in the hands of the young man standing, oar in hand, at the flatboat's stern.

"The negroes were in this state of hope and fear when one fine April day, while floating down the gentle currents of the beautiful Ohio, I called on deck the whole part, young and old," Coles would recall, years later.[17]

So now comes Ralph Crawford, and his wife Kate, 43 or 44. Their children, the teen-aged Betsey, Thomas with his withered arm, Mary and little William, all gather round. Ralph Crawford's much younger brother Robert, just 25, is there. So is their unmarried little sister, Polly, just 16 or 17 years old. From below is the still-feverish Manuel; with Manuel, his wife, Sukey, who carries Wilson, a babe in arms, born just a few months earlier. Their daughter Frankie, son Alfred and little Elizabeth, just five, come, too. Coles had purchased Manuel, the only man he ever bought, just before starting west—Frankie "was not large enough yet to nurse the youngest ... with so large, helpless and, at the same time increasing family, I felt it my duty to assist her [Sukey], as far as it was in my power; and I knew no more effectual way of doing so than by purchasing her husband." With them come Nancy Gaines, 16 or 17, and her new husband, Tom Cobb, also shaking with fever—"poor Tom," Coles wrote his mother, a few days later, "had taken a pleurisy such as prevailed in your neighborhood before we reached the boat, and was very ill."[18]

They stand, silently, before the man who owns them.

"I commenced by saying it was time for me to make known to them what I intended to do with them," Coles would remember afterwards. With perhaps more than a few shivering with fear as well as fever, they waited. Then: "By the turn of a sentence, I proclaimed in the shortest and fullest manner possible that they were no longer slaves, but free—free as I was, and at liberty to proceed with me or go ashore, at their pleasure," Coles would write.[19]

Of the hundreds of thousands of Americans who owned or would own slaves, only a handful would ever do what Coles had just done. His slaves did not have to buy their freedom, with the hoarded savings of years of extra work. They did not have to wait for him to die, and hope some distant cousin would not contest the will that set them free. They were not his children, or his nephews and nieces, or his half brothers and sisters, whom some might think conscience would command be freed, though surprisingly few Virginia planters ever did. There were about 10,000 free blacks in Virginia at this time, nearly two centuries after the first of their parents marched in chains off a ship from Africa, and more than 20 times as many still in bondage. While a Virginia law of 1782 formally allowed manumission—granting slaves their liberty—few slave-holders seem to have taken the opportunity. The Quaker planter Robert Pleasants' efforts, setting his slaves up as tenant farmers on his estate, brought him fines and his ex-slaves beatings. His friend James Madison dissuaded Pleasants from introducing legislation to the state legislature to emancipate all slaves in 1791, already seeing a changing climate that would, in 1798, lead the legislature to enact a law banning any member of an abolition society from sitting on a jury considering lawsuits involving the freedom of a slave. In 1806, Virginia legislators declared it was against the law to free slaves and let them stay in the Commonwealth, even if their owners wished to follow the example of George Washington, and grant freedom with their wills. The words "You are free" were rarely spoken to a black man, or woman, or child, in America, in 1819.[20] Coles spoke them.

"The effect on them was electrical," Coles recalled. "They stared at me, and at each other, as if doubting the accuracy or the reality of what they had heard. In breathless silence they stood before me, unable to utter a word, but with countenances beaming with expression which no words can convey and no language can describe." Time stood still. Then, "with a wild and hysterical laugh they gazed alternately at me and at each other, looked as if they thought they ought to say something, and yet at a loss to know what to say." Coles, too, would be swept away by feeling he could never describe in any of his later, written recollections of the moment. It took some time, he would recall later, to "mutually become a little composed."[21]

The boat drifts on. "At length, simultaneously, in broken sentences, they poured out their gratitude and praises." And once they do, Coles has more to tell his former slaves. He wants to be sure they understood what he has just done for them, the changes that freedom will bring. If, perhaps, what he is about to tell them will seem a bit presumptuous (for Coles is about to give the freedmen plenty of good, if completely unsolicited, advice) his goal is something other than to savor his own generosity or enjoy the delights most men might indulge in when granting a gift: the joy of proclaiming wisdom, of basking in appreciation. He wants them to know that they now are really free—and to know that liberty means they are free to go wherever they might want to, that he will set them off on the Ohio shore, if they so choose. He wants them to know that they can never again be compelled to work for no pay, that they need no longer fear a whip or

Edward Coles liberating his slaves. This mural in the Illinois State Capitol shows an anachronistically dressed Coles liberating more slaves than he owned, as they travel on two unlikely looking flatboats (courtesy Abraham Lincoln Presidential Library).

an overseer. He has set them free a few days' journey west of Pittsburgh. The hills to the right are the hills of Ohio, and in 1819 Ohio is, along with Vermont and Massachusetts, one of the few places in America that have formally banned slavery (although its Black Code laws of 1804 and 1807 would require freedmen post bonds of $500 for their good behavior and be prepared to produce court papers to prove they were not runaways from another state). It is a real offer he is making for any who might not wish to follow him farther west.[22]

He has still more to tell them, though. "I described duties, obligations and consequences incumbent to freedom ... I assured them, as long as they behaved themselves well, they should find in me a friend." He tells them to learn to read and write. "And in all things (I) urged them to be honest and industrious. I particularly dwelt upon the good effects, not only to themselves but to their relations and friends in bondage, from their conducting themselves in such a manner as to show that the Black race were not inferior to the White and were equally qualified to enjoy all the blessings and perform all the duties inducement to freedom."[23]

Later, his most bitter critic will say that what Coles did that day was nothing but a calculated political move. The dour New Hampshire transplant Hooper Warren, an abolitionist Illinois newspaper editor who would be an unwilling political ally and a lifelong enemy of Coles, would say he really didn't free his people, but kept them in secret bondage for years afterwards. There would be rumors that Polly, or Betsey, or Kate was his mistress. Recalling "an elderly colored woman, who I understood to be the mother" of two kitchen maids he employed, Warren slyly noted she worked as a cook on Coles' farm and "had with her two younger children, a boy and a girl, *mulattoes*." As for the men Coles freed, Warren airily declared he had no recollection of them for all that, decades later, he so carefully remembered the skin color of Thomas, Mary and William. Even when reminded that Coles' adopted Illinois county sued him to demand a bond it said he owed because he freed his slaves, Warren would not credit him for a love of freedom. It was, he said, merely "a mark of his shrewdness, to make all the capital he could out of the performance of a praiseworthy act."[24] The editor's animus and the way in which he gives it voice, perhaps, speak for themselves. Warren would always suspect Coles had come to Illinois, presidential commission to run the new Edwardsville Land Office in his pocket, to play a complicated, and probably national, political game (as, indeed would a later governor of Illinois, Thomas Ford). But if freeing his slaves was to be seen as merely a political gesture, it was also a costly one: "for I not only emancipated all of my negroes, who amounted to one-third of all the property my father bequeathed me, but I removed them out here at an expense of between five and six hundred dollars."[25]

It was, in fact, a gesture of a different kind than either bitter editor or the professional politicians whom Coles would later battle would ever understand, clear though it would prove to be to his fellow Illinoisans in the years to come. As they came to know him, those farmers and backwoodsmen would understand that Coles' actions grew from a politics of ideals, a politics of belief pursued to an inevitable end despite the cost, the kind of politics that can shake a nation and that would shape the State of Illinois, stalwart as it would become in the struggle against slavery, for decades to come. "A remarkable man," Judge Joseph Gillespie would recall, who "devoted himself to the propagation of the sentiments of freedom." Even his opponents for the most part would understand that, and honor him for it, too—though Illinoisans would also brush off his later, hesitant feelers for other offices. Some have seen in that rejection evidence that Coles was ineffective and naive, others an almost-populist resentment of his wealth and supposed arrogance.[26] When Coles calls on his former slaves to be examples, when he preaches that they should work hard and be honest, that they should learn to read and write, when he says they should prove that the color of their skin was no badge of shame or inferiority, he is saying things that virtually no American then, and hardly any Americans for many decades yet to come, would ever think to say.

For Coles calls his former slaves his friends. He will call them his friends for the rest of their lives and his. He will count on Robert Crawford to run a farm for him, years after he leaves Illinois, and he will boast about their achievements on the prairie. If he sounds presumptuous, if he sounds sententious when he talks to them, it is worth remembering that what he presuming to do is to give voice to the sentiment that all men should be free.

Presumptuous or not, there is still more that Coles will tell the freedmen that April morning, because there is still more to the gift he is giving them. Coles is, of course, the child of a wealthy man, though his share of the estate, the farm at Rockfish, was worth roughly $17,000—far from the being the prize of his father's estate. Rockfish, several miles to the south and west, with just seven slaves, was a near-frontier farm with a clapboarded-over log cabin to live in. While Coles was far from struggling for money, his father's estate, divided amongst his widow and his nine then-living children, did not leave his youngest son a rich man, merely a well-connected one. Knowing presidents, though, does not always mean knowing where the money is. In Coles' case, his supposed wealth was in land he could sell and slaves he wouldn't. It would take years to find a buyer for Rockfish—and in the end, it would be his older brother Walter who shouldered the burden of the farm and bought Coles out. The proceeds from selling the land his father left him have paid for this trip and for the land, the swaths of land, Coles has been buying in the Military Tract of Illinois, the bonus lands for veterans of the War of 1812, in the wedge of rich prairie and bottom land between the Illinois and Mississippi Rivers. On a trip the year before, Coles spent a large fraction of his inheritance, about $2,300, buying more than 3,500 acres in the Tract and in Madison County, across the Mississippi from St. Louis, where he has also been buying.[27]

Now, he tells his former slaves, he will give each adult, man and woman, 160 acres, the standard quarter section on which so many settlers in the new west would get their start. More pandemonium. "After some confused and embarrassed expressions of astonishment and thanks, they said I had given them enough in giving them their freedom and that it was unreasonable and that they did not wish me to give them more." Coles brushes aside their offers to pay for the land from future harvests, saying that they had worked, as slaves, for him far longer than he ever wanted, and that the land is his way of trying to repay them for that. "Judging from Ralph's countenance, he was more pleased, or surprised, I know not which, at the land than at the freedom."[28]

Ralph Crawford, of course, might well have guessed at Coles' plans to free his slaves, after accompanying him on two earlier trips to Illinois. During their last trip, in the summer of 1818, Coles had stopped in Kaskaskia, Ill., the tiny capital at the bottom of the Mississippi River bluffs, keeping a careful eye on the deliberations of the convention that wrote the constitution for the soon-to-be created State of Illinois, leaving the sweltering little village only when he was satisfied—prematurely, as it would turn out—that slavery would be barred in the new state. Crawford, too, would have been watching and listening to the deliberations in Kaskaskia; a man who had seen something of the world and of the way blacks were treated, freed or slave, in the west, Crawford might well have thought that talk was nice but land was real.

Officially, each plot of land Coles is giving his former slaves was worth $320, a price far beyond what many an American pioneer had been able to amass in half a lifetime of hard farm labor, which was why so many simply squatted on tracts in wilderness and why most others went deeply into debt—and which would be why, in a few years, Congress would cut the price of public land by one-third and the size of the minimum purchase in half, a move that Coles, virtually alone among Illinois politicians, would support, though it enraged the state's powerful, politically-connected land speculators.[29]

Coles will himself be farming in Madison County, he tells the freedmen. He will need to hire hands to clear the land and plow his fields; a wealthy child of a plantation owner, he has no intention of scrabbling a bare subsistence on a few acres. The land, after all, is wilderness. Coles tells his former slaves they need to remember this because they will need tools and stock animals and cash to carry them through the first year or two on their new farms. For some, not all, he can offer work, and pay. He gives the names.[30]

This disconcerts the ones he doesn't name. Property all their lives, it is hard to take to heart the notion that they no longer have to do what Coles might want, that they no longer need a white man's permission, tacit or expressed, to do what they need or want to do. "They expressed fear that they should be ill-treated, seeming at the moment to forget they were free, and at liberty to change their situation at pleasure," Coles would recall. "On my reminding them of this, it was gratifying to see their countenances brighten." He tells them there is plenty of work to be had. Hired hands were always hard to find on the western frontier, and the backbreaking chore of clearing woods or of plowing the tough prairie sod with its thick, closely-entwined mats of bluestem grass roots or of building fences or of digging drainage ditches meant there was plenty of work of to do. The fast-growing town of St. Louis is near to hand, as well, this early investor in city lots reminds the freedmen, and still more jobs are going begging there. With that, they seem reassured.[31]

They shouldn't have been, for the lot of freedmen, as Ralph Crawford knew but Coles did not stress that morning, was a hard one in America in 1819. In cities, north and south, they were barely tolerated; shunned by most, relegated to the worst work, paid hardly enough for survival. In the country, farming was not an option, for few had the legal ability to buy land and fewer the money; hired hands in most of the nation were assumed to be runaway slaves. They had little recourse to the courts if they were wronged, under the Black Codes that many states, including Illinois, enacted, with little protection even if kidnapped by slave-takers. Coles knew this, too. And he knew that real freedom for his people would require the independence that a farm would bring, especially for men and women who had so far known only farm work. Events would prove him right. While some of the freedman later found work in Illinois, "offered by ill-disposed neighbors $20 a month to work in town making bricks" only to find they would be paid in devalued paper money worth a fraction of each note's face value, "they were compelled to acquiesce to whatever terms their lordly white brothers would deign to allow them." Coles would step in; if they felt they needed the brickyard work to earn the cash they knew they needed to buy seed, livestock and tools, he would provide those necessities instead, on credit, in return for half their produce. That turned out to be enough to get them started growing corn, raising cattle, discovering, with Coles, the new art of farming prairie land at a time when most other settlers shunned the grasslands as desert.[32]

But it was a hard life. Within three years, Ralph Crawford, Tom Cobb and Nancy Gaines would be dead: Crawford of "bilious fever" and Cobb by falling down a well. Kate Crawford persevered, raising her family and eventually marrying her younger brother-in-law, Robert. They expanded their holdings, renting Coles' Edwardsville farm from him, buying land nearby. Manuel, Sukey and their family would settle in St. Louis, but fared less well. Manuel fell ill, and was unable either to repay Coles for purchasing the Virginia indenture that allowed him to marry and leave the state, or for the money Coles offered the struggling family, including a doctors' bill for a then-staggering $96.50. Manuel ended up hiring himself out temporarily to the doctor to settle his bills.[33]

Yet, "in despite of the prejudice against the Negroes, and the disposition to oppress and ill treat them, there has never been a charge brought against one of them for harboring slaves (the most likely complaint they would face) or keeping bad company or disrespectful conduct to the whites or of any violation of the laws or of any immoral or improper conduct of any kind whatever," Coles would note years later. For many years, the Crawfords would manage his farm in Illinois, in addition to owning their own 80 acres (they bought two already-improved tracts, opting for them rather than the uncleared 160-acre tracts Coles gave them). Concerned about the prejudice that the freedmen faced, Coles offered Robert and Kate any financial help they'd need if they wanted to sign up for the newly-popular (among white abolitionists, that is) notion of colonizing Liberia. "They are, however, so happy and content where they are that they seem reluctant to change their situation." Crawford would be ordained a Baptist preacher and settle happily in Illinois, "where he has a large farm, and is 'well to do' in this world."[34]

Now, though, the long-hoped-for day of liberation having at last come, his slaves free men, Coles and the people he now calls friends continue down the river. After eight more days, "remarkably fine weather for floating," Coles and his freed slaves reach the Falls of the Ohio, near Louisville. All have decided to stay with him. Their health improved, their spirits high, Coles has taught them how to use the oars and steer the boat, to watch for snags and sandbars. "For you know, they are old mountaineers and had never before been on water," he wrote his mother from the Kentucky shore. Early on, he added, they weren't much help: "I was reduced to but two who were well enough to stand to the oars and myself had to work pretty hard for two or three days and nights"—but not to worry, for "since then, Commodore Coles has lolled in his cabin, or walked his quarterdeck with all the exceptions and dignity becoming his station."[35]

Coles would sell the flatboats in Kentucky for $50, buying another strong horse and a wagon, before sending the freedmen and their families on ahead to Vincennes, Indiana, on the national road that cut west though the woods to Illinois. They would have a 12-day trek but the way was marked and he promised he would join them soon in Edwardsville. To his mother, he would jot one more comment: "You must not conclude that I have made up my mind to spend the rest of my days in Illinois, far from you and all my beloved friends, and out of that kind of society in which I have moved all my life and of the pleasures to which I am so much attached. So my dear mother, this is what I cannot consent to do. My heart recoils at the idea. I feel so many particular ties and so strongly the attractions on your side of the mountains that I cannot bring myself to believe that I shall ever been a permanent inhabitant of this."[36] There was still much to do in Illinois, though. Coles did not yet know how much.

CHAPTER 2

Youth

"I was born in the very bosom of negro slavery, have seen it in all of its bearings, reflected well upon the nature of it, and, having found it impossible to reconcile it with either my political or my religious creed, I abandoned my native state, my aged parents and relations," Coles would recall to his friend Richard Flower, of the "English Settlement" at Albion in eastern Illinois.[1]

A child of gently beautiful, genteel Albemarle County, Virginia, Coles was the eighth of Col. John Coles' 10 children and the youngest of his five sons, born on December 15, 1786, at the family's plantation, Enniscorthy on Green Mountain, in the rolling hills just north of the James River and just below the Blue Ridge Mountains, a few hard hours' horseback ride south of Jefferson's Monticello and Madison's home at Montpelier. Though not as wealthy as his neighbors, the colonel was well off, with more than 70 slaves working his lands on Green Mountain and up the valley of the Rockfish River on into what is now Nelson County. It was a holding of thousands of acres, assembled over decades and at enormous expense, a testament to the wealth that comes from other people and to the power of single-minded reinvestment over many years in the red clay soil of Albemarle.[2]

John Coles' father had come to Virginia from County Wexford, Ireland, early in the 18th century, settling amongst the small, slow creeks and low hills of Hanover County, not far to the north of Richmond. It was an out-of-the-way country, several miles beyond convenience from the landings on the James and Pamunkey rivers, where the big planters' slaves rolled their hogsheads of tobacco onto the ships from London and Bristol— the kind of country where a young man with little money would have to seek his opportunities, the part of the colony left over for the Dissenters, Quakers and Germans who were just starting to make their way across the Atlantic to the New World. He soon settled in to win an important place in this back country community; in 1739, the county named him a

"Processioner," commissioned to pace the boundaries of new-bought land. But John Coles would not be content with just farming and a county sinecure. The young immigrant and his brother William, who had followed him to America, would eventually marry two prosperous Quaker sisters, Mary and Lucy Winston, whose father Isaac, a leading member of the Cedar Creek Meeting, had settled nearby, clearing a large farm of several hundred acres and already well on his way to becoming a wealthy man by wheeling and dealing in land.[3] John Coles never became a Quaker, but his children and grandchildren would know and remain close to many Friends, despite the isolation and hostility that that disregarded religious minority, opposed to slavery, suffered in a Virginia where an easygoing, eventually disestablished Church of England still held the loose allegiance of most. Still, while John Coles would not follow his father-in-law into the Meeting House, but the young immigrant from Ireland did take up Winston's lead in business matters, buying acreage in Henrico County, to the south. It was land eventually sold as 14 lots in the city of Richmond, then just beginning to supersede the colonial capital Williamsburg as a center for trade in the upcountry (though it was still a few decades from becoming the political capital as well). It would be in Richmond where the first John Coles would make his fortune. A commission merchant, he grew rich trading wheat from his farms and his neighbors, exporting grain to Europe and the Lower South and using the hard cash he earned (as scarce in colonial Virginia as it would be in frontier Illinois) to buy a wide range of goods to be imported from England. When he died in 1747, just 42 years old, he left his daughters a stock of goods for sale worth £800, as well as two tracts of 500 acres each. His real wealth, though, was the land he had steadily been buying, and he left a plantation and 15 slaves to his oldest son Walter. The youngest, John, just two years old when his father died, got 3,000 acres in the still-wild Blue Ridge foothills.[4] With that not completely promising inheritance, his son John, the colonel, would eventually set himself up as a great squire at a place he called Enniscorthy (named for his father's birthplace in Ireland) in Albemarle County—Albemarle, which (as Edward Coles' close friend, the banker Nicholas Biddle, would later joke) raised presidents the way the French did wine-grapes.[5]

It was no vineyard that John Coles the younger found, though, when, just 17, he finally claimed his land in 1766. Southern Albemarle County was still forest, a place where cougars could still be spotted. Coles (and his slaves, of course) started with the heavy work of clearing virgin forest, giant oak and poplar; the timber made him some money; the cleared red earth (its color promising a wealth from iron that never materialized) produced a little more. It helped that Coles, like his father, married wealth. His wife, Rebecca, Edward Coles' mother, was a Tucker, from a blue-blood family of Bermudian immigrants. Her father was one of the biggest merchants in the port of Norfolk. Born to a life far different from a frontier plantation, her affectionate and lively nature was undaunted by what should have been a lonely life but that, with 10 children (nine surviving infancy), never was. The close-knit family drew Edward Coles to his Blue Ridge home at least once a year until he was well into his forties; the family's letters make clear that he and his brothers and sisters regularly turned to one another for advice, help and love. At home in the self-contained if isolated estate John Coles carved out for his family, they had all they needed, and more. Each time the colonel sent a hogshead of tobacco—the giant barrel making its own wheel as his oxen it dragged along what would be called Coles' Rolling Road down to the James River at Scottsville—a little more cash came back. John Coles, like his father, carefully reinvested his funds. The free-spending ways of the big Tidewater planters that so often landed them in debt, the kind of debt that creates revolutionaries, were not for him. As the years passed, and more planters moved to the Blue Ridge country, John Coles of Albemarle would also become a trader and by way of a banker to his neighbors. He bought land, and more land and more land: 1,455 acres in 1771, 706 in 1780, a grist mill on the Hardware River soon after; eventually, more than 14,000 acres in several counties. Edward Coles grew up never wanting for anything.[6]

But the tobacco that made the Old Dominion rich and that John Coles hoped to raise at Enniscorthy and at his other farms in the valleys of the James and Rockfish Rivers was a crop long past its prime. Prices were low, and falling. After the United States won its independence, smokers in Virginia's traditional British market tended to turn to other sources for their leaf. The cool air and heavy red soil of Albemarle didn't particularly favor the crop, either: the "bright" leaf British smokers demanded likes to bake in the August sun of Tidewater and prefers the scrubby, sandy soil of the coast. So John Coles, like most of his neighbors, eventually and gradually turned to raising grain and livestock, produce for the beleaguered Tidewater planters who stuck with the sot-weed, grain for the fever-ridden coasts of Georgia and the Carolinas, where the slave-worked crops of indigo and rice still had steady markets. Though a new and rising demand for cotton must have tempted some Albemarle County planters to try their hands, that crop, like tobacco, indigo and rice, preferred a warmer climate and lighter soil. The corn and wheat and pigs that farmers like Coles raised brought in nowhere near the cash their estates consumed. The trend was slow to develop, but clear. By the time John Coles died, in 1808, the family's real wealth, like that of most Virginia plantation owners, was not to be found in tobacco. Nor was it really in land. It was in slaves.[7]

They were property, but they were also the people he and his children passed most of their days with, isolated as they were in the middle of Coles' huge landholdings. When Edward was ready for his first schooling, he boarded at the home of a neighbor, Cary Nichols, who had hired a tutor for his own children, since it was too far to go back and forth every day. That would have been the first time in his life when he would have played with children other than his brothers and sisters and the sons and daughters of his parents' slaves. His tutor was the first adult, other than his parents and their slaves, with whom Coles would spend any extended amount of time, for while slaves worked John Coles' fields, they helped to raise his children, too. "Although he was a highly educated and accomplished gentleman, yet his talk on common subjects, when he was not on his guard, was exactly that of an old Virginia negro, such was the force of early habits," one of Edward Coles' friends in later life remembered.[8]

Schooling opened a world for all the Coles children. At the Nichols plantation, Edward Coles' first tutor taught him some French and Latin, as well as arithmetic. When he was a little older, his parents sent him to a Mr. White's Academy, near Dwyer's Store, to prepare himself for college. John Coles' five sons all went away to school; all eventually finished up at the College of William and Mary. Edward, though, made a slight detour. In 1805, he went away to little Hampden Sidney College, a small Presbyterian school then located to the north of Richmond.[9] Founded in 1774 with the aim of teaching Calvinist virtue and the practical skills that upcountry Virginia's Dissenter leaders would need, Hampden Sidney's students took the mission seriously enough that, in the 1790s, they forced their professors to junk the school's classical curriculum. But the new regime of science, surveying and skeptical analysis didn't last long. By the time Coles enrolled, eager to plunge into just those courses of study, in the full flush of a youngest son's hunger for the practical knowledge he would need to earn a living and a young skeptic's impatience for abstract pronouncement, a new president had taken office at the college, promising to crack down on his free-wheeling charges. Church elders demanded still more religious discipline, insisting that the school establish a theological seminary, while a series of revival meetings the year Coles enrolled helped fuel the fire. Dozens of students left. Within a few months of entering college, Coles and a small group of friends were complaining to school officials about the curriculum changes and the conduct of the lecturers, winning promises, or so they thought, of a return to the way things had been before. "The very men that threatened to expel us ... and represented it to us as the most rebellious and unpardonable behaviour, now say that we have done ourselves a great deal of honor and showed a great degree of public spirit," Coles wrote to his father. Still, he complained, the library was poor. He had no plans to be a preacher and, as a young man who was seeking a livelihood more promising than a relatively small plantation way up in the hills, he wanted the surveying and mathematics courses that the college still would not offer. College president Archibald Alexander, appalled when one student shot off a pistol near the building where he had hoped to establish a theological seminary and then displayed "utmost contempt of the Board by leaving their presence ... telling them they might do what they could," had decamped to Philadelphia. His successor, Thomas Rice, was unswayed from his goal of creating a denominational college. The number of students fell by roughly a third, to 55. Coles gave up. The next year, he went to William and Mary, as his older brothers had.[10]

Coles worked hard at William and Mary, not then a school renowned for its hard-working scholars. He didn't like it much, at first. "They have no library worth anything," he complained to his father, adding that he saw "nothing very prepossessing either in the town or College." A bad fall from a horse in 1806, his first year there, fractured his leg so badly that his family feared for a while it would have to be amputated. Coles missed months of classes, yet made up for that by studying on his own. A letter to his father strikes what would be a characteristically light note: his leg is strengthening, the young man writes, "let it suffice when I say that I was tempted to dance."[11]

Coles and his dancing. "Why Edward you are quite a romantick lover," his older sister Mary Eliza would tease, a few months later. For two decades, he and his sisters would joke, but only partly in fun, about his ballroom escapades and about the young women he would not quite court and would not just ignore. He was happy to flirt, delighted to dance, but would not marry. He was, it seems, concerned with something else.[12]

It was in the years after he broke his leg, still at William and Mary, pursuing "a political course of studies," rooming with "a very good scholar ... more moral and less dissipated than young men generally are here," that Coles turned serious. Now, delving deeply into the Enlightenment writers whose political essays were the intellectual underpinning of the American Revolution, Coles would find he "had my attention first awakened to the state of master and slave."[13] It happened in a class taught by Bishop James Madison, president of the college and Episcopalian Bishop of Virginia. Nothing he had seen on his father's farms, no laments of slaves, no nostalgia for the companions of his childhood nor remorse for their fate, would move him in quite the way that the gently murmured lectures of the bishop would—although Madison, second cousin to President James Madison, was no radical and would never have intended his teaching to forge such a stern opposition to what was, after all, the very foundation of Virginia's economy. But he was perhaps the only college president in the first decade of the 19th century who would have asked his charges to read the work of such democratic radicals as John Locke, Thomas Paine and Jean-Jacques Rousseau, without seizing upon the text of a blood-soaked French Revolution to preach the danger of too much democracy. A gentle man, as well as a gentleman, Madison was never one to discourage his charges or to snap too sharply on the reins when he might feel they were headed astray. Beloved by students, "his manner to all the inmates of the college was kind and parental, and his reproval offered in the gentlest tones," one former student (and classmate of Coles), President John Tyler, would later recall. "No one who attended the college during the time he presided over it, has failed to acknowledge him as a second father."[14] For Coles, the bishop's "goodness and purity of ... character shone clearly," as did "that peculiar meekness of deportment and philanthropic feelings, which characterize the true Christian." The bishop would be a decisive figure in Coles' life, a man who sought to marry an Enlightenment vision of a life of reason with religious faith: there is, he held, "everywhere a system, upheld by laws, both physical and moral, which never err; and which, the more they are investigated the more they evince the beneficent [sic] design of the Creator." His fundamentally liberal view was that if God dictated morality, reason revealed it, and logic demanded virtue of governments and men. The bishop's message that men—young men at a college, say—must resist corruption, vice and tyranny and strive for virtue would be deeply appealing to many students, not just Coles. Inspired, the bishop's charges "acquire more liberality & more ambition than at any other place in the world," as Coles' brother Isaac would write, adding that they "shine forth with a splendor that dazzels [sic] the continent" even though they risked taking their liberal and democratic principles too far.[15] But for Coles, as for many young Americans of his time, it was perfectly logical to go on to say that the pursuit of virtue was only possible when men were free to chose to pursue it. That was rational religion. That was what Coles, and the bishop for that matter, would have called "republicanism." It was, in their view, what America was all about. "It is reason, it is patriotism, it is gratitude to our God, which persuades," Madison would say. Heaven, he declared, was a republic.[16]

They were hard days for the bishop, though. A teacher at the college since 1773, president of William and Mary since 1777, he was ordained first Bishop of Virginia in 1790, just four years after the church had lost its position as the established state religion and was seeing its influence and authority slip away. The college, too, faced hard times. It closed for a year when the final campaign of the Revolution brought the main British and American armies to the Virginia Peninsula, while the removal of Virginia's capital to Richmond sucked out much of the life of the town of Williamsburg itself. "Truly a great and good man" though he may have been to Coles, the bishop (like many Virginians in the first decades of American independence) said he was troubled by the immorality of owning other men—yet, when the financial distress of the college seemed to require it, in the 1780s, the bishop seemed to have had little trouble cashing in human property, putting some of the college slaves up for sale along with the lands the King had long ago granted it.[17]

In his final years at William and Mary (the bishop died in 1812), it was beginning to be difficult even to talk about the morality of slavery. Things had changed since 1782, when the General Assembly of Virginia enacted the first law allowing slave-owners to free their slaves. Early on, many of the most ardent Revolutionaries soon found, on closer examination, that the cost of liberating their property was simply too high. The Quaker John Payne, for instance, who married Coles' aunt Mary, freed his slaves in 1783, moved to Philadelphia and was bankrupt within six years, despite the sale of his plantation at Coles Hill, Virginia. By 1786, the year Coles was born, when the New Kent County slave James would "humbly intreat" the Virginia General Assembly for the "inestimable favor" of freedom, he would find that the postwar fervor for freedom had already started to be tempered by economic concerns—for, even though James noted that he had enlisted under the Marquis of Lafayette during the final campaign against Cornwallis and served as a messenger carrying items "of the most secret & important kind" through British lines, "which if discovered would certainly have endangered my life," he made sure to ask the legislature to reimburse his owner, Will Armisted, for his liberation.[18]

"This unfortunate difference of color, and perhaps of faculty, is a powerful obstacle to the emancipation of these people," Jefferson himself wrote in his *Notes on Virginia*, in 1782 (the year Virginia first formally allowed people to free their slaves).[19] The *Notes*, a standard text at William and Mary even in Coles' time there, encapsulated Jefferson's basic view on slavery and slaves, held through his life. The obstacles to emancipation loomed larger in the eyes of the Sage of Monticello's fellow Virginians, and grew more daunting still after an attempted slave uprising outside of Richmond in 1800, led by Gabriel Prosser, which was stopped only by a torrential near-hurricane. The entire state was panicked; and the entire state noted that freedmen had helped while the state militia seemed unable to contain the rebelling slaves. Not even the immediate execution of 35 rebel slaves could calm those fears.[20] In 1804, Richmonders Benjamin DuVal, H.Y. Dabney and 52 others complained "Many Captains of Northern trading vessels" trading on Chesapeake Bay and along the rivers of Virginia were engaged in "a clandestine and marauding intercourse and traffic with the slaves" that in some cases would "beguile them to comit [sic] Robberies on their masters," and in others inspired "a spirit of discontent, tending to insurrection." In 1806, the same year Coles entered William and Mary, the legislature enacted a new law that said any newly freed slaves would have to leave Virginia.[21]

Virginia was afraid, and Virginians were less and less willing to talk about slavery, to say nothing of criticizing it. But Coles knew the bishop well, and the bishop, who had taught all of Coles' older brothers, knew and indulged the young man. "This intimacy emboldened me before the class to ask questions" and allowed him to spend hours "conversing privately with the mild old bishop," Coles would recall. But the comfort of that connection and the warmth of the old bishop's friendship notwithstanding, Coles had hard questions to pursue. "I can never forget his peculiarly embarrassed manner, when lecturing and explaining the rights of man, I asked him in the simplicity of youth and under the influence of the new light just shed on me—if this be true, how can you hold a slave—how can a man be the property of man?" The bishop neither dodged nor lost his temper: "He frankly admitted that it could not be rightfully done, & that slavery was a state of things that could not be justified on principle & could only be tolerated in our country, by our finding it in existence & the difficulty of getting rid of it."[22]

So said many Virginians, Jefferson and Madison among them. But new light Coles now saw—whether the revelation and inspiration his Quaker relations so named, and sought, in their meeting houses, or the Locke and Voltaire and Paine the bishop had his charges read, or simply the ever-fresh message of the Declaration of Independence that all men are created free—was not to be satisfied with mere pragmatism.

"As to the difficulty of getting rid of our slaves, we could get rid of them with much less difficulty than we did the King of our forefathers," Coles would argue.[23] That, after all, took a war; the war in which his father served, the war whose leaders said was fought to end their own enslavement by the crown, the young man said. The fact that slavery existed did not justify it.

"In class and in private I would ask was it right to do what we believed to be wrong because our forefathers did it?" Coles recollected much later. It did not matter, he would argue, that "they may have thought they were doing right & their conduct may have been consistent with their ideas of propriety," for those ideas were changing and he and his contemporaries had grown up in a different time, liberated through revolution from tyranny. "Far different is the character of our conduct if we believe we do wrong to do what our forefathers did," Coles would say. "Such inconsistency on our part, & such injustices to our fellowman, should not be tolerated because it would be inconvenient or difficult to terminate."[24]

The bishop told Coles he, too, wished to see slavery ended. Virginia, and the nation, needed to move in that direction, the old man said. For now, though, slavery was the law. America was a land of law, and it was a republic whose citizens could change the law, but it was a republic whose citizens were obliged to obey the law, the bishop said. Coles, though, replied that an individual could act without waiting for his fellow citizens to change their constitution: "[F]or what was the law of the land—nothing more than the will of the majority—and was every individual citizen bound to do what the law permitted him to do—not compelled him to do, but permitted him to do?" Coles asked. If the people of a state "neglected to do their duty & tolerated a state of things which was in direct violation of their great fundamental doctrines," what was he to do? "I could not reconcile it to my conscience & sense of propriety to participate," he declared, "[and] being unable to screen myself under such a shelter from the peltings and upbraiding of my own conscience and the just censure, as I conceived, of earth and heaven, I could not consent to hold as property what I had no right to, & which was not and could be property, according to my understanding of the rights and duties of man—and therefore determined that I would not and could not hold my fellowman as a slave."[25]

The passionate language suggests a near-if-not-quite religious fervor, something little in evidence in Coles' youth or among others of his family, an uncomfortable intensity in a Virginia more famed for partying than for praying. It was a belief, though, as much in what Coles would have called "republicanism" as in the dictates of heaven, a view that would not fade as the decades passed ("Often have I most devoutly wished that I had either talents or wealth which would enable me to take a stand ... restoring the blacks to their liberty and the whites to the consistency of their republican and Christian virtues," a 58-year-old Coles would write).[26] It is a view that ties human rights to moral law, not surprising for a student of the bishop's, but that unlike the bishop, sees a two-way linkage, arguing that immorality, in this case, the immorality of slavery, must inevitably lead to the loss of other men's rights, not just those of the bondsman. If virtue demands freedom, freedom in turn demands virtue.

He was terribly out of step with his times. Washington freed his slaves with his will, but the first president died in 1799. His Richmond neighbors were shocked by the murder of the great jurist George Wythe in 1806, and likely nearly as surprised to learn his will also provided for his slaves to be freed. When the death in 1796, at age 26, of Richard Randolph (who styled himself Citizen Randolph because of his admiration for the French Revolution) freed his slaves, his widow had to struggle for years to fend off legal challenges to keep them on the 400 acres her husband had also willed for them to live on, in a last testament in which he wished to "humbly beg forgiveness" for having held them in bondage. Abolition, even for the boldest, was something for after death.[27]

By 1797, Virginia delegates to the American Convention of Abolition Societies were complaining that a new law barring their members from sitting on juries in cases involving slaves' legal status was "calculated to destroy almost every suggestion of hope that any person ... can obtain liberty by due process of law, however valid their claim."[28] Three years later, the Alexandria, Va., society would complain it had been infiltrated and disrupted by pro-slavery men.[29] For men like the Quaker miller and merchant William Hartshorne, the collapse of the Alexandria society, its resources drained by writs sworn out against it, meant having to set aside for many years a strongly-held belief that slavery must be confronted and overthrown. Through the first decades of the 19th century, Hartshorne's opposition would be a private, choosing to neither own nor hire slaves, though he did unhappily invest in businesses that hired slaves. That was, he would write in an 1816 report to the Quaker Alexandria Monthly Meeting, something a Virginia Friend should try to avoid in order to live up their faith's rule that they could not own slaves.[30]

Considering the growing unease the opponents of slavery were feeling at this time, the confidence and the boldness with which Coles talked to his bishop are striking. The classes that he took with the bishop, though, were a kind of capstone of his studies at William and Mary, a kind of special seminar for Virginia's young leaders-to-be, intended to be a special part of their final year of schooling. Coles' hard work after recovering from breaking his leg had allowed him to catch up with his classmates, and hold his own in debate with one of the most prominent men in the state. Yet it left him struggling, too: for what was he to do? He "greatly preferred general to individual action, and was anxious for it," but knew, deep down, that someday, he would have to act. When? How? Still wrestling with these questions that last year at William and Mary, word reached him that his father was ill. So, too, was his older brother, Tucker, upon whom the colonel had relied the most to help run the main farm. His family needed him, the colonel wrote: "For as I do expect you will be a farmer, it will be necessary to attend something to the business." Unhappily, Coles returned to Enniscorthy.[31]

Back home, he kept his counsel. He did not talk about his feelings about slavery, at this point known to "but a few of my fellow collegians." Coles quickly saw that if his father knew his youngest son would not own slaves, he would change his will. The colonel's other children would get the slaves he had intended to give Edward, the colonel would give his youngest son more land, or cash or some other asset to make of the difference. "The difference," said Coles, "would be the same in perpetuating their bondage, as if I had sold the portion of them which I should otherwise have inherited." He could not do it.[32]

But when his father died, in 1808, Coles told his family he wished to free his slaves. He had inherited 20, but only three were old enough and strong enough to work in the fields of the farm his father left him in the Rockfish River valley: Ralph and Robert Crawford (though he was just 15 years old) and Thomas Cobb. (Besides Ralph Crawford's wife Kate and their four children, Ralph and Robert's little sister Polly, Nancy Gaines and Sukey and her two little children, the rest were small children or too elderly to work.)[33] He talked openly of his feelings about slavery to his family and to his friends and to some of his father's friends nearby, saying he hoped to get his slaves their freedom papers soon. All were appalled. His family feared for him. Coles' inheritance would be "barely enough to enable you to live as a gentleman, even with your Slaves," and his slaves might well be worth more than the farm his father left him at Rockfish. Yes, Coles replied, he understood the economics. "But, said they, you have no other profession. You have been brought up & intended to follow the occupation of a planter, how can you carry on your plantation and support yourself without slaves?"[34] He thought he might be a doctor, "but as soon as I assertained [sic] positively that my breast was effected, I immediately delayed."[35] Freeing his slaves and hiring them to work for him was no answer. Legally, it was barely possible. Coles thought he might be able to manage by "not having three free papers recorded, & by making my Will supply and defect in form." The issue was the Virginia law, enacted just two years earlier, that said anyone freeing slaves had to move them from the state, although the legislature could decide, in individual cases, to let freedmen stay in the Old Dominion. In the rare cases when it was asked, the legislature generally agreed. But petitions were rare, for opposition to the very idea was strong and growing stronger. "I found it would to a great degree render me odious," Coles would write. His friends thought his opposition to slavery was merely the not-completely-unprecedented posturing of a young Virginian who had read his Declaration a little too seriously and

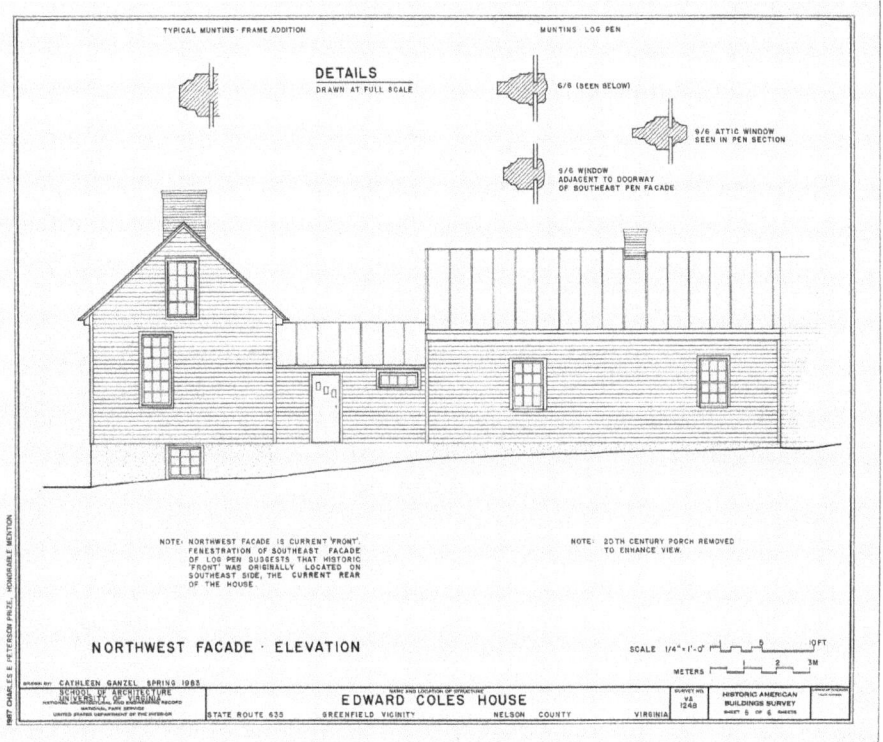

Rockfish. This modest house was the farmstead Coles inherited in Nelson County, Virginia (Library of Congress).

whose father, alas, had died before the realities of life had had a chance to sink in. But when Coles proposed running his farm with hired freedmen, it was too much. "Upon presenting my plan to some of my friends, I found they were indignant at the idea, and if I attempted it, I should incur not only the displeasure of my relations and neighbours but I and my poor unfortunate negroes would be considered as pests of society and every effort made to persecute, to injure and to exterminate us."[36]

Beyond mere property, Coles' family and friends, like most Virginians, primarily saw their slaves as threats now, their fears not calming in the years after Gabriel's Rebellion or the rising of slaves against their masters in Haiti. Virginians' slaves were no longer the people who raised them, no longer former playmates. Attitudes had hardened further. In an 1809 petition to the legislature, one Samuel Templeman complained that his task of settling the estate of his neighbor William Hutt, who "died considerably indebted," had been complicated by the flight from Hutt's plantation of a slave named Joe, "a young dark and likely negro man ... whom, your petitioner believes, he might have sold for £100," and who had been hunted down by a county patrol after a notice from the governor of Virginia advised "of the alarming intelligence, that, on the day preceding Christmas, a massacre of ourselves & of those more dear to us was intended by the negroes." The patrol found Joe—astonishingly enough, at the cabin of his wife, on a nearby plantation—on Christmas Eve, when, "on hearing the voices & enquiring of the patrollers, he was alarmed, and attempted to escape by flight ... he was commanded to stop, but continued to run when a gun was fired at him, and he died of the wound which he received." All things considered, because of the financial loss to Hutt's creditors, and "dictated by a regard for the welfare of the state," Templeman thought the General Assembly should pay Hutt's estate for Joe. The legislators, with the traditional Virginia concern about profligacy with public monies, disagreed.[37]

At the same time Virginians' fears grew, so did the value of their slaves. As promised in the Constitution, the United States had recently banned the import of slaves, perhaps for care of tender conscience, perhaps for reasons that had more than a little to do with laws of demand and of supply, and the impact that a restriction on imported supply would likely have on the price for slaves born in the United States. Between the time Coles' father started farming with his slaves and the ban on importation, slave prices roughly tripled, with one series of data from South Carolina showing a rise from $125 to more than $380. They would soon rise still faster: the explosive growth of cotton cultivation would keep driving the price of slaves higher. Coles' neighbors, even the humanist and democrat Jefferson, believed they simply could not afford to do without their slaves.[38]

So Coles would, he was beginning to understand, have to leave. In August 1809 he set out for the west, spending four months looking to see if he could settle himself and his slaves in Kentucky, Ohio or Indiana; upon his return, he advertised his land for sale. There were no takers; there'd be none for years. And so he stayed, 22 years old, his father just buried, his family unable to hide their fears for him, still hoping for a way to avoid the pain of leaving his home and going to live among strangers, even though, as he tried bravely to tell his mother and brothers, "this is as dust in the balance when weighing the consolation and happiness of doing what you believe right."[39]

Green Mountain had become a gloomy place. "It was with much concern that I read in your last letter that you had heard the whole of my family, at least the female part of it 'were extremely exasperated against (me),'" Coles wrote to an old college friend, assuring him that that was not in fact the case.[40] Still, to another friend Coles would complain, "[M]y situation, my dear Hawkins, presents a sad and melancholy reverse ever since I left Williamsburg, that Paradise of modern times."[41] He was stuck. He knew he had to act, but could not.

Fate saves him from action at this point—or, if not fate, a quiet word from his worried older brother Isaac to the man who had just taken office as the nation's fourth president, James Madison. Isaac, who had been in Washington as President Jefferson's private secretary, had promised to continue in that position with Madison, but had had to resign after attacking a member of Congress over a personal matter; Isaac, too, was also eager to start his career in Virginia politics, for his older brother John was urging him to run for governor. If Edward could take his place, if Isaac could be "rid in a decent manner" of his obligations to Madison, he would be free to return to Virginia—and it might distract his younger brother from the untenable dilemma his objections to slavery had posed.[42] Isaac Coles, as it would turn out, would have no luck dabbling in politics, but instead would have to content himself with managing the estate an Enniscorthy, digging a fish pond which "here among the wild mountains ... cannot but be considered as a vast acquisition. I shall feel happy indeed, if I may contribute by my example to the introduction of little improvements of this sort"[43]; with 1,250 acres at Enniscorthy and an additional 1,000 to come when his mother died, he had plenty to keep him busy on Green Mountain, but within a few years would be itching to sell out. But for the moment, he was impatient to seize the prospects in Virginia, and thought his youngest brother could provide the means. "As he had nothing to do at home, he had perhaps as well amuse himself with novelties of such a situation until the close of the session, when he might give it up and return to his more sober occupations," Isaac would write to his older brother, John, a few weeks after setting the plan in motion. Edward was unaware of all the maneuvering.[44]

When, then, a letter "most unexpectedly" came from the president-elect, inviting the Coles family's worrisome youngest son to come to Washington and become his private secretary, Coles wrestled with the question of what to do. For days, he was unable to decide. Finally, unable to put aside the idea that he had to set his slaves free, suffused with an almost theatrically urgent need to sacrifice himself if necessary, he wrote declining Madison's offer. "I can assure you Sir nothing has ever more flattered me my vanity or given me more gratification than this token of your esteem and confidence in me," this never-to-be-sent letter said. "While I am penning this, I feel sensibly a struggle between my inclinations and my reason. The former propels me to accept, the latter withholds its assent." Coles added that he felt he did not know enough and did not have the time he would need to properly prepare for the job, preoccupied as he was with his plans to take his slaves to the west.[45]

On his way to the Charlottesville post office, though, full of both high feelings and remorse for the sacrifice he would be making, Coles crossed paths with James Monroe, another old family friend, who was then serving as Secretary of State. Monroe, perhaps, knew about the family plot to send Coles to Washington, perhaps not; in any event, Coles was moved to tell about the letter from the president-elect, and to add that he intended not to go to Washington but instead would turn all his efforts to bringing his slaves west, where they might live in freedom. Monroe had different advice.

"He urged me by all means to accept," Coles recalled later. The older man, who like Jefferson and Madison, had often expressed his dismay about slavery, talked not only about the honor Coles proposed to shun, not only about duty and about old friendships, but said as well that time spent in the inner circle of power in Washington would let Coles make contact with members of Congress from the western states, who could offer the best advice about settlement and emancipation.[46]

The possibility of a political life, the possibility that engaged so many Virginia planters, would have seemed an obvious one to Coles and to the men who became his sponsors in Washington. Coles was born for it. The Virginians who led the country were neighbors. They were friends of his father. Many had known the young Coles since he was a child: "I congratulate you on the very promising appearance of your two sons. They are fine boys indeed," Patrick Henry wrote to the colonel after a 1797 visit to Enniscorthy and meeting then 10-year-old Edward Coles.[47] His friends and his family could not understand why Coles would not jump at Madison's offer. Nor could James Madison and his wife Dolley (who were married at Enniscorthy—Dolley was a cousin—when Coles was not yet three years old). They would be perplexed, now as in the years to come, at Coles's hesitance to begin building the career in public life they saw as such a natural path for him, and one they were happy to launch from inside the White House itself. His brothers, especially Isaac, closest to him, were simply irritated. "What has he decided to do? Will he come on and make an experiment?" Isaac complained. "If he does not like it he has only to go back when he is tired—I have been waiting to hear."[48]

CHAPTER 3

The White House

Coles did go to the White House.

He became private secretary to Madison and, as Dolley's cousin, was a part of the president's family. At formal dinners, Coles sat at the foot of the table, opposite the First Lady, to help make the conversations flow. At Dolley Madison's Wednesday soirees, it was Coles who diplomatically steered the president to the guests he needed to see. "A thorough gentleman and one of the best-natured and most kindly-affectioned men it has ever been my fortune to know," William Preston, a young visitor at the White House, would recall of those early days.[1]

The young man from Green Mountain, still fretting about what to do with his slaves, was more than decorative: Coles was, in fact, Madison's only aide. In a tiny capital, just 6,800 residents, a small Cabinet and still-rudimentary organization in Congress, he found himself in the middle of everything. Greeted by the president with "two handkerchiefs stuffed full of papers," a request to sort them and a warning that it would be "work that will require no small quantity of labour or time," Coles' central role was clear from the beginning.[2] He saw virtually every official paper the president did. He carried the president's messages to Congress, and lobbied there for the president's proposals. Not quite a year into his first term, with Napoleon's wars still raging and both Britain and France trying to stop one another's American trade, Madison was having an ever-more difficult time hewing to the neutrality policy set by his predecessor and patron, Thomas Jefferson. British warships routinely stopped American merchant vessels, impressing seamen, offhandedly dismissing their American citizenship. The Royal Navy's patrol of the American coast was so tight as to amount to an undeclared blockade. The west pushed for war, the cities of the east for something, anything, to reopen commerce. Madison's support in Pennsylvania and New York was eroding, even his fellow Virginian, John Randolph, led a faction attacking him. There were fences to mend in Congress, and it would be for Coles to help.[3]

One way was, as ever in Washington, the schmooze. Although he would feel it an "ordeal of embarrassment" at first, Coles would eventually form ties of friendship, or at least mutual regard, with the capital's main political actors. It was a work of many evenings, countless pleasantries, a game of wit and manners. Dinners and dances and, most especially, a social evening at the White House created a neutral ground where politicians or their go-betweens could sound out their opponents and, completely unofficially, completely safely, explore ways to settle their differences. Coles' fine Virginia manners made him a star on the capital's social circuit. His daily contact with the president, the messages he carried to and from Congress and the foreign diplomats stationed (usually reluctantly) in Washington gave him both gossip and hard information to retail. Key, too, to winning friends in Congress: Coles managed patronage matters for Madison, dealing directly with some of the nation's most important politicians on the matters that lay closest to their hearts, men like soon-to-be Attorney General Richard Rush of Pennsylvania or Joseph Story, speaker of the Massachusetts House of Representatives and soon, possibly with a quiet hand from Coles, to be named an associate justice of the U.S. Supreme Court.[4] He came to know and to ally himself with William Crawford, the Georgia senator who had, in just five years, risen to be elected president *pro tem* of the Senate, a key ally of Madison's in that body.[5] (Later, when Crawford became Secretary of the Treasury under President James Monroe and would aspire to succeed him in the White House, he would appoint Coles as registrar of lands in the new federal Land Office in Edwardsville, Ill., the post that Coles took up after he freed his slaves in 1819.) From Crawford, a financial conservative who was unable to carry his case in 1811 that the First Bank of the United States should be re-chartered, Coles likely picked up a suspicion of the kind of easy-money, state-chartered banks that so many Illinois politicians would dabble with and that Coles would try to rein in. Coles, too, would support Crawford when he ran for the presidency in 1824, which would not be a popular move with many of the Illinoisans who had by then elected him their governor.[6] Like Crawford, Coles was impatient with political parties, a failing that would affect both men's careers. Attorney General William Pinckney, meanwhile, would push Coles hard for a federal appointment for a Maryland ally, a "real out party man" named Howard Goldsborough. But then, lobbying, and being lobbied, was part of the job. An old college friend, Joseph Hawkins, asked Coles for his help winning an appointment as major in the Army, while his new friend Nicholas Biddle, the Philadelphia banker, asked Coles to do what he could to win his father the appointment of commander of the Pennsylvania militia.[7] Lobbying for the admission of what eventually would be the state of

Louisiana, Julian Poydras, delegate to Congress from Orleans Territory, "insisted" Coles dine with him every Sunday.[8] And it would be Coles who would take on the delicate task of trying to calm down a furious Robert Fulton, feuding with the head of the patent office, who had taken sides against the inventor in a long-running lawsuit over patent rights.[9] He made friends for the president and kept a careful eye on enemies: Maryland Senator Samuel Smith's family, he warned Madison, "are said not to directly vent their spleen" but still "spur on their relations & friends, many of whom are extremely abusive of The President." "A good deal of feeling has been excited here by some military appointments," he wrote Madison from Philadelphia, adding that some were political opponents and suggesting "that the Secretary of War [John Armstrong] thinks too highly of [Madison opponent and newspaper editor William] Duane and his friends, and suffer them to have too much influence over him."[10] He was subtle, he was sharp. And the work never seemed to stop. "I am kept continually hurried and continually behind hand," Coles complained.[11]

Immersed in the social whirl—"it is enough to say, I have not dined at home in family way, more than three times in the last fortnight"—he felt he had little time for anything.[12] He found that Dolley Madison's Wednesday evening levees, open to all, the regular round of balls and dinners of the capital consumed hours and hours of every week. "I am sick, yes heartily sick with the number of our parties," wrote the young man whose accounts of flirtations and dancing had so entertained his sisters just a few years before. "I have not been out of company one evening from more than two weeks."[13] Still, though he may have grumbled privately, in public he remained the soul of decorum, a light-hearted ornament to public life whose response, when the Navy Department needed a hand with an appropriation bill before Congress, arranged a ball held on the gleaming white decks of the frigate U.S.S. *Constellation*, where, with "utmost concord and hilarity," undimmed by the rare appearance of the as-always black-suited president himself, the Navy convinced Congress it needed the money. In fact, a happy Congress voted to increase the fleet by a dozen vessels.[14]

It was now 1812, going on four years since his father died. He had, he feared, missed his chance to go west and to free his slaves. Now 25, still unmarried, he felt he was missing other things as well. "You have no doubt received before you left home my letter announcing the change in my matrimonial prospects ... I do not *altogether despair*" for all that the conduct of the young lady, a Miss Swann, "is a perfect riddle and uncomprehensible to me," he wrote to his older brother John. In the event, Coles and Miss Swann would decide they did not have the money to go out on their own and live the kind of life each wanted. A few months later, though, he was courting another young woman, identified in his letters only as "Miss A.," winning the promise that she would "unconditionally engage herself" and set a wedding date. But that match, also, was not to be.[15]

There was little encouraging in what his family wrote back to him, either. Things at Rockfish were not going well; the markets for his wheat, tobacco and hemp were in a deep slump, his toying with horse-breeding more a folly than a business. Any sale of the indebted property would be at a distress price, Coles knew. "I had supposed you all understood my wishes with respect to the sale of Rockfish," he complained to his oldest brother, John. "Although I am disposed to sell, yet I am not so much bent on it as to make a sacrifice. My idea is, that it is worth $15,000." A Mr. Coleman had offered even more, and Coles dryly noted that "without a twitch of conscience for setting aside my judgment, I would accept $2,000 (more)—or $17,000."[16] It appeared that this would be his best chance to sell for years; ultimately, his brother Walter would buy him out. (In contrast, his brother Isaac did quite well; with the 13 slaves he inherited, who by 1816 would be worth $10,000 to $12,000, he figured, and 1,250 acres he valued at $44,000—though was unable to sell—he was in far better shape than Edward with his smaller, more remote farm; Isaac sold tobacco at $11 per hundredweight, compared with Jefferson's $5. In his first year as a planter, he turned a profit of $4,340.)[17] Prices for tobacco and other farm produce would remain depressed. His harvests would be poor. "I am so much surprised at the amount of my flour that I really suspect you must have made a mistake and wrote 23 when you meant 33 barrels," the overworked presidential secretary wrote to his brother John at the end of his first year in Washington. There would be little improvement as the years passed, and the War of 1812 ravaged American trade. "Yet was it mortifying and to me quite melancholy when I reflected, that I had commenced my operations as a farmer more than four years ago with a debt of $500" and yet despite "my utmost economy" Rockfish was unable "to pay off this small debt and support itself," he wrote again to John that last spring before the war. "If I cannot do better on Rockfish, I must move elsewhere."[18]

But he neither moved nor married. Perhaps that was because Coles was too distracted that summer. The years of tension with Britain over the blockade, the seizure of American ships, and the impressment of American sailors into crews of British men-of-war, were coming to a head. Helping fuel the rush to war were suspicions the British had incited Tecumseh and his brother, the Shawnee Prophet, to resist American authorities in the Indiana Territory and eventually fight them. Madison was pushing now for war. In June 1812, Congress finally gave Madison the declaration of war he sought. By July, American troops had crossed from Detroit into Canada. And in October, British soldiers crushed a force of U.S. Army regulars at the Battle of Queenston Heights, north of Niagara Falls, as New York State militiamen watched from the American side of the border, saying they had not signed up to invade anyone but only to defend their own homes. Coles' president needed him.[19]

It all wore on him. The work in wartime Washington would be unrelenting. He fell ill in the fall of 1812, and went home to Green Mountain to try to recover, with little luck. He wrote to Madison that September, saying it would be three to four weeks before he'd be well enough to return to Washington.[20] In November, back in Washington, he wrote to tell his brother John that the ulcer on his chest was not going away, despite treatments by two prominent doctors.[21] He languished through the winter, until, at Dolley Madison's insistence, he headed to Philadelphia to be treated by the Philip Syng, the renowned Dr. Physick, who removed two growths from his lower colon.[22] It was a major operation, and Coles stayed in Philadelphia for weeks, writing Dolley Madison in late May to say he expected to be fully recovered in two weeks.[23] That summer, he fell ill yet again, and in September, Dr. Physick repeated the operation, leaving Coles feeling little better.[24] He moped for months, still complaining of feeling bad into the fall. When, frustrated, feeble, he would finally ask the president to relieve him of his post and name a replacement, Dolley Madison replied that her husband "can do very well without a secretary until your health is reestablished," sounding the usual mix of reassurance and anxiety that marked so many of her letters to Coles. Suspecting that what ailed Coles was as much his frustrated desire to head west and free his slaves as anything else (a suspicion no doubt later confirmed by Coles' letter to her son, Payne Todd, which concluded "I must therefore in the spring, however reluctantly, retire to the woods of the west"), the First Lady reminded her young cousin that "the winter is not the season for emigration, so that next summer you will be better able to make your election—to go or not to go."[25]

But the war was on and his place was Washington, even then not a place or situation to foster patience and calm. Why was it, he complained to his brother John as the war clouds gathered, "that so much time should be lost in useless debate, to gratify the vanity of self-imagined orators"? [26] As the war came and continued, ingloriously for the United States, his frustration mounted. "Every bone," he said of Madison's antiwar opponents, "their public speeches, in their prints in all their proceedings, clearly show their desire of blowing up in the tempest of discord and Civil War."[27] He would growl to his friends that Congress, balking at appropriating war funds, had acted "ever since the war commenced, on the very verge of treason, throwing every difficulty in the way." And yet, for all he felt Congress had collapsed into a morass of pointless argument and inaction, he kept faith: "Great as are our difficulties, they can all be surmounted.... The pure, highminded spirit which led to war has not been and cannot be killed, either by disaster or difficulties."[28] This is, it is needless to say, not exactly the voice of a young man who will respect legislators and the lobby men who whisper to them in the corridors of power, whether a marble Capitol or a frontier State House built of rough-sawn timber.

The war did not go well. Victory at the Thames River in western Ontario did not offset the fiasco of that autumn's failed attempt on Montreal. By December, the British had taken Fort Niagara, on the American side of the Niagara River, and would hold that key choke-point on the Lakes until the war's end. Andrew Jackson's push for Mobile, Pensacola and the British-held Gulf Coast of Florida was stalled when the Creek Indians of Alabama took up arms and rose against the United States. A British blockade of the Chesapeake and Delaware Bays bit hard. In August of 1814, a British force of 4,000 soldiers took Washington, and burned the Capitol and White House before contemptuously returning to their ships and leaving the ruined city behind. The president and Dolley Madison had had to flee. On Doctor Physick's instructions, Coles was away from the city, still trying to recover from his lingering illness.[29]

His absences weighed on the president and his wife. While Coles recuperated from his second operation in Philadelphia and was beginning to think yet again of resigning his post and heading west, Dolley Madison anxiously wrote him that a mutual friend had assured her husband "that you will soon be well in spite of yourself. We indulge this pleasing hope in addition to that of your remaining with us to the last ... there are none who feel a more affectionate interest in you than Mr. Madison and myself. I hope you will believe that such is our regard and esteem for you that we should consider your leaving us a misfortune."[30] As fond of his cousin as she was of him, Coles, too, had grown close to the president after years of working by his side. "Few men possessed so rich a flow of the language, or so great a fund of amusing anecdotes, which were made the more interesting from their being well-timed and well-told," he would describe his mentor, many years later.[31]

Coles was close enough to Madison to be able to say things to that that prim and very proper statesman that others could not: "On occasion of seeing a group of Negroes, some in irons, on their way to the southern market, I have taken the liberty to jeer him, by congratulating him, as chief of our great Republic that he was not then accompanied by a foreign minister & thus saved the deep mortification of witnessing such a revolting sight in the presence of the representative of a nation, less boastful perhaps of its regard for the rights of man, but more observant of them."[32]

The edge in Coles' voice here, allowed by the kind of indulgence a fond older man grants a favorite protege, reflects the unusual self assurance that would be such a strong element of Coles' personality—as well as the frustration and anger he obviously was feeling at this point because he was still unable to do anything about his slaves. The demands of the president left him little time to do much but play with ideas for how to free them or spin fantasies that somehow, someone might figure out an answer for him. It was during this time that Coles wrote to Jefferson, asking him to take a stand for a general emancipation of Virginia's slaves. "I will only add," Coles told the ex-president, "that from the time I was capable of reflecting on the nature of political society, and of the rights appertaining to man, I have not only been principled against slavery, but have had feelings so repugnant to it as to decide me not to hold them, which decision has forced me to leave my native State, and with it all my relations and friends."[33]

Well, not quite, of course. Coles lived in Washington because he held a political plum; and though he spent much of his free time in Philadelphia, his letters to his mother and sisters remained warm and friendly and carried the implicit promise of his eventual return home. In any event, he had little encouragement from Jefferson, who wrote back from Monticello, as his slaves started picking the first fruits of his orchards and hoed the weeds from his grain fields and extensive gardens, that it was heartening to learn the flame of liberty still glowed within younger Virginians. But, Jefferson continued, slaves "brought up from their infancy without necessity for thought or forecast, are by their habits rendered as incapable as children of taking care of themselves." Even worse, the great democrat added, "in the meantime they are pests in society by their idleness, and the depredations to which this leads them." Coles should, Jefferson continued, try to make sure his slaves were fed and clothed well, were protected from ill-usage and weren't worked harder than were men who were paid for their labor. "I hope then, my dear sir, you will reconcile yourself to your country and its unfortunate condition."[34]

As private secretary to the President, charged with shepherding appropriations through Congress, with managing favors to politicians in such critical states as Pennsylvania and Massachusetts, companion at the family table in the White House, perhaps it is no surprise that this young man could find it within himself to chastise a former president—but then, it was not as if he was over-awed by presidents. On an 1811 fence-mending

Left: James Madison, whom Coles served as private secretary during the War of 1812 (Library of Congress). *Right:* Dolley Madison. A cousin, Coles would maintain warm relations with her and her husband through their lives (Library of Congress).

mission for Madison in Massachusetts, Coles made a point of heading down to the seaside farming town of Quincy to see crabby old John Adams, taking it on himself to give the one former president another's—Jefferson's—views on an election Adams still felt the Virginian had unfairly won. Returning to Virginia, Coles visited Jefferson to report back. The two old enemies soon began corresponding. Coles would, in later years, claim it was he who had brought them together and convinced them to put aside old enmities.[36] True or not, the story suggests that Coles was, or at least saw himself as, an important actor in national politics.

Coles' own enemy and supposed ally, the editor Hooper Warren, would later contend that Coles "greatly magnified the importance of his office as Private Secretary and seemed to think it second only to the Presidency itself." During Coles' 1822 campaign for election as governor of Illinois, added Warren, "I had represented him, although not invidiously, as a sort of upper servant in the Presidential mansion"—but when Coles, soon after his election, asked newspaper editors to drop the title "Excellency" when referring to him, Warren pounced. He published a sarcastic little piece in the *Spectator,* reminding Edwardsville readers of an innkeeper there whose wife owned a boy slave, named Jo. "Frequently during the day, the mistress would call out 'Jo!' The boy in the street or yard, as quick as lightning, would answer 'Coming, Madam,'" as Warren told the story. Perhaps that, too, was how Coles answered his own master's wife, during his days in the White House, the editor slyly speculated. In any event, Jo was well known throughout the small town, so it must have stung, said Warren (still, decades later, obviously pleased with himself). Warren added that he could easily understand Coles' reluctance to accept the title for "the phrase 'His Excellency,' applied to himself, seems so very odd in contrast with his former position in Mr. Madison's family. But time and practice will soon make it as familiar to his ear, as the response of 'Coming Madam' was then to his tongue."[36]

Clearly, though, both of the Madisons saw Coles' role much differently. More than an aide, he is at this time a young man whose marriage Dolley tries to plot, and to whom she would turn when worried about her son, Payne, and his excesses with wine and with women. Even after the war was over, and Coles resigned his position to begin preparing for a move west, it would be to his young former secretary that Madison again would turn for a particularly delicate diplomatic mission. "Circumstances have arisen," the president wrote in a confidential note to his protege, "make it expedient to forward communication to St. Petersburg by a special hand." The allowance was $6 a day, the president thought, "be so good as to let me know as soon as you can." With nothing "to engage my attention at home," replied Coles, "and being desirous of seeing Europe, I have no objection to availing myself of this occasion to do so."[37]

Madison wanted the Russian Minister to Washington, one J.M. Daschkoff, and the Russian Consul in Philadelphia, a man named Kostoff, recalled. Kostoff had been convicted of raping a 12-year-old servant girl. Daschkoff's contention that this violated his Consul's diplomatic privilege had led the Tsar to refuse to let the U.S. Charge d'Affaires, the consul in St. Petersburg, come to see him in Moscow. It was more than a minor spat; Russia's intervention had been critical to keeping British and American diplomats negotiating during the long sessions that eventually brought an end to the War of 1812. Madison was about to send a minister to the Tsar's court, former Attorney General William Pinckney, and needed to be sure he would be received and accredited. Coles' job would be to make sure this happened, and, if possible, to get Daschkoff out of the United States. Commission in hand, Coles hastened to St. Petersburg on the U.S. warship *Prometheus*, although Madison had originally proposed he take the easier route, by commercial packet across the Atlantic, and then through London to the Continent. His haste, in any event, would soon seem pointless: Coles had to cool his heels in St. Petersburg for three months, trying not to fume over the petty officiousness of the Russian officers who kept him there—one of whom, he complained, insisted on poking a fork into the confidential letters and despatches Coles was carrying.[38] Coles passed some of the time he had to wait traveling the Russian countryside, finding that while Russian serfs could be bought and sold they were "inseparably connected with the soil" and therefore "not so much an object of traffic" subject to being torn from their spouses or children at an owner's whim. While a master could force a serf to work, "the situation of the vassals is gradually improving," and they did not have to work all the time and only for their owners. "Nor are the duties they are required to perform or the treatment they receive anything like so severe or oppressive" as American slaves. Upon his return to the United States, Coles pointedly shared his findings with his fellow Virginians.[39]

When the Tsar finally returned from a tour of Poland, at last consented to see Coles, his ire over the supposed insult to Daschkoff was apparently assuaged by the president's gesture in sending an extraordinary envoy, one whom Secretary of State James Monroe's letter of introduction carefully noted had been the president's private secretary and was a "very respectable and amiable young man." Dropping any hint of his own impatience, Coles was able to make his case that Kostoff's conviction was not intended as an insult to Russia, and would delicately point out that Daschkoff's own behavior in Washington left much to be desired. "His conduct in relation to the late war between the United States and England was that which seemed most displeasing to those connected with the court, whose feelings, it is well known are not at all favorable to England," Coles reported. The Tsar took the hint. He politely asked Coles how Daschkoff should be punished; Coles demurred and asked only that the minister be recalled. And so he was.[40]

Coles returned to the United States by way of England, after traveling overland through Poland, Germany and France, a ten-month trip. While in England, he would meet Morris Birkbeck, of Wanborough, in Surrey, an early experimenter with new techniques of farming, whose writing on scientific agriculture—and on the inequities of English land law and England's antique limits on the right to vote—had won a trans-Atlantic renown. A tenant, farming an astonishing 1,500 acres on a long lease, who despite his wealth and wide following as an agricultural expert, was not entitled to vote in England simply because he did not own his land, Birkbeck, though in his fifties, planned to uproot himself for America and its democracy. "He took me over every part of the estate, and pointed out and explained everything peculiar, or in which the English agriculturalists excelled," Coles recalled many years later. "With a heart beaming with the republican and philanthropical feelings congenial with our political Institutions, it was natural that he should be partial to the United States."[41]

The two had much to talk about. By the time they first met, both men already had been thinking hard about the Illinois country. Coles had been there once already, seeking a place to settle his slaves, Birkbeck was planning to sail soon to America to scout for land for a new farming colony in the west. Both detested slavery.

More than that, their anti-slavery views, grounded as they were in their most basic political views, were distinctive at a time when abolitionist sentiment in Britain and the eastern United States was still largely a Quaker phenomenon—although the camp meetings of the southern frontier beyond the Appalachians (such as the great Camp Ridge, Kentucky, revival of 1801, at which more than 10,000 gathered), had already sparked a slow rising of religious fervor that would soon flower into a Second Great Awakening that would energize the abolitionist, temperance and social reform movements that swept the northern states in the 1830s. But though it would be a decade before northern believers took up the cause that already preoccupied Coles and Birkbeck, a linking of religious faith and opposition to slavery was occurring in the obscure and still somewhat inchoate transformation of church life on the frontier. In those camp meetings, earnest Methodist circuit-riders and Baptist preachers declared that believers need not resign themselves to the idea that a Calvinist God determined their destiny on Earth and their fate in the afterlife, but rather that people could exercise their own free will to find salvation and to do good. In the Scripture, as many newly inspired frontier men and women read it, there was no justification for owning human beings. Instead, as the Awakening's greatest preacher, Charles Grandison Finney, said: the Bible demanded that "to the universal reformation of the world [true Christians] stand committed."[42] In contrast, a pastor from the Calvinist tradition, Robert Finley, had just a few months before Coles and Birkbeck met given form to a different kind of Christian vision for American slaves. Joining forces with the American political leaders who, hoping for a way to finesse the growing strain between free North and slave South, had by this time started pushing for sending freed slaves back to Africa, Finley organized the American Colonization Society. It was formed in late December 1816, at a meeting chaired by Henry Clay and involving James Monroe, Andrew Jackson and Daniel Webster. The federal government would soon contribute $100,000 to the cause—but despite the prospect of a subsidy to get his slaves out of Virginia, and the temptation of a painless way, sanctioned by some of the most respectable public figures of day, to solve the problem of how to free his slaves, Coles would remain focused for the next few years on taking his slaves west, and settling them as free men and women on the frontier.[43]

In the end, chewing over where and how to settle a group in the west—whether English tenant farmers or American slaves—to turn them into republican landowners, Coles and Birkbeck would spend five days together, forging a firm friendship. Coles seems to have convinced Birkbeck that Illinois was a likely spot, and the Englishman and his friend George Flower later that year would end up buying 26,400 acres in Edwards County, in eastern Illinois, for the settlement. Flower would return to England to recruit emigrants, while Birkbeck churned out two promotional books, *Notes on a Journey in America* in 1817 and *Letters from Illinois* in 1818, which painted a glowing picture of prospects on the prairies and which, despite somewhat sour ripostes from William Cobbett and other less prominent pamphleteers, would encourage tens of thousands to migrate to Illinois. Coles would later claim he had convinced Birkbeck to look at Illinois; both men were attracted because, they thought, Illinois was Free Soil territory, and both men hated slavery. "I saw two female slaves and their children sold by auction in the street," Birkbeck would write of a visit to Richmond, hosted by some friends of Coles.' "I could hardly bear to see them handled and examined like cattle; and when I heard their sons and saw the big tears rolling down their cheeks at the thoughts of being separated, I could not refrain from weeping with them.... A traveler told me that he saw, two weeks ago, one hundred and twenty sold by auction, in the streets of Richmond; and that they filled the air with their lamentations."[44]

Kindred spirits, Coles and Birkbeck would meet again, in Illinois, as embattled allies.

Chapter 4

To the West

West of the Wabash, the new post road across Illinois grew menacing. The sunless forest, the empty prairies, the glum, heavily armed men at the crude log inns terrified many a traveler. Tales of murder and robbery filtered east, tales of sullen tavern-keepers who let dirt-floored rooms by night and gallop on ahead before the next dawn to wait in ambush for their guests. The wise emigrant listened carefully to these stories and kept a watchful eye out for these men. Emerging from the dark woods into the clearing of one inn, the traveler Richard Lee Mason remembered looking carefully for one such innkeeper: "Saw his wife, a handsome, young dejected-looking woman, who appeared very uneasy at her husband's being inquired for by a man almost as well armed ... saw a bloody cravat at the end of the log of which his house was built."[1]

It took months to get to this empty land. Coles, for instance, riding in a horse and buggy, of all things, took much of the spring and all of the summer of 1815 on his second trip west seeking "a spot on which to locate myself for life"—and discouraging it was, too.[2] His friend, Secretary of State James Monroe, "disapproves of it in toto," a mutual friend relayed to Coles, warning that the soon-to-be-president felt sure his young protege "will not be satisfied ... to set down in the midst of rough unpolished people, perfectly uncongenial to you in habits and manners." Even as he set out for the west, Coles found, for all he felt he needed to take his slaves west if he were to free them, that "my partiality for my relations & friends ... still continues to perplex and disturb me."[3] It was not the best frame of mind for finding a place for which he would have to pull up all his roots. And as he trekked on, week after week after month after month, he would have little luck in this search. "I have seen no country yet I should like to make my residence," he wrote to his brother John that June; on the way back to Virginia in September, he complained to his sister Sally: "I know not where to settle myself or even if I give over my western views, I know not what to do with myself," while to his brother Isaac he complained, "I have not get been able to find any country N.W. of the Ohio River which was healthy, fertile and well-watered."[4]

But he pushed on, heading for St. Louis and a boat that would carry him down the Mississippi River to New Orleans, where he planned to purchase passage by ship back to Washington.

What he found on the Illinois shore opposite the then-tiny river port was the lush American Bottom. Those flat bottomlands near St. Louis looked a little more promising—a country where the German traveler Ferdinand Ernst would note, "I found maize from 12 to 15 feet high on an average. The gardens which have sufficient age for fruit settings are luxuriant with peach trees and other fruit trees ... so full that branches have to be propped." But, in at least a purely business sense, Coles at this time seemed more intrigued by the possibilities on the other side of the Mississippi. He bought land, in partnership with two of his brothers: 6,000 acres in Lincoln County, Missouri, crowing that "10,000 dollars in the hands of only a tolerably judicious man will be five years be worth 100,000 dollars."[5] Though he wrote to his friend Nicholas Biddle of the pleasing prospects in the American Bottom, saying that "I still think it is very probable I may yet make it the place of my residence," he also seemed inclined to take up Biddle's suggestion that he should become a landlord, not a farmer. If Illinois was the promised land, its promise was, at best, a whispered one—it would be another two years before Coles would make his first, tentative purchase of Illinois land, two small tracts to the south of St. Louis and near what was then the capital of the territory, Kaskaskia. Perhaps even then he was thinking as much about politics as planting. "A man must have some occupation, something to engage his attention, or else he cannot be happy," he wrote to Biddle. All in all, having seen Illinois now, he was, he added, "disappointed in the impressions I had form[ed] of it."[6]

What Coles had found in Illinois at the end of his six-month journey west was a raw frontier, tiny settlements strung out along the Ohio, Wabash and Mississippi rivers, smallholdings cleared, sort of, in the dreary woods and swamps. When the road through Illinois broke out of the woods, it took emigrants through a kind of country few had ever seen before: the open grasslands of the prairie, "where one all day long sees no house, no, not even a tree, so that protected from the burning heat of the sun, one could rest in its shade," the German traveler Frederick Hollman would record in his diary. "If the traveler from the coast of the Atlantic Ocean to this point has grown weary of the endless journey in the forests then he believes himself transferred to another region of the world as soon as he crosses the Wabash."[7] As Mason, Hollman and many another traveler found, the wilderness of central Illinois on either side of the trace linking

Vincennes, in Indiana, with Saint Louis, in Missouri, was forbidding and forlorn, with only a handful of newly-cleared farms or "groceries" (what frontier Illinoisans called their general stores-cum-drinking places)—and many of them not places a stranger might care to stay. "Rutherford and three sturdy fellows, armed, entered the house, all half-drunk," Mason recalled of one such place. "Some of their private consultations were overheard. Robbery and murder was contemplated. They would frequently whisper and pinch each other, wink, eye us ... about the break of day the signal of rising was given by our visitors. We were on our feet in a minute, and our hands on our arms."[8] The newly opened country, in fact, had not yet been completely relinquished by the Indian peoples of the Illinois River valley (which would happen only with the cession in 1819 of the claims of the Kickapoo people).[9]

Coles shared neither the desperation nor the hope that led settlers down those dangerous trails through the empty, eerie prairie land. The Virginians, Carolinians and Kentuckians—camp meeting people—who struggled to carve out farms on the Illinois frontier (giving it its markedly Southern feel) stuck to the woods and bottomlands instead, resignedly trying to make do. They thought the grassy stretches of prairie were desert, and in the shadowy, swampy bottomlands they favored, felt far less optimistic about their prospects than the Yankee settlers, bit by the "Ohio Fever," who were filling wealthier Ohio, and just beginning to eye the Illinois grasslands. The fever that the Illinois settlers got, they called the "Illinois Shakes," the ague, "a terror to newcomers," the bane of those already struggling to scrape by, making them pale and yellow, the way frostbite does. It was almost emblematic of bottomlands life. "You felt languid, stupid and sore," an old settler recalled, "Your back was out of fix and appetite was in worse condition than your back. Your head ached, you thought the sun had a kind of sickly shine about it. About this time you came to the conclusion that you would not accept the whole state of Illinois as a gift."[10]

Sick or not, though, the newcomer had to throw up a shack to live in, clear a patch to plant in and somehow or other, get a crop in the ground. "Frequently a little wet smoky cabin or hut is erected with the floor scarcely separated from the ground and admitting the damp and unwholesome air," the missionary John Mason Peck remembered, "All hands that can work are impelled to labor beyond their strength, and more land is cleared and planted with corn than is well tended." They were sloppy little fields, corn sprouting among the stumps and dying trees: "They have two modes of clearing land; one by cutting the trees round, so as to kill them, and afterwards clearing away the underwood," Peck explained, adding that it was for those who "to use their phrase, are 'weak-handed.'" Less common was cut the trees, drag them into heaps, and burn them—"this operation is almost always the subject of what they term a frolic or a bee," Peck remarked, and it was a procedure that produced one of the few items Illinois exported in its early days: potash, used to take the sting out of acid soil. There was little enough else to sell. Few had the cash to buy tools or food or to hire hands; those who did, most likely had only the shoddy shin-plasters and yellow-backs issued by the wildcat banks of Ohio, Kentucky and eventually Illinois, paper worth only a fraction of its face value when it came time to head to town and pick over the dry goods, hardware and tools in a musty little general store, with its tiny selection of goods costing many times more than back east. It was far from the kind of country life Coles would have know growing up in Albemarle County.[11]

Still, the settlers came. "They came in an old-fashioned Tennessee wagon ... women, children, beds, buckets, tubs, old fashioned chairs ... a chicken coop, with two or three hens and a jolly rooster for a start, tied on behind, while under the wagon trotted a full-blooded long-eared hound ... the boys walked ahead, with rifles on their shoulders, at half mast."[12] Others, like Braxton Parrish, a North Carolina youth who would spend his last two dollars on a Bible for his new wife, would have only a "wallet"—two connected sacks, one slung over his back the other hanging over his chest. "When I arrived here I had but 18¾ cents in money—it troubled me to know how to dispose of it to the best advantage, more than any money has troubled me since," he remembered.

> I cleared my own farm; cut and split the rails and carried them on my shoulder and made a fence, as I had no wagon to haul them. There were no plows to be had any nearer than Shawneetown, fifty miles away, and I had no money to buy one had they been nearer. I borrowed a 'bull-tongue' plow ... it had no iron about it ... for harness I had a shuck collar, hickory bark traces, raw deerskin back band, and hickory bark lines. With this rigging I broke my ground, and covered my corn with a cooper's adze, having no better tool for the purpose.[13]

"They are," wrote Coles' English friend Morris Birkbeck, "a migrating people, and even when in prosperous circumstances, can contemplate a change in situation, which under our old establishments and fixed habits, none, but the most enterprising, would venture upon, when urged by adversity."[14] For the better off, men who weren't as desperate as Parrish was, what impelled them west was the chance to sell their Kentucky or Tennessee or Piedmont holdings to the monied slave-holders looking for new land to plant in cotton. Poor or not-so-poor, they came to Illinois for cheap land—the same thing that intrigued Coles, in part—for public land cost just $2 an acre, a quarter down, the rest due over four years for most, with outright grants in the vast and barely settled Military Tract for ex-soldiers. And when they came, many found good, black earth; grain grew with little effort, orchards flourished. "Such is its luxuriancy that one acre in that bottom has yielded its cultivator 110 bushels of Indian corn ... a more congenial

MAKING A CLEARING.

Settlers clearing a farm in frontier Illinois (Northern Illinois University Library).

soil for general cultivation I believe no where exists, it may be called the Elysium of America," wrote one correspondent to the *Illinois Intelligencer*, shortly after Coles' 1815 trip, describing the American Bottom.[15] Pigs and cattle wandered free, growing plump on the mast of the forest floor and grasses of the prairies. "Hogs will live & get fat in the woods & Prairies. I have seen some fat upon Hickory nuts, Acorns, Pecans & Walnuts, as ever I did those that were fat[ten]ed upon corn ... there are places in this territory where cattle & horses will live all winter & be in good order without feeding ... most of the people cut no hay for their cattle & Horses," the new settler Gershom Flagg wrote to his brother back east.[16] Illinois was a place for the self-sufficient, Thomas Ford would recall: "[T]he farmer's sheep furnished wool for his winter clothing, he raised cotton and flax.... His wife and daughters spun, wove and made it into garments. A little copperas and indigo, with the bark of trees, furnished dyestuffs ... and a log cabin made entirely of wood, without glass, nails, hinges or locks, furnished the resident of many a contented and happy family."[17]

It was not a land that needed slaves, and that suited the Southerners who made up the majority of Illinois' first settlers just fine. "I had a young and growing family of children, two sons, and four daughters, was poor, owned a little farm of 150 acres," recalled the Methodist circuit rider Peter Cartwright, writing of his decision to move from Kentucky to Illinois in 1823:

> I saw, or thought I saw, clear indications of Providence that I should leave my comfortable little home, and move to a free state or territory, for the following reasons: First, I would get entirely clear of the evil of slavery. Second, I could raise my children to work where work was not thought a degradation. Third, I believed I could better my temporal circumstances and procure lands for my children as they grew up.[18]

Cartwright was not the only young Southern farmer detesting slavery and looking west: "[O]f my neighbors, friends and kindred, nearly one half have left the state since I was old enough to remember," the North Carolinian Benjamin Hedrick would remember. "Many is the time I have stood by the loaded emigrant wagon and given the parting hand to those whose faces I was never to look upon again. They were going to seek homes in the free west knowing as they did that free and slave labor could not both exist and prosper in the same community."[19] Franklin county settler Parrish was even blunter: "[B]eing disgusted with slavery, I wanted a home in a free state."[20]

But slowly, as the forest traces turned into something more like roads, and as more and more steamboats ventured down the Ohio River, new kinds of settlers began to drift into the Illinois country, with new kinds of aspirations. A handful of men, as Coles himself would eventually do, came with money in hand and ambition in mind. More and more were coming from the states of the northeast: Pennsylvanians, "Yorkers" and even a few New Englanders. Their habits, their speech, their politics did not make a smooth fit; though a young nation, the United States already seethed with ill-feelings between Yankee and Southerner. These new settlers were men in a hurry; they were not men to shoulder their own axes and sleep in mud while clearing a small field and throwing up a rough cabin—they dreamed on a different scale. In Illinois, as in Kentucky, Ohio and the backcountry South, they simply paid for land others cleared. "The improvements of a backwoodsman are usually confined to building a rude log cabin, clearing and fencing a small piece of ground for raising Indian corn. A horse, a cow, a few hogs and some poultry comprise his livestock, and his farther operations are performed with his rifle," said the Scots economist James Flint, after a three-year tour of the western frontier. In time, Flint added, came the commercial farmer, a man who (as Coles was planning) "immediately builds a larger barn than the former and then a brick or frame house. He either pulls down the dwelling of his predecessor or converts it into a stable." Such a venturer "fattens cattle for the market and perhaps erects a flour-mill, or a saw-mill or a distillery. Farmers of this description are frequently partners in the banks, members of the State Assembly, or of Congress or Justices of the Peace."[21] Elias Pym Fordham, an English settler, noticed these new emigrants, too; a group, he said, "composed of enterprising men from Kentucky and the Atlantic States. This class consists of Young Doctors, Lawyers, storekeepers, farmers, mechanics & c., who found towns, speculate in land, and begin the fabric of society." These men looked for help clearing and draining the wet bottomlands by the rivers that they favored, and they looked for hands to mind the large herds of cattle and hogs they were starting. They had different concerns, different needs and different politics from the older, southern settlers, and they would be expressed in surprising ways.[22]

Some emigrants, of course, did not come willingly. When Ninian Edwards, one of those enterprising Kentuckians, swapped his post as chief justice of that commonwealth's appeals court for a colleague's unwanted appointment as governor of the new Territory of Illinois, he came to the country with his slaves in tow. Son of an influential Maryland lawyer and planter, who "until he was twenty-one or twenty-two led a dissolute life; he indulged in dissipation and gambling to an extent that alarmed his friends," Edwards became a legislator, a leading western lawyer, and a wealthy man. By the time he was 31, he was sitting on Kentucky's highest court. He was a man whose friends loved him for his generosity and his kindnesses, whose enemies detested him for his double-dealing and high-handed manners.

Edwards (soon to dub himself "The Old Ranger" for his role as territorial governor during the Indian skirmishes of the War of 1812) would always swear he hated slavery for all that he owned slaves. "I am no advocate of slavery," he wrote, in vetoing legislation that would have repealed a law allowing slaves to be brought to Illinois and indentured there. "If it depended on my vote alone, it should never have been admitted into any State or Territory not already cursed with so great an evil." At the time he owned two dozen men, women and children. As territorial governor, as leader of a political faction, as a U.S. Senator who toyed, relatively ineptly, with king-making, Edwards would play a major part in the first Congressional battles over slavery, when the issue would erupt over the question of the admission of Missouri to the union, and the Illinois statesman would help derail an effort to ban slaves from the lands beyond the Mississippi River—a battle that would later set the stage for Illinois' own bitter fight over human bondage. For Edwards, generosity and his opposition to slavery, in any event, were not enough to keep him from carefully registering indentures on the slaves he brought with him from Kentucky: the court house records for Randolph County show him registering 15-year-old Maria to bind her for a term of service of 45 years; another slave, 21-year-old Jesse, was bound for a term of 35 years, as was 23-year-old Rose. He would also take care to register 18-month-old Joseph after bringing his mother to Illinois, thereby binding him to service until he turned 35.[23]

The peculiar status of Edwards' slaves (and hundreds more brought by the other Southern planters and lawyers venturing into the Illinois Country in the first decades of the 19th century) reflected peculiar law—a body of law that, as events would prove, Coles may not have fully understood. Part of the old Northwest Territory, ceded by Virginia to the new national government in 1784, Illinois' basic law before statehood in 1818 remained the Ordinance of 1787, which Coles would argue in a lengthy 1856 paper on its history, "finally passed Congress with such extraordinary unanimity" and "ordains that there shall neither be slavery nor involuntary servitude" north of the Ohio River. The Congress, in fact, went even further than Thomas Jefferson had proposed, Coles would note, since Jefferson had proposed delaying the ban on slavery until after 1800, a suggestion which was cut out of the Ordinance as it was enacted.[24] But the Ordinance did nothing to change the status of the slaves already in Illinois. Men and women had labored in bondage there for more than six decades when Congress enacted the Ordinance, the children and grandchildren of slaves owned by the French farmers who drifted into the Illinois country, especially once the French colony of Louisiana formalized its control of the area in 1717. Although some of the French, in the words of

Gov. Thomas Ford, "made no improvements in anything," spending spring and fall "paddling their canoes ... in pursuit of deer, fur and wild fowl," others buckled down to farming—farming with slaves, that is. In the years before the American Revolution, the British Royal Army Captain Philip Pittman mentions a M. Balet, the richest man in the Illinois country, with 100 slaves "besides hired white people constantly employed," as well as a M. Beauvais, with 80 slaves on 240 arpents (a bit less than 300 acres) of land. Of 1,600 people living in Illinois in the 1770s, about 600 were slaves.[25] For the French community, large sums of money were potentially at issue, if the Ordinance had really freed their slaves, as at least some in Congress had wanted. They found reassurance in the Ordinance's second article, declaring that "no man shall be deprived of his liberty or his property," which was read as protecting the French settlers' property in slaves. More than that, even, for the political leaders of the Territory felt it protected a supposed property interest in the children of those slaves. From there, it seemed a trivial step to feel the law could protect the property interest of wealthy new settlers in the slaves that they were bringing in. While the intent of Congress seems clear in the Ordinance's sixth article, which flatly declared that "there shall be neither Slavery nor involuntary Servitude"— and was clear enough to Congresses that rejected a series of petitions from slave-holding westerners demanding its repeal—by the times Coles and his freedmen would arrive at their new farms in Madison County, Illinois, there would be two more generations of men and women and children held in bondage. The French settlers "being ignorant of the English language and laws ... continued to hold and treat their late slaves as if the Ordinance had not emancipated them," Coles said. They were allowed to do, he said, because "many of the officers in whose hands the law had placed the power, were themselves claimants of the negro services, and interested in continuing the then existing state of things."[26]

By 1800, census takers found 135 slaves remaining in Illinois and Indiana, then joined in a single Territory of Indiana, a sharp decline from the number that had been living in the Illinois country when Pittman did his survey. With the American Revolution, many of the French settlers decamped for the other side of the Mississippi River. "This state of things continued for a long time, in consequence of the ignorance of the negroes of the English language and of the mode of obtaining their rights, and from fear of punishment if they attempted it, and also, from the odium which attached to those who should aid them," Coles would remark, four decades later. The laws of the Territory provided that slaves might not leave their masters' lands without permission, that they could be whipped for laziness, that anyone who hid a slave must pay the master a dollar a day for each day the slave or indentured servant was so protected, and that to trade with a slave risked a fine of four times the value of the items or service sold. "The long and extraordinary acquiescence in the continuation of the bondage of the French slaves (as they were then called) encouraged those who can always find reasons for doing what will promote their own immediate interest, or what they like to do," wrote Coles.[27]

That interest was to own slaves. The number of slaves in Illinois, now separated from Indiana, rose to 168 by the Census of 1810, as wealthy Southern office-seekers and power brokers like Edwards started arriving.[28] They were men who, like Edwards, as the political need arose, could contend they opposed slavery and yet with apparently clear conscience legally bind their indentured servants for 30, 40 or 50 years of unpaid labor. They blithely ignored territorial, and later state, laws that sought however ineffectually to contain the abuse inherent when men own other human beings: The law said men over 35 years of age, and women over 32, could not be held in bondage; yet one Jack Bonaparte in 1816 did "agree and freely oblige himself to serve ... Joshua Vaughan, his heirs and assigns ninety-nine years as a good and faithful servant"—in the margin of the deed book recording this, the Madison County clerk, perhaps sarcastically, jotted the annotation "Jack Bonaparte to be a free man on the 15th of March, 1915." Slave-owners bought children, such as Frank, 13, whose 22-year indenture was recorded the same year as Jack Bonaparte bound himself to servitude. That same year, 15-year-old Sam bound himself to serve 50 years, as did 16-year-old Willis the following year. The year after that, 17-year-old Peter and 24-year-old Dilsey indentured themselves for terms of 99 years, as did Sarah, 19, the year after that. Slave-holders also registered babies and children under 12, and bills of sale recording the purchase of women's indentures made clear that their children were part of the deal. When Lucy, 28, bound herself for 20 years, she also bound her seven-year-old son Frank, six-year-old Reuben and two-year-old Silvey to serve until they turned 35.[29]

In Illinois, it soon was clear, a black skin increasingly meant bondage. Freedmen had to record their certificates of emancipation in the county courthouses; those who could not were held and advertised as available for hire from the county for a year's service. The Black Code, as refined, made clear that indentured servants, like the French slaves, could be whipped if they were idle and could not leave their masters' farms without permission; if they did, they were obliged to serve an extra two days for every day they were away. It was a felony to hide a runaway servant. They "were to be punished with thirty-five lashes for being found ten miles from home without a pass from their master." A landowner could give slaves or indentured servants ten lashes on their bare backs for coming onto his property without permission; those landowners who might have been tempted to allow slaves to gather on their land to dance and make merry were to be fined $20. "It was made the duty of all sheriffs, coroners, judges and justices of the peace, on view of such an assemblage, to commit the slaves to jail, and to order each one of them to be whipped, not exceeding thirty-nine stripes, on the bare back," Governor Ford recalled. Any man who brought slaves to Illinois in order to set them free could be fined $200 for each person emancipated.[30]

By 1820, there would be more than 900 slaves and indentured servants in Illinois, roughly two percent of the state's population and a more than fourfold increase in number in just a decade. The tally of free blacks, however, declined from more than 600 in 1810 to about 450. (Eight of them were Coles' former slaves: Robert and Kate Crawford, Kate and Ralph Crawford's four children, sister Polly Crawford along with Thomas Cobb and his wife, Nancy Gaines.) The trend was quite clear. Its meaning for Coles' freemen would be, as well: Cheated by Coles' neighbors, paid for the hard work they did on those neighbors' farms and brickyards with almost-worthless paper notes, they had had to turn to Coles for the grubstakes they needed to turn the land he had given them into farms. Madison County, at that time home to just 33 other "free people of color" and another 77 slaves, did not welcome them and would eventually sue Coles for bringing them to the farms in Madison County's Pin Oak Township.[31]

Coles missed the uncertain legal state of free blacks in his 1815 trip to the west. The concerns he had about Illinois and the west did not seem to include the status of slaves there. He still seemed completely reassured that they could live the life of free farmers there; instead, he worried more about how he would afford life in the west and what that life might be like, especially on a frontier even more isolated than his father and mother first found, getting started back on Green Mountain. But Ohio was too costly, nearly as bad as Kentucky. Indiana and southern Illinois were isolated swampy woods, poorly drained, hard to clear. Missouri, where the uncertain writ of the Northwest Ordinance did not run, was clearly headed for admission to the Union as a slave state. It looked as if it would have to be the American Bottom. "Were I a married man," he wrote plaintively to Biddle, "I think I could set myself down and be very happy in the Illinois Territory, especially if I could induce some clever sociable fellows to accompany and live near me." That prospect seemed dim, though. Nor, for that matter, was he courting any woman who might want to venture to the west: country girls were more practical than city women, he had advised his friend Tench Ringgold; but Coles himself saw sophisticated, intelligent women as more likely life partners for himself. "Whether I shall dwell in the wilderness, or abide in the city," he wrote to another friend, "is still to be decided by future circumstances."[32]

Was he just dithering, unable, unwilling to take a decisive step? His hesitancy, his clearly-stated preference for the city life he had come to enjoy in Washington, Philadelphia and Boston, suggest he felt himself cut out for a better life than scraping his livelihood from an Illinois farm. There is the slightest sense of, what?—perhaps some would call it snobbery? Or perhaps that is just a little unfair. Coles was clear-eyed enough to see how hard, how grindingly, unendingly hard, life on a frontier farm could be; clear-eyed enough, too, to sense that, even from the tamer, no-longer-frontier fields of Rockfish, he had not shown himself to be the best of farmers. He had hoped to sell his farm in 1810, though not quite willing enough to do so for a price one third of what his brother Isaac figured his own farm was worth—but then Isaac never got his price, either, giving up in 1819 and relying instead on the retained profits from his years of running Enniscorthy to make his own flier in St. Louis real estate. Edward Coles was able to cash out only because his brother Walter agreed to buy him out. How long it took to convince him to do that, how hard he had to argue for it, the family's remaining letters offer not even the smallest hint.[33]

While he pondered, came the commission to Moscow and his visit on the way back to the United States with Birkbeck, who was becoming an enthusiast for Illinois and its prairies—"rich natural meadow," he opined, where "in their irregular outline of woodland and their undulating surface, these tracts of natural meadow exhibit every beauty, fresh from the hand of nature"—a land for free men to farm and prosper by virtue of their own work, not the sweat of slaves. Memories of his 1815 trip fading, the Illinois that Coles contemplated from afar in 1817 might well have seemed intriguing in a way it could never have before. Perhaps it isn't too far a stretch to wonder whether the prairies, or the memory of them, reminded him of the sweeping lawns and tiny islands of trees that had become the favored style of grand garden in England; surely, they seemed to remind enough Englishmen of lush, Old World manor parks: "Bruised by the brushwood and exhausted by the extreme heat we almost despaired when ... a beautiful prairie suddenly opened to our eyes," the almost-giddy English traveler George Flower would write, "under the warm light of an afternoon's summer sun, its indented and irregular outline of wood ... clumps of oaks of centuries growth, its tall grass, with seed stalks from six to ten feet high waving in a gentle breeze."[34]

Or maybe it was less about looking back than looking forward. Barely settled but now a stage on which a nation's passions for wealth and anger over missed chances played out, Illinois was beginning to look like a place where ambitious young men, like Coles, could make things happen, in ways they could no longer have done back east. By the time Coles had returned from Europe late in 1817, knowing by then (and at last) that "I could encounter anything sooner than hold slaves," the frenzied race that would give Illinois its statehood had started.[35]

It started almost on a whim—or perhaps a fit of pique. Upset at failing to win President James Monroe's nod to become Secretary of the Territory of Alabama, the young Illinois lawyer Daniel Cook grew sick of hanging around in Washington for a plum and stalked back to Illinois, grumbling, "I am advised by my own judgment ... to return to the West, and remain there until an opportunity presents itself for my advancement."[36] He burned to do great things. He always had. Ambition had led Cook, as a teen-age boy, to reject the soft spot his father had found for him with an eastern Kentucky storekeeper; ambition, and a canny eye, had directed him to the law office of John Pope, then among the most prominent lawyers in that commonwealth. Ambition had transformed the young clerk into a politician of rare ability, a small, proud man who stood erect and whose kind and sincere nature gave "his manners a grace and charm which the highest breeding will not always give."[37] His urgent ambition, perhaps somehow knowing what he himself could not, which was how short a time he would have to act upon his plans, could hardly bear to wait. Within days of his return to Kaskaskia late in the autumn of 1817, the young lawyer had declared war on the territorial form of government for Illinois. "We are laboring under so many of the grievances of a territorial, or semi monarchial government," he grumbled in the *Illinois Intelligencer*, the newspaper he had helped found before heading off to seek his fortune in Washington.[38] A week later, he was thundering: "Crimes of the blackest dye (even murder itself) have defied [the territory's] feeble powers and laughed in guilty triumph at its suffering victims. Honest labor has had the bread taken out of its mouth, and injuries of all kinds have implored relief in vain."[39] Within three weeks after the would-be Territorial Secretary of Alabama had fired off his first blast against the "semi monarchial" territorial government, Cook had inspired the legislature, already seething quietly over the antics of Territorial Governor Ninian Edwards, and his delight in exercising his unchecked veto over their acts. The legislators fired off a Memorial to Congress that complained that Illinois' territorial status was "a species of despotism in direct hostility with the principles of a republican government" and urging that it "ought to exist no longer than absolute necessity may require."[40]

The isolated people of the Illinois Territory had not so far been much troubled by the limitations of their government, except, possibly, for those few who had the evidently frustrating experience of trying to settle disputes in the rudimentary courts. Impatient judges on infrequent tours of the circuits, accompanied by members of the tiny Bar of often ill-prepared and poorly-educated lawyers, made going to law a frustrating, unsatisfactory experience. The state of the courts was a sore point for those farmers or town merchants who felt the need of them. But few did. And few farmers were much troubled by the haphazard tax collections of the territorial government, or of the yearly call to pitch in and repair the public roads. Crimes were a matter for a posse, not police. While politics was always fine entertainment on the frontier, the settlers of Illinois seemed little bothered by the notion that the limited powers of government had a real impact on their daily lives. Statehood had not even been a subject for speech-making in the elections of 1816.[41]

But now that the harvest, a good one for once, was in, and now that the settlers could give themselves a break from the heavy work of clearing fields in the forests, they found they rather liked the idea of a State of Illinois. They had, they told themselves, as much right as any to run their own affairs, agreeing with Cook's regular diatribes on Illinoisans' subservience to the national government. The courthouse gangs of lawyers, merchants, and, above all, land speculators, meanwhile, quickly stepped to the fore. All saw opportunity in statehood. Almost all felt that opportunity depended on allowing slavery—the leaders of both major political factions, Gov. Edwards and his arch-rival, Judge Jesse B. Thomas, brought their slaves with them to Illinois. The biggest enterprise in the state, the Saline River salt works, employed as many as 2,000 slaves at a time, most of them hired from their owners across the Ohio River in Kentucky. Their job was boiling down the weak brine from the area's salt springs in huge black iron kettles, each large enough to hold 100 gallons, standing in long rows over trenches of fire that burned day in and day out. It was hot, hard work in a malarial area. As far as Illinoisans were concerned, it was work too unhealthy for a white man to do. The salt works were, far and away, the most important enterprise in the state, producing 200,000 to 300,000 bushels of salt a year, a critically important item for the meat-packing business, farther up the Ohio, as well as for frontier settlers hoping to lay in supplies of salt pork for the winter. To keep the salines viable, the federal government reserved a tract of woods 10 miles wide by 13 miles long, to guarantee a supply of wood; the salines were probably the primary economic concern of politicians from the eastern part of the state, around Shawneetown.[42] Whether they counted on bondsmen to clear their fields, hired them to make their salt or merely wanted to keep their political allies happy, Illinois' political movers and shakers all believed that well-off migrants were bypassing Illinois, because those emigrants could not be sure they could keep their slaves in Illinois. "Our country is thinly settled, and the great desire is, to see it filled," wrote Cook, an opponent of slavery himself. "The cry is, admit slavery, and the forests will immediately be converted into the cultivated habitations of men."[43]

But the advocates of statehood for Illinois walked a careful line. The old, informal rule that, roughly speaking, new states should come into the union in pairs, one slave, one free, opened up an opportunity for Illinois—an opportunity that, strictly speaking, its still-tiny population did not entitle it to take. With Mississippi's admission to the Union in 1817, there was now an equal split between slave states and free in the Senate, and fast-growing Missouri was already lobbying for admission to the Union as a state that everyone understood would allow slavery. From far-off Washington, few men could have noticed the slaves laboring in the French settlements of Illinois, or the hundreds of "servants," with their indentures running for decades to come. The Illinois men pushing for statehood understood the territory's situation was more ambiguous, but in the capital, what seemed obvious was that if the northern states were to retain at least the power to deal in the Senate, they needed a State of Illinois, and the sooner the better. And they needed a free soil Illinois.

Which was what many Illinoisans were starting to want, as well. As the rush towards statehood picked up still more speed, territorial legislators Charles Matheny and William Bradsby, who were among the four who had written the Memorial to Congress requesting statehood, joined forces to propose a repeal of the indenture laws then on the books—the ones that allowed those "voluntary" contracts. Both men hoped to resolve the issue before a convention to draft a new state constitution convened. Bradsby would be low-key and lawyerly; the issue, he said, was "whether the legislature which passed the law which is the object of this bill to repeal exercised its legislative power within constitutional limits," the limits, that is, of the Northwest Ordinance's ban on slavery. Matheny, too, would be mild, making a point of saying the bill, if passed, should have "no influence on contracts that have been heretofore made." In reply, the Speaker of the territorial Assembly, Dr. George Fisher, said it was up to the courts and not to the legislature to say if indentures were illegal. "I see no impropriety in leaving it to the convention who shall frame our constitution," he said. "We then perhaps may do something which will lead to a gradual emancipation of slavery in a partial degree, and so ultimately benefit them in their condition ... if we can better their condition and gradually emancipate them by bringing them to our territory, we are doing a laudable thing."[44]

Still, and despite that heavy hint from the speaker, the repeal passed.

But Gov. Edwards balked, saying his sense of democratic proprieties obliged him to veto the bill. "I cannot think it either proper or necessary, to impute to our predecessors, a total disregard of their oaths, and an intentional violation of their duty," he declared. Two weeks later, perhaps feeling some pressure from anti-slavery voters, he complained that the legislature could have responded to his concerns with a less obnoxious bill, noting: "The object could have been completely effected by the passage of the law alluded to, by limiting the period of service to one year only."[45]

It wasn't much of a hard line against slavery that Bradsby and Matheny had pushed, leaving unchanged, as it did, the status of the French slaves and of the bondsmen already under indenture. But the ease with which Edwards smothered it, apparently offending neither those Illinoisans who owned slaves now nor those settlers who felt, if perhaps not very strongly, that slavery was wrong, carried with it a message. The relatively small number of Illinoisans for whom slavery was the most important political question, on which statehood itself must rise or fall, were now badly isolated, and isolated at a critical time. Seeing the ease with which Illinois' political leaders brushed aside the indenture law repeal, "Caution," a St. Clair county anti-slavery man, urged his fellow citizens to slow the rush towards statehood: "The wealthy Southern planter will not part with the Plantation Gods, which he worships, starves and whips, for the blessings of the western woods, while we are a territory and doubtful as to the future of slavery," he wrote to the *Illinois Intelligencer*. "At present, although it might be doubtful if at this time a majority could be had in favor of the barter of human flesh, and placing a part of mankind in equality with brutes, yet a few years patience, in our present state, will certainly preponderate the side in favor of humanity and freedom."[46]

Illinoisans did not want to wait for a flood of outsiders—Yankee outsiders—to come in and perfect their territory; they rather resented the idea, once it was pointed out to them. Most had come from the South themselves, and cared little for Yankees and Yorkers, whether they had had a chance to meet any or not. "An old hard shell Baptist preacher, called Daddy Briggs, was once holding forth on the richness of God's grace," went one favorite story of Judge Joseph Gillespie, recalling this time. Preacher Briggs told his congregation, the judge's story went, that grace took in the isles of the sea and the uttermost parts of the earth, "It embraces the Esquimaux and the Hottentots and some, dear britherin, go so far as to suppose that it takes in these poor benighted Yankees, but I don't go that far." Or, as one woman settler who moved from Tennessee to Illinois, told Christina Holmes Tillson (just arrived from Connecticut herself): "I am getting skeery about them 'ere Yankees. There is such a power of them coming in that them and the Injuns will squatch out the white folks."[47] Suddenly eager for statehood, Illinoisans would have no patience with anyone who told them they were not ready. Political leaders who owned slaves and who wanted their right to own them to be clarified in Illinois law were now able to link the idea of statehood, and of the self-determination it implied, with the idea that the citizens of a new state had the right to make whatever rules they chose on slavery at its birth, the Northwest Ordinance notwithstanding: "The people here are utterly regardless of ordinances, and will take up the subject in their own hands, and say they will make a treaty with Congress as an independent state," wrote Elias Pym Fordham.[48]

Into this confusion came Coles. Back from his mission to Moscow and his long, pleasant journey through Europe, he

Ninian Edwards, as territorial governor, brought his slaves with him to Illinois, saying he personally opposed slavery but had to veto the legislature's effort to ban it. Later U.S. Senator, he led one of the new state's two political factions (courtesy Abraham Lincoln Presidential Library).

made his second trip to Illinois, for another look at whether it might be the place he had picked to settle himself and his slaves. He spent part of that spring and summer of 1818 in the hamlet of Waterloo, in the western part of the territory, and much of the rest of those months at the capital, Kaskaskia, in its little loop of Mississippi River, well to the south of St. Louis. He continued scouting for land—it was that spring that he bought the bulk of the land he would eventually own in Illinois, a total of twenty-one 160-acre tracts and one 320-acre half-section he purchased from a St. Louis speculator named Charles Moulton, paying $2,300, or a fraction of the federal Land Office price of $2 an acre. (He was still at least as interested, at least for land speculation, that traditional generator of American fortunes, in Missouri, for at the same time, he snapped up 2,250 acres along Bryants Creek, in Pike County, Missouri and six 1¼ acre town lots in St. Louis, for a total of $6,500.) But his main interest at this point was watching the election for convention delegates, for, if he felt Missouri's prospects were a better investment, he also believed Illinois was about the only place in the west where he could afford to settle his soon-to-be-freed slaves.[49]

Scores of Illinois' political leaders, and aspiring movers and shakers, jammed every free bed in the tiny riverside capital they nicknamed "Kusky." Coles immersed himself in all this, excited, almost giddy, as he watched a new state taking shape. "We boarded together at a hotel, and for several months lodged in the same room," recalled Hooper Warren, who was by this time editor of the *Intelligencer*. "During this time, as he was very communicative, I learned his inmost heart, morally, politically and socially ... he was exceedingly loquacious, and, although his conversations were generally interesting (our couches being side by side) he more often than once talked me to sleep." Coles seems to have been oblivious, as he was to the increasing resentment sparked by his stories of a life spent far from the hardships of Illinois. "The subjects of his narratives were, his management of the etiquette of the President's House, while Private Secretary of Mr. Madison, and the adventures of his European tour. The incidents of the later were sometimes very amusing," the sarcastic Warren recalled. "They consisted of accounts of his dining and sporting with the Lords and Nobles and the great respect and attention paid to him, particularly while at London, Paris and St. Petersburgh; of his gallanting the Ladies of the Courts— and how they offered to learn him the 'Twelve Positions.'" Oh, he did talk, Warren said. It took months for Coles to slow down enough, and let the tart-tongued Warren get enough of a word in edgewise, to realize that he had mistaken the editor, a New Hampshire native, for a Kentuckian—"and for all he knew to the contrary, I was entitled to fix the initials 'FFV' to my name," the editor grumbled. Warren was far from being one of the "first families of Virginia" and, like many New Englanders, resented the preeminence of the Virginia grandees in national politics, a resentment that soon focused on Coles: "I found him to possess an inveterate and unconquerable prejudice against 'Yankees' and his aversion to them could only be allayed by the hope or prospect of using them to the advancement of his purposes," Warren complained. "In politics, 'The South' was all to him ... Southern statesmen only, appeared to be in his view has having a right to the management and control of public affairs." Another settler, meeting Coles at around that time, would grumble that he "worships but one idol and that is himself" and that he was merely "two and one halfpenny animal."[50]

Blunt, hard-headed Warren was not a man to let what he saw interfere with what he believed, whether in his roommate in Kaskaskia that decisive summer, or in the hearts of his fellow citizens. Like Coles, Warren opposed slavery. For both men, that opposition was rooted in a deeply felt morality and a passionate attachment to the rights promised in the Declaration of Independence and in the Bill of Rights. Neither one of the mutually irritated roommates could see how any true democrat would take any other stand. Neither would catch the more uncertain feelings of their fellow citizens on the slavery issue. And neither would understand how skillfully their opponents—particularly Judge Thomas and his brilliant young Yorker lieutenant, Elias Kent Kane—would be able to shepherd a compromise through the soon-to-be-convened constitutional convention that would continue to allow slavery in Illinois.

Slave-owners themselves, each owning five, and based in the old French towns of Kaskaskia and Cahokia, on banks of the Mississippi, where their strongest supporters and closest connections owned slaves, Thomas and Kent now saw a way to tap the kind of popular fever that could let them wrest control of the constitutional convention and the new state from Gov. Edwards and his faction. Like his arch-rival, the governor, Thomas was a native Marylander—but, born a poor farmer's son, had a much different style as his built his potent political machine. "Plain in dress, in language and in manners, exceedingly social and affable," he had the kind of easygoing style that frontier voters appreciated, as they remembered him "in the streets, joking and laughing at the public table."[51]) He was also a politician who did much of his business behind closed doors. "[I]t was a maxim with him," recalled Gov. Thomas Ford, "that no man could be talked down with loud and bold words, but anyone might be whispered to death." Even before coming to Illinois, Thomas had forged bonds with the French settlers and Southern land speculators of Kaskaskia: In 1805, as a member of the Indiana territorial assembly, he had joined with wealthy Pierre Menard and Dr. George Fisher of Illinois (who in 1817 would lead the fight against the effort to repeal Illinois' indenture laws) as well as with the aristocratic William Henry Harrison, then the territorial governor of Indiana, in a Memorial to Congress urging the legalization of slavery his Illinois friends so badly wanted. It was a stand Thomas took even though his constituents in the eastern Indiana county of Dearborn were staunchly opposed to slavery—so much so, in fact, that they would that same year petition Congress to complain about Indiana's new indenture law and to ask that their county be attached to the state of Ohio, where free soil principles had never been questioned. Despite the opposition to slavery back home, Thomas backed the reenactment of that troublesome indenture legislation, a law that Illinois' later

Jesse Thomas, leader of one of Illinois' two factions. His close connections with the state's French slaveholders ensured him a solid political base (courtesy Abraham Lincoln Presidential Library).

version would be modeled on, in the 1807 legislative session. That, though, was not enough to satisfy his Illinois allies, who continued to push for separation from Indiana. In 1808, Thomas secretly agreed to vote for dividing the territories, in exchange for their promise that he would become a judge in a separate territory of Illinois.[52]

Though a newcomer, Thomas soon made a splash in Illinois politics. He quickly created a powerful new faction, backed by allies like Kane, the New York City native and Yale graduate who was his main lieutenant (Kane, "a man in a mask," clever, calculating and cold, could act as "the chief of the faction whenever he chose," in one historian's view).[53] The faction included John McLean, a big land speculator from Shawneetown, a quick-to-anger man, known for his bitter outbursts and vindictive nature, narrowly elected the first congressman from the state of Illinois, as well as Thomas Sloo, a legislator from Hamilton County, in southern Illinois, and Thomas' half-brother, Michael Jones. They were big operators—with land holdings in the hundreds, even thousands of acres—and they weren't content to leave the best pickings in Illinois to the lawyers and speculators who had arrived before them. Nor were their backers. "Edwards had the aged and sedate leaders of the people friendly to him, but Judge Thomas had the young, ardent and energetic men supporting him, who were mixing every day with the people," John Reynolds, one of the those young men, who would later become governor of Illinois, recalled many years later. And for such men, the question of slavery was ambiguous, at best. "I would not have on my conscience the moral guilt of extending slavery over countries now free from it," wrote the English settler Elias Pym Fordham, speaking for many. "But if it should take place, I do not see why I should not make use of it. If I do not have servants, I cannot farm; and there are no free laborers here, except a few so worthless, and yet so haughty that an English gentleman can do nothing with them."[54]

Still, Thomas and Kane would handle the question of slavery gingerly. They did not campaign for slavery during the campaigns for election to the constitutional convention that summer; Kane, in fact, declared that if one fellow candidate were elected, he "would consider himself instructed to vote for introduction of slavery, but if Mr. McFerron was elected as his colleague, then he would consider himself instructed to vote against." (Two years later, Kane would lose his bid to be Illinois' sole Congressman decisively, tagged as he was as a proslavery man.)[55] Though it was the biggest issue looming over the convention, few candidates for election to that body would declare themselves openly for slavery; John Copeland, a slave-owner from Johnson County, in the south, who had argued that the new constitution should tolerate slavery, was the only candidate from his county to be defeated, while two of the four men defeated in southern Union County were men who had argued for slavery. Most candidates simply waffled. "On this important point," grumbled "A Citizen" to the *Intelligencer*, "It may be well for every man to enquire before he gives a vote and enquire of the candidate in the presence of those of the opposite opinion to himself, so that he may not flinch and act the camelion, as, I fear, some of our candidates are doing."[56]

But most settlers, wrote "Candor" in the *Intelligencer*, at about this time felt "opposed to the toleration of slavery, yet I fear this majority will be defeated by the cunning of those who have a contrary interest." Reading this, perhaps after consulting with Warren, Coles seems to have decided he would try to stiffen Illinoisans' resolve to oppose the wealthy employers of indentured servants—and so, apparently taking up his pen as the *Intelligencer* correspondent "Agis," would declare that "already have the advocates of slavery taken the field ... murmuring because this territory is not permitted to enjoy the *inestimable blessing* as well as in some states and territories," a sarcastic turn of phrase that closely echoes Coles' aside to Madison as they saw that Washington slave coffle. Apparently hinting that, though an outsider, he would not be for long, Agis (or Coles) wrote with what he hoped was appropriate delicacy that: "I trust you will not deem it premature or improper" if he, "whose interests are united with yours," would call attention to "a subject of utmost importance to individual and national happiness—I mean the momentous question whether this shall be a free or slave state." Coles would never claim, and never deny, that he had been Agis (and some historians suspect he may not be, believing his ego too large to foreswear the credit),* but the style is very much his, as are the arguments, for, as might be expected from a good student of Bishop Madison, Agis still linked individual happiness with a society that gave freedom to pursue virtue, though perhaps the relationship was less clear to readers of the *Intelligencer* than to Coles. Agis picks up another favorite theme of Coles when he says he is "one of those who consider the present Laws of this territory, admitting slavery under certain restrictions & regulations, as not only unjust, but as plainly inconsistent with the law of Congress which declares that there shall be 'neither slavery nor involuntary servitude in this territory.'" Agis appealed to the anger of Illinoisans over Edwards' recent vetoes, noting that: "It must be a subject of regret to every lover of liberty that although our last legislature passed an act to repeal the odious law for the admission of slavery, yet the repealing act has been defeated by the veto of his excellency the governor," and sought to link Illinoisans' characteristic distrust of highhanded authority with opposition to slavery. "Let us hail the approach of that Period when we shall be delivered from the trammels and shackles of territorial bondage—when it shall not be in power of an individual, in whose appointment we have no voice, to set aside the will of the people, as expressed by their representatives."[57]

It was a direct attempt to confound those, like Thomas and Kane, maneuvering to tap two separate strands—resentment of Edwards and resentment of Yankees—and to link the popular despite to create a more democratic government with a tolerance of slavery. But it was a position that would bring its author in opposition to adversaries far more skilled in dancing away from firm declarations of principle than he.

Still, Coles, or Agis, kept writing. As the polling dates—July 6, 7 and 8—for election of delegates to the constitutional convention approached, he resumed his attacks on the still-discreet advocates of slavery, hard as it was to pin them down. "For my own part," said Agis, "I would rather see our rich meadows and fertile woodlands inhabited alone by the wild beasts and birds of the air, than that they should ever echo to the sound of the slave driver's scourge, or resound with the cries of the oppressed Africans." It was not a sentiment that seemed likely to appeal to farmers busily trying to turn those fields and forests in farms. But, Agis continued, "I would

---

*Coles was widely believed to have written the "Agis" anti-slavery letters; see, e.g., Solon J. Buck, Illinois in 1818 (Urbana: University of Illinois Press, 1967), 242. But Kurt Leichtle, "Edward Coles: An Agrarian on the Frontier," 73, 82, believing it "inconceivable" that Coles would not have claimed credit, reports that George Churchill had noted in his diary delivering an "Agis" letter on the subject of secret ballots to the newspaper a month earlier. Churchill made no similar note about the much more important slavery series. The style of the letters, though, seems to suggest Coles was in fact the author.

rather that our citizens should live fearlessly and contentedly in their peaceful and modest cabins, than that, surrounded by a host of slaves, and inhabiting splendid palaces and gilded domes, they should live in constant apprehensions of an attack from those who are, and who ought to be, their mortal enemies." There was a risk, this Virginian knew, to keeping slaves; and not just the danger from rebelling bondsmen, for the police power needed to keep control in slave quarters was inimical to others' freedoms, too. Even beyond that, though, said Agis (sounding still more like Coles, if that were possible):

> As the love of liberty is dear to your hearts—as you would preserve yourselves and your posterity from the miserable fate of the once opulent inhabitants of St. Domingo—as you respect the commands of Heaven and the dictates of your own consciences, let me beseach you to be cautious to what persons you confide the important task of framing your state constitution. Let no friend to slavery, however great his talents, enjoy your confidence.... Let no one enjoy your confidence who will not zealously advocate the entire exclusion of slavery from the state.

A wonderful way, to be sure, to ingratiate oneself with political faction leaders all pushing, as hard as they could, to allow slavery, especially if you continue with the thought and argue that some—Kane perhaps, waffling as to whether or not he would vote to allow it—might not be entirely trustworthy, while others "hope to divert your attention from the great question of slavery or freedom. Place your confidence in men who are in *practice*, as well as in *theory*, friends to liberty—men whose interests are blended with your own—who have no aristocratical desires to gratify."[58]

In the end, that call had little impact. Illinoisans voted for the men they knew even if they knew little of where they stood on slavery. They elected three of their judges, two more lawyers, two sheriffs, a land office official, a minister and three doctors. Four of the 33 delegates were involved in the slave-worked Saline. Once assembled in Kaskaskia, they quickly elected Thomas to preside over the convention. Elias Kent Kane took control of the committee that would actually write the constitution, though he modestly declined any title. Some kind of authorization of slavery was clearly in the works. "We are informed," a group of anti-slavery citizens wrote to the *Intelligencer*, "that strong exertions will be made in the Convention to give sanction to that despicable evil in our state ... at a crisis like this, thinking will not do, acting is necessary." But the acting was happening on the other side.[59]

Kane moved quickly. The convention opened August 7, rejecting on its first day a petition from the anti-slavery Covenanter sect in Randolph County that asked for a declaration that "Jesus Christ is the heart of the government, and that the Holy Scriptures were the only rule." That done, the Covenanters' rebuffed pastor, a Rev. Wiley, rode back home and the church's members forswore any acknowledgment of what they called a heathen and unbaptized government, refusing to come when called once a year for their few days of community road work, declining even to vote—until the time, six years later, when they would come to the polls, at a critical time for Coles.[60]

For now, though, with the Covenanters' request quickly tossed aside, the convention elected 15 members to draft a proposed constitution for them to mull, when the rest politicked and lobbied one another. Lifting whole chunks from the Indiana, Ohio and Kentucky constitutions, the committee slapped together a draft in just five days—although Sidney Breese, later a judge, would later insist that as a clerk for Kane, he had learned that the whole document was written in Kane's office "sometime before the meeting of the convention."[61]

The governor would be weak, without even the right to veto legislation on his own, instead exercising that power through a "Council of Revision" on which he and the justices of the state Supreme Court would sit. The General Assembly would appoint the Attorney General and the Auditor of Public Accounts, as well as the judges and officers of the circuit courts. On the question of slavery, a wholesale lift from Ohio's basic law banned slavery but allowed indentures if the bondsmen entered the contract freely and voluntarily. But key sections in which Ohio set strict limits on the term of such indentures and the ages during when men and women (not children) could bind themselves were left blank. "The question of slavery is not yet decided," the *Intelligencer* commented. "A majority, however, are said to be opposed to it."[62]

For legislators from the eastern counties, a key group, it seemed as if it would all come down to salt. Any government of Illinois the convention might agree upon would have few sources of revenue, except land taxes and royalties from the salt works. One letter to the *Intelligencer* put it plain: "[T]he exclusion of slavery will annihilate a source of public revenue ... white men cannot be procured in sufficient numbers to convert these salines to extensively valuable purposes."[63]

On second reading of the draft, August 18, the delegates started reworking the section on slavery, amending it to say "neither slavery nor involuntary servitude shall hereafter be introduced into this state ... under any indenture hereafter made." Slaves already in Illinois were to be out of luck. Another amendment proffered on second reading specifically exempted the salt works from the ban on importing slaves from other states. The delegates approved, by a 17–14 vote. The representatives from Madison County,

LOWER SALT-WORKS.

The salt works of Illinois. Hundreds of slaves worked here, and the 1818 state Constitution's ambiguity on the issue of slavery was in part meant to ensure they would continue to do so (Northern Illinois University Library).

whose citizens generally opposed slaveholding, joined with those from Gallatin County, home to the Saline, and Randolph County, where most of the old French settlers lived, in favor of these refinements. Holding St. Clair County and much of the western part of the territory for the antislavery cause was the tough old Baptist preacher James Lemen.[64] He was, it seems, a man who embodied much of the pragmatic but modest spirit of Illinois, and, like many of his fellow settlers, not much of a talker. A common story of the day says much about this preacher who would become a key ally of Coles': Once, when his son had hidden a plow-horse collar in the hopes of avoiding an afternoon in the fields, the old man "mused for a few minutes," wordlessly, before "very much to the disappointment of his truant son, he deliberately pulled off his leather breeches, stuffed the legs of them with stubble, straddled them across the neck of his horse for a collar, and ploughed for the remainder of the day as bare-legged as he came into the world."[65]

But for Lemen now, there was no straw to fashion a legislative plowhorse collar. His moral authority and quiet, if resolute, stance against slavery were not enough. For him and his allies, the effort to ban slavery from the new constitution would be futile. The day after the salt works amendment passed, Leonard White, of Gallatin County, proposed one more, to say that existing indentures and slave-hire contracts must be completed as written; it, too, passed by a 17–14 vote, although a handful of delegates from each side shifted their positions. One, Abraham Pritchet, of Madison County, who perhaps had not realized the import of amendments from the day before, moved that the whole section on slavery be thrown out, but the other delegates brushed him off. On third reading, though, they did decide that the children of indentured servants should be considered to be free, when the young men turned 21 and the women, 18.[66]

The advocates of slavery had won all of what they had wanted: No change in the status of the French slaves, no disruption of indentures, even those with 99-year terms, and slaves to work the salines, at least through the year 1825. Illinois would be the only state formed from the old Northwest Territory that did not simply ban slavery in its new Constitution. It would be under this basic law that Coles believed his slaves would have the legal protections they would need, once he freed them. He seemed unworried that the constitution made no specific provision on the status of freedmen, and unaware of the savage Black Code already in force in the territory. That code would be confirmed by the first legislature of the state, after Coles had returned to Rockfish to prepare for his move west. The Assembly would also quickly enact a law that banned free blacks from settling in Illinois without a certificate of emancipation. It passed another that prohibited slave-owners from bringing their slaves to Illinois for the purpose of setting them free, unless the posted a hefty bond.

All Coles saw was that the long-awaited day when he could set his slaves free was approaching. He had now decided Illinois was the place where his slaves could live in freedom, he had bought land. Despite the murky language in the new constitution, he remained certain that he saw in Illinois a place whose people agreed they wanted to see no slaves. But because he didn't see the Black Code, because his circle at the convention centered on such men as Warren and Lemen—the Yankee who believed in human rights, two Southerners whose religious convictions convinced them that slavery was wrong (Lemen had moved to Illinois to establish an anti-slavery Baptist church)—Coles may not have fully understood the compromise that Illinoisans struck on slavery. That wish to see no slaves, of course, in a nation where slaves were black and blacks were mostly slaves, could mean two things.

CHAPTER 5

A new home, a new challenge

The park-like prairies of western Illinois, the open sweep of grass, framed by dark groves of oak and hickory, now seemed promising to Coles. Like the carefully cultivated estates he had seen in England and that his former neighbors in Albemarle County were creating on the edges of the Blue Ridge Mountains, it was a landscape that promised riches and great possibilities to him. "The air there," he wrote, "is sweetened by a more free and uninterrupted circulation," unlike the woods and soggy bottomlands by the rivers where, "in the dusk of evening, after a warm day in the summer and fall, you have no doubt often encountered the disagreeable smell of the miasma."[1] He was thinking hard about the challenges of farming the prairie, with its tough sod and need for new techniques. He was reassured that the much-delayed liberation of his slaves was possible. He was eager to get to work.

But he had other obligations. Coles' commission from President Monroe as registrar—he and his contemporaries called it "Register"—at the newly opened U.S. Land Office in Edwardsville imposed duties that would take up much of his time in his first years in Illinois. It had taken some trouble to get: even before heading out to Illinois in 1818, he had written to Territorial Governor Ninian Edwards seeking a position. Edwards said he preferred a man who already lived in the state. Once in Illinois, hanging around in Kaskaskia and watching the wrangling over the new state constitution, Coles learned that the registrar's post in Edwardsville was open. He dashed off a note to Monroe: "You must be aware that the life I have led for many years past, whilst it disqualifies me in many respects for the enjoyment of the dull pursuits of a Farmer, qualifies me in some degree, and has given me a taste, for the sedentary occupation of the desk and of the bustling routine duties of an office." He knew the land well, having "been almost incessantly moving to and fro examining the different parts of the Illinois Territory," and planned to settle in Edwardsville because of the land he'd been buying in the Military Bounty lands. Back east, he hastened to

Washington to lobby for the job, was confirmed by the Senate, and appointed by Monroe on March 5. It was only when he had his commission in hand that he was, at last, ready to pick up stakes and move with his soon-to-be-freed slaves to Illinois.[2]

The work as registrar would keep him busy, if not as well paid as he might have wished ($500 a year plus a one percent commission on each land sale, out of which he paid the expenses of the Land Office). During that first spring, he was able, though, to begin experimenting with prairie farming, difficult work that had daunted and discouraged almost everyone who tried before him. The ground was "so tough and hard, that it required my whole team to pull one plough," he complained to Madison—even though he bought a supposedly already improved tract of some 470 acres, with several enclosed fields and a deserted log cabin, just three miles east of Edwardsville. He called it Prairieland.[3] With four horses to plow, and hiring the Crawford brothers, Ralph and Robert, as well as Thomas Cobb, Coles planted more than 50 acres. By early July, with that done (and a bit late, too), they cut hay and planted a crop of winter wheat. Coles paid his former slaves cash wages, bought them bacon and beef, corn meal and potatoes, covered their bills with doctors and local merchants. He hired Kate Crawford to keep his house. He bought her a dress, and cloth for her to make clothing for the men and for her children. That fall, Coles bought hogs, and the men tended them. They kept busy, too, trying to break unimproved prairie, building split-rail fences, tending hogs. It was a hard slog. Ralph died of his bilious fever that first October.[4]

He died a free man, though. Coles had written out the formal deeds of emancipation that liberated his slaves, on the Fourth of July, no less. In the deeds he carefully explained that "I do not believe that man can have of right a property, in his fellow man, but on the contrary that all man kind were endowed by nature with equal rights." The view that black men and women had rights, and rights equal to all other citizens, of course, was not commonly held, even by the handful of Americans of the day who bothered to speak out in opposition to slavery. That evening, at the Independence Day dinner at W. C. Wiggins' tavern, as the men of Edwardsville drank and sang patriotic songs and carefully, if a bit woozily, stood to make their toasts, Coles proposed raising glasses for the Rights of Man—"They appertain equally to him, whether his complexion be white, red or black."[5]

Perhaps the townsmen merely thought him foolish. Freeing slaves, farming prairie: Most Southern men kept their bondsmen, most newcomers didn't bother with the prairie, unless by bad luck they drew a quarter-section in the Military Tract lands, where the bulk of Coles' own Illinois land-holdings were. The traceless expanses of grasslands, thought to mean poor, infertile soil, daunted many. The tough prairie sod discouraged the few who were willing to try, especially those who had only their own muscle and a single horse to work the land. Coles spent nearly $500, on top of the cost of his land, moving to Illinois and setting up his farm. He made $600 selling his corn; with the $720 he cleared in commissions from the two-week August land sales, covering some 33 townships in western Illinois, and the sale of his winter wheat, Coles calculated that he broke even in his first year in Illinois—pretty good for man who could not clear his $500 debt at Rockfish—and pretty typical of the kind of fuzzy, rosy-colored financial calculation that keeps so many farmers on the land even nowadays. Still, it was better than many of the men who recorded their land with him, for once grain prices started slumping after the Panic of 1819, most settlers had to scrape for four years just to pay for their land, their tools and their stock.[6] By his second year in Illinois, though, Coles felt he had figured out how to deal with the hard prairie earth: "In the months of May and June last, I broke prairie, on which there was a thick sod, by first ploughing it with a plain knife coulter, such as is generally used to break new rooty lands," he wrote. That wasn't enough, of course. "I then immediately ploughed the land a second time, with a small bar shear, obliquely across the first ploughing, in order to reduce the size and diminish the number of clods; this was followed by two harrowings with an iron tooth drag, which effectively broke the land, pulverized it, and put it in an excellent state of preparation for a crop of corn." In contrast to the four-horse plowing he had tried the year before, the approach of repeatedly carving away at the heavy land took only a single pair of horses, Coles said, and they were able to do the work "with ease." It took far more time, however, and required more implements than most new settlers could afford, as they scrambled to clear a few acres and put up a small house. Of course, he had help.[7]

And he would need it. As land office registrar, he arrived in Edwardsville just before a scheduled sale of thousands of acres of public land. Hundreds of people poured into the tiny town for what would be a three-week epic; the taverns and rooming-houses were jammed, often with several men to a room. The auction was a major event for a frontier farmer laboring through a dull round of days, miles from any neighbor; it would mark the day many a new arrival would consider the starting point of his family's adventure in Illinois; it was what many a would-be speculator hoped would mark the start of a new fortune. The crowds drew peddlers, shopkeepers, lawyers, politicians and townspeople curious to see the show. On May 3, 1819, they all filled Edwardsville's main street; Coles, Land Office Clerk William P. McKee and the auctioneer marched through the milling crowd, clambered up a rickety, temporary platform outside the Land Office, and called out the first quarter-section of land for sale. Throughout the next three weeks, it was Coles' job to officially record each purchase: buyer, tract description, amount paid (usually the minimum downpayment of $16 for a $2-an-acre quarter section) and the amount owed. While Receiver Benjamin Stephenson (a business partner of Sen. Ninian Edwards, and unabashed owner of eight slaves) collected the farmers' hard-earned specie, it was Coles' job to keep track of the subsequent installments: the first one, $64, due 40 days after the sale with three $80 payments due each year after that. There were discounts for early payment, three-month reprieves for missed ones, to make note of. He had, as well, to maintain plat maps for a region comprising the entire northern half of the state, keeping track of what was sold and what was to sell. In the evenings, buyers sought him out for his wisdom on where the best land was to be found, or to celebrate what was for many one of the biggest days in their lives. It was a prominent role in a tiny town of less than 170 residents, where the Land Office, the Bank of Edwardsville (a shaky little thing, despite the backing of Governor Edwards and a new-minted designation as a government depositary, with just 10 percent of its capital actually paid in), Warren's *Spectator*, two stores, a hotel and a flour mill were the only businesses—besides a slew of taverns, that is.[8]

It would be difficult for Coles to concentrate on farming, even if he had been inclined to. Hoping to focus on the Land Office during his second year at Edwardsville, Coles offered Robert Crawford and Thomas Cobb "half of all they made" selling Prairieland's produce, if they would work the farm for him, staking them "stock, tools and food" as well as covering their doctor's bills. But the Land Office business slumped, with sales in the summer of 1820 barely one fifth the level of where they had been in Coles' first year there, in what would turn out to be the best year ever for the Edwardsville land office. They would remain low for years—even 1828, sales at Edwardsville and the new Springfield Land Office accounted for less than one-quarter the 1819 total.[9]

Even so, Washington had plenty of work for him. He spent most of the summer and fall of his main prairie-breaking year, 1820, sorting out a table of land claims in the old French village of Peoria. In May, as Coles' teams of horses dragged the coulter through the sod of his Pin Oak Township farm, Congress passed an Act calling for the settlement of land claims at Peoria, where, as Coles carefully noted, in 1812, the French and Metis settlers were forcibly removed, their homes razed and farms burnt, by a Captain Craig of the Illinois militia "on the ground, as it was said, that he and his company of militia were fired on in the night while at anchor in their boats before the village, by Indians." The Illinois River valley and the woods north of Lake Peoria in that time of war were still Indian country, where traders from Montreal and agents of the British crown freely roamed and where most Indians, "with whom the inhabitants [of Peoria] were suspected by Craig of being too intimate and friendly," were inclined to be hostile to the United States.[10] It would be Coles' job now, as the federal official responsible for recording claims and purchases of public lands in the northern half of Illinois, to sort the mess out.

Mess it was. There were no maps and no records. To verify Etienne Bernard's claim to an arpent of land in the village, described merely as "situate about forty or fifty yards south of the lot of Joseph Graveline," for instance, Coles had to consider testimony from Graveline and another neighbor, Tousant Soulard, who both agreed that Bernard had in fact held an arpent or two off the road by the Lake Peoria shore. Graveline and Soulard swore that Bernard had cultivated the plot for about three years, beginning in 1778, until driven off by increased tensions between the villagers and nearby Indians. But, it turned out, some years later, in 1788 or 1789, one Francis Wilette built a house on roughly the same land and began improving a half-arpent of land, according to the testimony of yet another neighbor, Drezy Blondeau. Wilette lived there until 1806, passed the house on his daughter, Angelica, and her husband, Louis Pilette, according to Blondeau and yet another neighbor, Simon Roi. The dispute, though, grew even more complicated, since part of Wilette's holding, an 80-foot-by-300-foot lot just to the south of Bernard's claim, was held by another Peoria settler, Felix Fontaine, who said he had purchased it from Antoine Deschamps in 1811, after Deschamps, supported by two of his friends, Hypolite Maillet and Pierre Lavassieur, swore he had purchased it from Wilette's widow around 1806. Thus, one claim. There were 70 such claims, some even more complicated.[11]

For months, settlers from Peoria trekked the 170 miles south to Edwardsville, to make their cases, or to speak on behalf of neighbors' claims to land. The disputes involved lots of just a few acres, sometimes less. "You who are acquainted with the illiterate [cha]racter of French settlers can form an idea of the time required, and the trouble attending the taking of depositions for seventy claims—many of which are supported by two, three & even four depositions," Coles complained in a note to Daniel Cook, who had recently been elected Illinois' sole Congressman.[12]

In the event, it was too big a tangle for Coles to formally confirm anyone's claim. "This village has been inhabited by the French previous to the recollection of any of the present generation," Coles reported to Treasury Secretary William Crawford, one of his patrons back in Washington. The inhabitants of Peoria were mostly Indian traders, hunters and voyagers of an "itinerate character" who, as far as Coles could tell, had settled there "without any grant or permission from the authority of any Government ... each person took to himself such portion of unoccupied land as he wished to occupy and cultivate, and made it his by incorporating his labor with it; but as soon as he abandoned it, his title was understood to cease." The village itself had been at two different sites, first by the southern end of Lake Peoria, later on the high western bluff overlooking the lake. For a time, the settlement had been abandoned. The settlers usually owned more than one piece of land, with a lot in the village and a plot farther out for hay or wheat. "I must add my regrets at the insurmountable difficulties I have met with," Coles wrote. The law did not say what kinds of claims he was to rule on, or set rules for saying one claim stood and another didn't. It didn't give any hints to any other law or custom by which he could be guided. "I have been at a loss to determine upon what principles to decide, and have, therefore, been compelled to omit making out a list of such claims as, in my opinion, ought to be confirmed." The result, not unknown in Illinois, was to let the current holder of land keep the land. And Coles would necessarily come to learn what some of his political opponents never would: the political importance of making it easy for a frontier family to stay on the land it cultivated.[13]

Buried by the Peoria claims, worried that the slaves he had freed were not yet able to start their farms in Pin Oak Township, Coles could only watch, with growing alarm, as the issue that mattered most to him erupted in that same summer of 1820. The issue was slavery. The spark was Missouri.

A New York Congressman, the ambitious and hot-tempered James Tallmadge, a lawyer from the upstate town of Poughkeepsie, had managed the year before to derail Missouri's bid for statehood, as he had nearly managed to put the brakes on Illinois' own frantic rush for admission to the Union, by insisting that slavery should have no haven in either place. Illinois' Constitution, Tallmadge had complained in 1818, did not in his words "sufficiently" ban slavery. Like Coles an abolitionist before there really was an abolition movement, Tallmadge was unable to convince more than a few others to share his concerns about Illinois. But Missouri would be different. Unlike Illinois, Missouri was clearly slave country, and had been ever since its first settlers arrived, with their slaves in tow, for the Northwest Ordinance did not apply on the far side of the Mississippi River. The French families that crossed to Missouri after the Ordinance's enactment and the scores of Southern farmers who came to the territory in the years after the Louisiana Purchase made it American territory, solidified political support

5—A new home, a new challenge

for slavery there. With a U.S. Senate delicately balanced between slave and free states, the political import was clear, even if the moral issue still seemed obscure to many.[14]

On February 13, 1819, Tallmadge stood in the House of Representatives to propose that Missouri should only be admitted as a state if its state constitution specifically prohibited the introduction of slavery and provided for the liberation of slaves' children born after Missouri became a state. Tallmadge feared a slave-holding Missouri meant a slave-holding west, and an entire section hostile to the interests of his own. Eager to make his mark, he and his family were convinced his stand put him, as his mother would write, "on the Side of truth and justice."[15]

No one had expected it. Missouri's territorial delegate to Congress, John Scott, only learned what Tallmadge was planning "at a late period, at second hand, through the medium of a foreigner, the Portuguese ambassador." Enraged, he thundered that Missourians "know their own rights," including the right to own slaves, "and if admitted into the national family, they would be equal, nor not come at all."[16] Scott and his backers in Missouri were hardly mollified when Tallmadge's proposed condition on the territory's admission died in the Senate.

It would be Jesse B. Thomas, now a U.S. Senator from Illinois, who would during the following year, 1820, find a way out of the challenge Tallmadge had posed. The District of Maine, then a part of Massachusetts, was also seeking statehood. Thomas proposed admitting it and Missouri at the same time, keeping the balance of votes in the Senate unchanged between slave states and free. At the same time, to reassure those who feared the whole west was about to turn slave, Thomas suggested banning slavery north of the latitude 36 degrees, 30 minutes north in the rest of the Louisiana Purchase (which is, roughly speaking, the line running along the Missouri-Arkansas border and extending west to pass just north of what is now Tulsa and along the southern boundary of the Oklahoma panhandle to the Rocky Mountains). Though it meant the bulk of the Purchase would be free soil, it was, most northerners felt, a giveaway to southern slaveholders, since most then believed the plains north and west of Missouri were desert. "It would have been happier for us," declared one disgruntled northern congressman, "if the Mississippi had been an eternal torrent of burning lava, impassable as the lake which separates the evil from the good, and the regions beyond it destined to be covered forever with brakes and jungles, and the impenetrable haunts of the wolf and panther."[17]

Back in Illinois, *Edwardsville Spectator* editor Hooper Warren was convinced that Thomas had been duped by his fellow senator from Illinois, Ninian Edwards; Warren had months earlier published a letter from Illinois congressman Daniel Cook, Edwards' soon-to-be son-in-law, denouncing the compromise and hinting that it was Edwards who had instigated the whole idea. The Missouri Compromise was about to become an Illinois issue. The two men had stopped speaking to one another; the faction Edwards led was paralyzed. And, as the election of 1820 approached, Warren now (with some help from Coles, though he would never acknowledge it) discovered a conspiracy.

Cook and Warren both had infuriated the Missourians already. The men from Missouri needed Illinois to back their bid for statehood, and Cook's outspoken opposition in the House of Representatives, along with Warren's regular reports of atrocities against slaves in Missouri, widely reprinted in the northern states, were galling: "A most impartial liar," the *St. Louis Enquirer* called Warren's paper, adding that "the sympathetic presses which copy its filth, have hardly time to take down their types from one lie, before the have to set them for another."[18] They wanted Warren to shut up. They wanted Cook out.

The way to do that, the Missourians decided, was to encourage proslavery agitation across the river in Illinois. It "would be nothing more than justice to Illinois (as its citizens were so violently opposed to Missouri, as a State, without restriction) to create a reaction by engaging your side of the river in a contest and home, which would prevent them from so particularly interesting themselves in our concerns," a St. Louis friend would write to Edwards. The idea gathered steam through that winter of 1819–1820. Joseph Street, a longtime member of the courthouse gang down in the salt works country of Gallatin County (and unsuccessful candidate for a U.S. Senate seat in 1818), quit a lucrative sinecure in state government to go to Washington and start organizing the campaign. There were other Illinoisans, too, quietly planning an push to allow slavery, "contend[ing] that you could, the next day after being admitted under an *antislavery* constitution, change the constitution so as to admit slavery, and in that way 'whip the devil around the stump.'"[19]

The effort—conspiracy, as Warren called it—didn't remain secret for long. "Through the medium of leaky vessels, both in Kentucky and Missouri," Warren recalled, "I was duly apprised of the project to make Illinois a slave state, and that the first move was to be, the bringing out of Elias Kent Kane, then Secretary of State, in opposition to Mr. Cook at the next election." Warren held his scoop; he checked with Cook, still in Washington, who said he already knew of the plan. A few weeks later, Kane formally announced he would be running for Congress. Warren itched to expose the plot, and to give Cook's campaign a boost, but as a client of Edwards, disgruntled with the former governor though he was over the Missouri issue, the editor needed to see how the factional land lay. Soon after Congress adjourned for the summer, and Edwards had returned to his home in Edwardsville, Warren came to call. "From his rupture with Mr. Cook, and the fact that he held slaves in Kentucky and Missouri, I had some misgivings as to his future course," Warren would recall. But Edwards, "with his accustomed frankness," told Warren that his position had not changed, that is, that he opposed introducing slavery to territories where it had been excluded and that, in particular, he opposed changing Illinois' Constitution to formally allow slavery. The faction would hold through the 1820 election, Edwards said, "seeing the new combinations for agitating the question of slavery, and that the first blow was to be struck in an attempt to put down Mr. Cook, he had cast aside all hard feelings toward him, and would support his re-election." Confident that his expose-in-waiting had the faction leader's backing, Warren went public.[20]

Kane was hot. He immediately issued a "furious handbill" accusing Edwards of making up the story—the "juggler behind the scenes"—and adding that he was "well convinced" that no such plot had ever been thought of. Edwards coolly replied by rattling off the names of eight leading citizens of Madison County, including Coles, as well as two men from St. Louis, all of whom, he said, could confirm that there had been talk for weeks that a pro-slavery press was to be set up in Illinois and run by Street. "Some of the gentlemen referred can testify that a change of our Constitution has at least been thought of' pretty seriously," Edwards wrote. "Knowing as much as I do upon the subject, in relation to certain individuals who are intimate with and support Mr. Kane, I am truly surprised that he should know of little as to believe that the change spoken of had 'never been thought of.'"[21]

The compromises of the 1818 constitutional convention related to slavery had, it seemed, resolved nothing. "The people in Illinois, in 1820, were ready almost to commit violence on one another," Judge John Reynolds, later governor of the state, would recall. Slavery "was the prominent issue" in the election that year, he added. But the pro-slavery men's ploy backfired badly, once exposed by Warren and Edwards. The election was a rout: Cook won by a margin of nearly two to one, carrying every county but one.[22]

Coles followed the election intently, but missed most of the action, preoccupied as he was with the Peoria claims, worrying about the expenses he'd incurred investigating them and struggling to finish his lengthy report on them as voting day approached. "I will not apply to Congress for compensation but I will say to you that I ought in justice to be paid, and liberally paid, too, for the trouble and labour I have been at in examining witnesses, taking their depositions, and transcribing two copies of the substance of the evidence," he complained to Daniel Cook, who having won the election had already returned to the House of Representatives in Washington. He was spending less and less time recording land sales, and more time tracking requests for reprieve and recording relinquishments, as more and more settlers found themselves unable to pay their annual $80 installments to buy their land.[23]

Coles seems to have treated the settlers who came to see him with unusual consideration—perhaps already thinking, as did so many Land Office registrars did, of how easy a jump it would be to go from recording land sales into politics. Unlike Stephenson, he didn't actually have to take their money, or have to insist that only hard-to-find coin or Bank of the United States bills would be accepted. In a place where the notes of state-chartered banks, discounted at will—and deeply, too—by merchants, the Land Office's restrictions would be a real burden on new settlers, barely getting by. Coles had the happier side of the Office's work, and there was plenty of business: new settlers checking to see where they might clear a farm, or coming back to claim and pay for their choice; farmers and speculators dropping by to check on the state of land sales. "When the settler reached Edwardsville, dressed in jeans and wearing moccasins, with his money in belt, having traveled on foot or on horseback long distances, and first presented himself to the Register of the Land Office, there he found Edward Coles," as Elihu Washburne, the influential congressman and senator from Illinois, summed up the common recollection of the days. Despite Coles' presidential connections, his "genteel" dress, his "somewhat awkward" manner, "[t]he anxious settler was at once put at ease by the suavity of his address, the interest he appeared to feel in aiding him, and the thoroughly intelligent manner in which he discharged his duty. No man went away who was not delighted with his intercourse with the 'Register.'"[24]

They were difficult years for settlers. There was little money and less credit, for the Panic of 1819 had driven good paper back east, leaving notes that storekeepers and bankers would accept only at deep discounts, sometimes for as little as one third the shin-plasters' face value. "All the notes of the Banks of the District of Columbia, and to the North and East ... are immediately bought up by the merchants and sent to the Eastward," Coles would note, "They are seldom in circulation." Secretary of the Treasury William Crawford's concern that feverish land speculation and out-of-control wildcat banks in the west risked financial collapse was something westerners couldn't understand, as they scrambled for the Bank of the United States notes and specie they needed to do business at land offices. Crawford's policy infuriated many of the most powerful men in the new state of Illinois; even Coles, long an admirer of the crusty old Georgian and a supporter of the hard-money policy, warned the Commissioner of the General Land Office, Josiah Meigs, that if at least some state bank notes were not accepted, noting that "little or no land ... has sold above two dollars per acre," then without a change in policy "much of the little that has been sold will be forfeited."[25]

Coles' hard-money stand set him apart from most Illinois politicians, especially after the state legislature, in 1821, stepped in and chartered a state bank. Authorized to issue notes of $1, $2, $3, $5, $10, and $20, each supposedly paying interest at 2 percent a year and redeemable by the state for specie in 10 years' time, the aim was supposedly to ease the strain on indebted settlers. But the bank had no money and was backed only by the untested credit of the state—basically, the ability of state officials to collect taxes. "Most of the people are in debt more than they can posably [sic] pay. Our wise Legislator [sic] have taken the matter into serious consideration and made a Bank without any specie to redeem their notes," settler Gershom Flagg sarcastically noted. The legislature elected all the directors and officials of the bank, and instructed it to lend $100 to any Illinois resident who applied, simply on his promise to repay. With a mortgage, a borrower could get even more. The notes could be used to pay taxes, and were what the state issued to pay state and county officials. And any creditor who refused the state bank paper opened himself up, under the so-called "replevin" law, to a three-year stay on any collection of money if the debtor declared he would replevy the obligation. But there was one key creditor a state replevin law

Elias Kent Kane, Thomas's most trusted lieutenant, owned slaves and worked to legalize slavery, while trying to mask his aim (courtesy Abraham Lincoln Presidential Library).

couldn't cover: "Gentlemen of de Senate," Lieutenant Governor Pierre Menard declared when the bill authorizing the bank was up for a vote. "It is moved and seconded dat de notes of dis bank be made land office money. All in favor of dat motion, say aye; all against it, say not. It is decided in de affirmative. And now, gentlemen, I bet you one hundred dollar he never be made land office money."[26]

They would not be. In the Land Office, Coles was worried about how settlers could keep up payments on their land, if state bank notes, on top of the yellowbacks and shin-plasters already flooding Illinois, drove still more hard currency out of the state. His boss, Treasury Secretary Crawford, like Coles (and unlike the frontier politicians who happily licensed wildcat banks, drew salaries from them and took out loans they never fretted about repaying) worried about how settlers would buy the land they needed to start their new lives in the west. At the same time he issued his hard-money orders to the nation's Land Offices, and over angry objections from frontier politicians, he and his allies pushed to rewrite the Public Lands Act, eventually winning legislation that ended sales on credit but that slashed the price of land nearly in half. Their reform also reduced the minimum amount of land that could be sold to an 80-acre, half-quarter section. For $100, a settler might buy enough of a farm to support himself and his family; a better deal, it seemed to the reformers, and to Coles, who spent much time helping settlers understand the new law, than the old system with the four annual installments, of $80 each, it used to take to buy a farm. The new law, of course, meant the large tracts of $2-an-acre public lands that many speculators had amassed were, overnight, worth much less. And so both of Illinois' senators, Ninian Edwards, with more than 6,000 acres, and Jesse Thomas, who had purchased more than 1,100 acres, voted against the new Public Lands Act. Coles' holdings, except for 368 acres of public land, were purchased privately, most for far less than $2; an average, in fact of 62.5 cents—unlike Edwards, Thomas or other political opponents such as William Kinney, who bought more than 9,700 acres of public lands, a price not dependant on a government-supported credit system. Nor was Coles enmeshed in the shady game of printing money that purported to have one value when paid out to a settler but that was worth less when the settler tried to use it for his own needs. Though Coles' farm at Prairieland was bigger than most, farmers saw wealth as an attribute of men who handled money: lawyers, merchants, bankers—and politicians. And that may be one critical reason why many newly-arrived Illinoisans took with a grain of salt pronouncements such as Thomas' declaration that cutting the price of public lands would encourage settlers to forfeit their holdings, while wealthy speculators would simply repurchase that land at the new, lower price, an option that smaller farmers would not have. "It certainly can never be a sound policy in any Government to act in such a manner as to make it the interest of its citizens voluntarily, and from a regard to their pecuniary interests, to incur forfeitures ... Such an example could not fail to have a baleful influence upon the public morality," Thomas told his fellow senators.[27] The difference between Coles and the rest of Illinois' political leaders on the land question would almost necessarily become a central part of his political appeal in the years to come, just as their ability to convince voters that a policy that happened to be in the self-interest of the wealthy and established was also in the interest of the struggling and aspiring.

For although western politicians like the two (normally bitterly-opposed) faction leaders from Illinois, Edwards and Thomas, cared little for the new land policy, the emigrants still flooding into Illinois liked the idea of cheaper land. And for the indebted small-holders still struggling to gather their annual installment payments, Crawford's land reform offered a helping hand, though it was not the easiest to grab hold of. The 1821 Relief Act allowed indebted settlers to relinquish some of their land, as long as they retained the 80-acre minimum set by the 1820 act. The act allowed a farmer who had paid some installments to hang on to at least some of the land he had originally claimed. The Relief Act also allowed farmers to clear their debt for 66½ cents for each dollar owed, and let widows with children apply for further credit. It was a complicated law intended to help thousands of desperate farmers refinance their holdings, but its application depended very much on the situation any particular farmer found himself in. Land Office registrars were the officials charged with helping the settlers use the Relief. Some were more interested than others: it meant listening to, often reassuring, anxious families who could not find the bank notes or specie they needed to make their latest installment payments on their farms in a few more months, helping barely literate men from hardscrabble farms look at what they'd paid already and where they stood, decide what land to keep, look where they could find funds by when they'd need to pay, plan how to run their farm to do just that. It was fussy, painstaking, case-by-case work "in which there is little to excite," Coles would remark, a day-in, day-out chore that would soon become "dull routine." But Coles plugged on. He did not make his usual spring visit to his Virginia family. When a series of complex new directives arrived from Washington that fall, Coles drafted and dug into his own pocket to pay to publish a lengthy notice on land surrenders and discounts of installment payments, "the only items which are important, at this late period, to be made known ... I avail myself of this occasion again to remind debtors ...

that unless they shall, ON OR BEFORE THE LAST DAY OF THIS MONTH, pay to the Receiver the whole balance due, or sign and file with the Register a declaration of acceptance or relinquishment, that they will not be entitled to any of the benefits of the act."[28] A partisan of Crawford, a backer of the cut in land prices and of the elimination of credit sales, Coles, of all the government officials in Illinois, was possibly the most effective, and the most public, in trying to help settlers deal with the new land laws. It was not a bad position to be in, as Illinois geared up for another election.

By February 1821, Joseph Phillips, chief justice of the state Supreme Court, had already declared himself a candidate for governor for the 1822 election, more than a year and half off. An Army captain who had settled in Illinois to pursue a career as a lawyer, Phillips had first won office as secretary of the territory, when Nathaniel Pope gave that office up to run for, and win election as, territorial delegate to Congress in 1814. Although a newcomer, the Tennessee native had fended off a bid for the same office that year from the one of the first American settlers in Illinois, the well-liked, if reticent, Shadrach Bond, who would go on to become the first governor of the state, in 1818. Phillips, by that point clearly in the Thomas camp, won the legislature's nod as chief justice of the three-member state Supreme Court, "being a lawyer and a man of high order of talent."[29] By 1821, with the two faction leaders, Edwards and Thomas, sitting in the U.S. Senate, and their top lieutenants focused on the race for the U.S. House, where Cook was sitting and where Kane still aspired to go (despite his dismal showing in 1820), Phillips seemed a natural successor to Bond, who was barred by the state Constitution from a second term. His early declaration was likely an attempt to scare off any challenger from lower down the factions' hierarchies.

But within six weeks of Phillips announcing his bid, letters in the *Edwardsville Spectator* were accusing him of being in favor of introducing slavery to Illinois.[30] As the attacks in the *Spectator* continued, his allies, perhaps remembering the furor that *Spectator* editor Hooper Warren and Senator Ninian Edwards had raised over the pro-slavery newspaper plot, tried at first to fend off the attacks. Then, suddenly, they seemed to have second thoughts.

In June, "One of the People" wrote to the *Spectator* that there were five potential candidates considering a run, including one anti-slavery man, raising the possibility that slavery could emerge as an issue to galvanize political support. Phillips' backers jumped. On July 3, they published a letter in the *Illinois Intelligencer* saying that their candidate did, in fact, favor slavery and that (in the words of the letter-writers) like most Illinoisans,

5—A new home, a new challenge 89

understood that introducing slavery to the state would be in its best interests. The idea was that wealthy Southerners, already flooding into Mississippi, Alabama and west Tennessee with their slaves, hoping to cash in on the still-frenzied cotton boom, might be wooed to Illinois, and willing to pay a premium for already-cleared farm land. That was, indeed, what many of the settlers who had bought their quarter sections on the $80-a-year plan had hoped for: they "paid out all the money they had on first installments," hoping to sell "before the other payments became due," one aspiring politician of the day later remembered.[31]

For two months, little else happened, at least in public. For all the passion that the slavery issue had stirred in the debate over Missouri's statehood, Phillips' pro-slavery stance did not embolden any of Illinois' ambitious young politicians to challenge him on that issue.

Coles must have itched to. Within weeks of Phillips' declaration he "was solicited by some of the first citizens in this part of the state to become a candidate," he wrote to one of his nieces, back in Virginia. But "in the first place, I am doubtful whether I am not too poor, and in the next place, whether it will not be productive of more trouble pain and vexation than of pleasure and happiness." But the lobbying continued, the ambition flowered, the fear that all the mutterings and plottings for slavery would succeed overcame whatever real reluctance he may have had. In October, Coles declared (in what had not yet become the usual formula) that he would "in compliance with the wishes of his friends" be candidate for governor.[32]

It was to be an uphill battle. Coles had become a prominent man in Edwardsville and in the northern and western counties, but few elsewhere knew him—less than a month after he declared his candidacy, "An Inquirer from Kaskaskia" wrote to the *Spectator* asserting that Coles was not running because he had asked the man and was told he was not. Apparently, "An Inquirer" mistook Coles for a Randolph County man named Cowles. The exchange pointed to one of Coles' biggest challenges: he was a newcomer. Coles would cast himself as a man of experience and connection, a friend of the nation's leaders, who had learned from them the arts of republican government, but it was a case that risked reminding voters of how recently he had come to Illinois. For all that many voters were furious over the roles both faction leaders, Edwards and Thomas alike, had played on the Missouri question and on the public lands acts, Coles' short stay in Illinois was a potential issue. It was one that *Edwardsville Spectator* editor Hooper Warren, whose dislike of Coles had only deepened with the years, seized on with glee: Coles wasn't really an Illinois man, the editor declared, he hadn't really moved to the state until the year before. A friend of Coles, writing under the name "Justice," fired back that Coles had moved to Illinois in year before he took up his office as register in the Land Office, that is, in 1818, evidently referring to the time when Coles was in Kaskaskia for the constitutional convention. Warren replied that Coles' long absences meant he was merely an office-seeker whose heart remained in Virginia. Coles, Warren continued, had won appointment as Land Office registrar over the objections of an unnamed member of the Illinois congressional delegation (the editor probably meant his own political mentor, Senator Ninian Edwards) who supposedly felt "our own state possessed citizens capable of filling the office," while Treasury Secretary William H. Crawford, an unpopular man in Illinois and bitter foe of Senator Edwards, was using Coles to promote his own campaign for the presidency in 1824. Six months after arriving in Illinois "he again went 'home' (the term is borrowed from his own expression)," Warren wrote. "And, moreover, it is fact, that it was his intention to have gone 'home' again last spring, to be absent during the whole summer; but the additional business at the Land Office, occasioned by the relief act, prevented the gratification of his object."[33]

But Warren was in a jam. As a partisan of Edwards, he had no real candidate to support in the race for the governor's office. Edwards himself seems to have toyed with idea of making a run for the office; frustrated in Washington, he was spending little time in the Senate, and feared he was losing control of his faction back home: "It cannot be supposed that I wished to transfer the right of nomination to the Senators," he wrote angrily to Treasury Secretary Crawford, after two of his supporters had been rejected for land office jobs. "It was well understood, however, that two parties existed in Illinois ... knowing that suitable persons could be selected from both sides for the office in question, I did not doubt that the distribution which I proposed could be made without any violation or surrender of power on the part of the President." While their leader dithered, Edwards' lieutenants back in Illinois were left hanging. Nathaniel Pope, the former territorial delegate to Congress, tried to move things along, pushing for John Reynolds, a "good natured, easy and pliable" judge and hero of the War of 1812. Reynolds wrote to Congressman Daniel Cook to see if Cook could convince Edwards, by now his father-in-law, to decide one way or the other. In February, faction member Thomas Reynolds tried as well. Edwards balked; already upset by an effort by Pope to argue him out of resigning the Senate seat, he was not at all sure he liked the idea of John Reynolds running for an office he half hankered for himself. Edwards would not commit his support; Pope finally, and half-heartedly, picked state Supreme Court justice Thomas Browne to run as the faction's candidate. "I understand you were dissatisfied with me," Edwards wrote afterwards,

5—A new home, a new challenge 91

hoping to mollify the still-peeved Pope. But by this point, his faction was near collapse. His backers had a candidate. They didn't have a campaign.[34]

At the *Spectator*, Warren had little idea what to do. "I was an admirer of Judge Phillips, for his great talents and urbanity of his manners," Warren recalled of this time. "But he was avowedly pro-slavery, and the candidate of the Thomas party." Browne, too, was an advocate of slavery for Illinois. But Warren couldn't, or wouldn't, take Coles seriously as a candidate, "and therefore adopted the burlesque ... and I succeeded in that composition far beyond my expectation." Warren had his first fun by tweaking Coles for a breach from the usual decorum in Illinois politics: instead of leaving it an ally to announce his bid for office, Coles himself declared his candidacy. "Mr. Coles observed to us," a sarcastic Warren noted, "that he came out on his own bottom; that he was neither Edwards' man nor Thomas' man and he had not the pledges of support from any individual in the state." "Justice" quickly fired off a letter to say Coles had plenty of support: "[H]e may not have received any pledge of support from either of the old parties," Justice wrote, but "he had received assurances of support from the great mass of people in his part of the state." Warren, nevertheless, couldn't resist again making sport of Coles' slip of the tongue the following week. "A portion of my friends remonstrated with me against it; others liked the fun, and between the two, I followed my own inclination," Warren wrote, somewhat smugly, many years later.[35]

In December, Coles headed down to southern Illinois to campaign, working the crowds in taverns, visiting local office-holders and the leading citizens of the older, downstate counties. For many, who would act as host for other candidates as well, his campaigning would be a welcome distraction from the dreariness of winter; some would be impressed by this man they hadn't met before. He headed east, where his old friend Morris Birkbeck's English Settlement was flourishing (despite Birkbeck's feud with co-founder George Flower; both wished to marry the same woman). "He appeared like some old acquaintance," one correspondent wrote to Vandalia's *Illinois Intelligencer*, "praised the children, and nursed little Joe, the same as you have done ... he is a fine man." Coles came across, to that writer at least, as neither a mere office seeker or a grandee whose time at the White House and in European courts gave him airs or made him arrogant. But "Neptune," writing from Vandalia and playing off Coles' now well-known line about coming to the country on his own bottom, remarked that "the new *flat*-bottomed boat Edward Coles will touch at Vandalia to take an additional supply of whisky and gingerbread" (two of the main types of ammunition in a campaign of the day). But the flatboat Coles, Neptune continued, "has been hastily built, and of the worst materials." Even those who liked Coles thought little of his prospects. "High Flyer," though impressed by Coles' "sovereign contempt for danger, for which he is famed" and "a voice seven times more terrific than the tornado," claimed the hardworking candidate was unable to win over one hostile southern Illinois crowd. Still and all, even before he finished this tour, there was, as even Warren would acknowledge, "no doubt of his being familiarly known, in every quarter, before the election."[36]

Few insiders expected Coles to mount much of a challenge. He talked of the need for a new canal to Lake Michigan, a project opposed by many in the southernmost counties as something that would cost them money but benefit only newer Illinoisans in the northern and western counties. Coles warned that the new state bank needed to take care not to flood Illinois with worthless paper, a warning little appreciated by the politicians and the influential speculators who served as directors and bank officers, or by the merchants who had received the $100, no-collateral loans the bank had been handing out, and were happily appreciating the advantages of using the notes at face value when buying produce from farmers, while taking them back at two-thirds off when the farmers came shopping a few weeks later. Though Coles tried to keep the slavery issue alive, he couldn't prod his opponents into coming out strongly on the question. His opponent Phillips' backers had already urged those "favorable to slavery to rally round" as he was the one "through whom their objects can be accomplished. Thomas C. Browne, a lawyer from the Saline region, had shrugged off the calls that mounted through that spring that the candidates declare their positions. But when the pro-Phillips *Illinois Gazette* briefly floated the idea of a new constitutional convention, reviving a notion the Thomas faction had tried in the 1820 campaign, Coles jumped. The issue he cared most about was now an issue in the election, and he spoke out with all the energy and passion he could bring to bear. In two letters to the *Illinois Intelligencer*, he told the story of how he freed his slaves. He had the paper publish the letters he had exchanged with Jefferson on slavery. Suddenly, there was real emotion and real energy in the contest.[37]

Warren quietly copied both the Jefferson letters and the emancipation story in the *Spectator*, knowing that it would help the man he so disliked, doing so, he said, "without request from anyone and without comment." But he still could not stomach supporting Coles. The issue of slavery, he wrote, "should not operate in favor of the pretensions of a candidate who may have *emancipated* half a dozen FREE negroes, with the sole view of thereby obtaining the votes of the Methodists and Yankees." Two weeks later, he printed an anonymous writer's declaration that Coles had only freed "six or eight old and worthless negroes, yet holds in bondage, in a neighboring state many young and valuable ones." That this author might have been Warren himself, blinded by his enmity to the situation of men and women who lived an easy stroll down the Marine Road from his office, is a suspicion that is hard to lay aside, for despite Coles' angry and detailed denial, and the ease with which the matter could be verified, Warren would again, years later, come out and formally charge that Coles had remained a slave-holder. Rumors and gossip that Coles had kept slaves, particularly young women slaves, dogged him for months, forcing him to write a lengthy letter to the *Intelligencer* in June (printed, after a surly delay, by Warren the next month) detailing the dealings that united Sukey with her husband, by buying out the six years remaining on Manuel's indenture so he could join his wife in the west, a debt Manuel had tried to repay. Coles added that an older woman slave had wanted to stay behind in Virginia, and that he continued to provide for her support to live there. "I not only emancipated my slaves from a conviction of the impropriety of holding them, but, from a desire to serve and befriend them, I removed, at my own expense, all those who were willing to come to this free, new and prosperous country," an angry Coles wrote. "If there be anything in my conduct ... in relation to any of the unfortunate descendents of Africa, which is in violation of my religious or political creed, I am not aware of it." Years later, Warren still savored the scandal over Coles and his slaves and continued to try to recycle the calumny.[38]

The sniping from the *Spectator* hurt. A last minute candidate, Gen. James Moore, also declared himself an opponent to slavery, threatening for a time to split the anti-slavery vote. Worse, many voters seemed unsure which candidates stood where—both Phillips and Browne had come to understand after several months of campaigning that saying anything terribly specific on slavery risked costing votes, one way or the other. "Some candidates for the office of governor ... are believed to be favorable to slavery and a new convention; that any are unfavorable is uncertain," complained "A Majority of the People" in a letter to the *Spectator*.[39]

Fun was fun, but Warren's anti-slavery friends were worried that Phillips was set to win the election in a landslide; his allies in the Edwards faction did not want to see a man so closely linked to Thomas win, either. The pressure on Warren mounted. "In the spring of 1822, four months before the election, Judge Pope came up to Edwardsville from Kaskaskia," Warren recalled. "Calling on me, he remarked with much earnestness, 'If you do not want Phillips elected, you must let Coles alone.' And he went on to demonstrate that such was the fact. This information alarmed me, and I held up."[40]

As editor of one of the four papers that circulated in the state, Warren's role was possibly not quite as decisive as his own recollection of the race suggests. But the campaign was a mess. Barely a month before Pope rode up to Edwardsville to lobby on behalf of Coles, he had been scrambling to rally the Edwards faction behind Browne. Pope's ride to Edwardsville signaled a major change in the character of the election, and, indeed, of politics in Illinois. Coles' independent run, and his outspokenness on the issue of slavery, had rendered the usual contest between factions irrelevant in the face of a far more important issue, and the people of Illinois responded. Oddly enough, Browne's own campaign seemed to reflect this, too. A Kentucky native who had settled in Shawneetown, Browne, like most politicians from the Saline region, felt slaves were essential to the financial health of the salt works. As he stumped and tried to distance himself somewhat from Edwards, Browne saw what Pope did, that the faction's waffling on slavery had rendered it irrelevant, and that the election of 1822 could well come down to that critical issue. Browne, though, mistook the feelings of his neighbors for the feeling of the state. Faction may have decided Illinois elections before 1822, but it would no longer: "Principles, not Men," as Coles declared in a well-publicized July 4 toast.[41]

Fueled by long speeches, sharply worded letters to the newspapers and much whisky, Illinoisans were engrossed by this new kind of election. Coles and Phillips stumped across the state, speaking at the little "groceries" in the county seats and tiny hamlets along the state's few, rude roads. The arguments among voters started long before either man swung through and continued long after the candidates had moved on. "The whole state is overwhelmed by a sea of politics," Nathaniel Buckmeister, a Madison County farmer, wrote to his brother John, that April. The ferocity of the debate was a shock to many. "There was probably never an election more warmly contested than our next election will be for all our state and national officers. Where ever you go, you hear of nothing else," Horatio Newhall, a Harvard-educated doctor who settled in Bond County, wrote to his family back in Massachusetts. But to some older settlers, what was remarkable was not the heat of the battle, but rather what they saw to be the main focus of it: for all that the new state bank was already looking shaky, even though the new public land policy still excited anger, despite the crying need for better roads and a canal to the Great Lakes, the biggest issue of all was something else. "No measure was discussed except the slavery question," Judge John Reynolds would recall, nearly 25 years later.[42]

That question carried Coles to victory. It was a squeaker: The final tally in the August vote was 2,854 votes for Coles, a mere 167-vote margin above Phillips' 2,687, while Browne won 2,443 and Moore, 622. Coles won more than eight in 10 votes in Madison County, the biggest in the state,

1822 Election

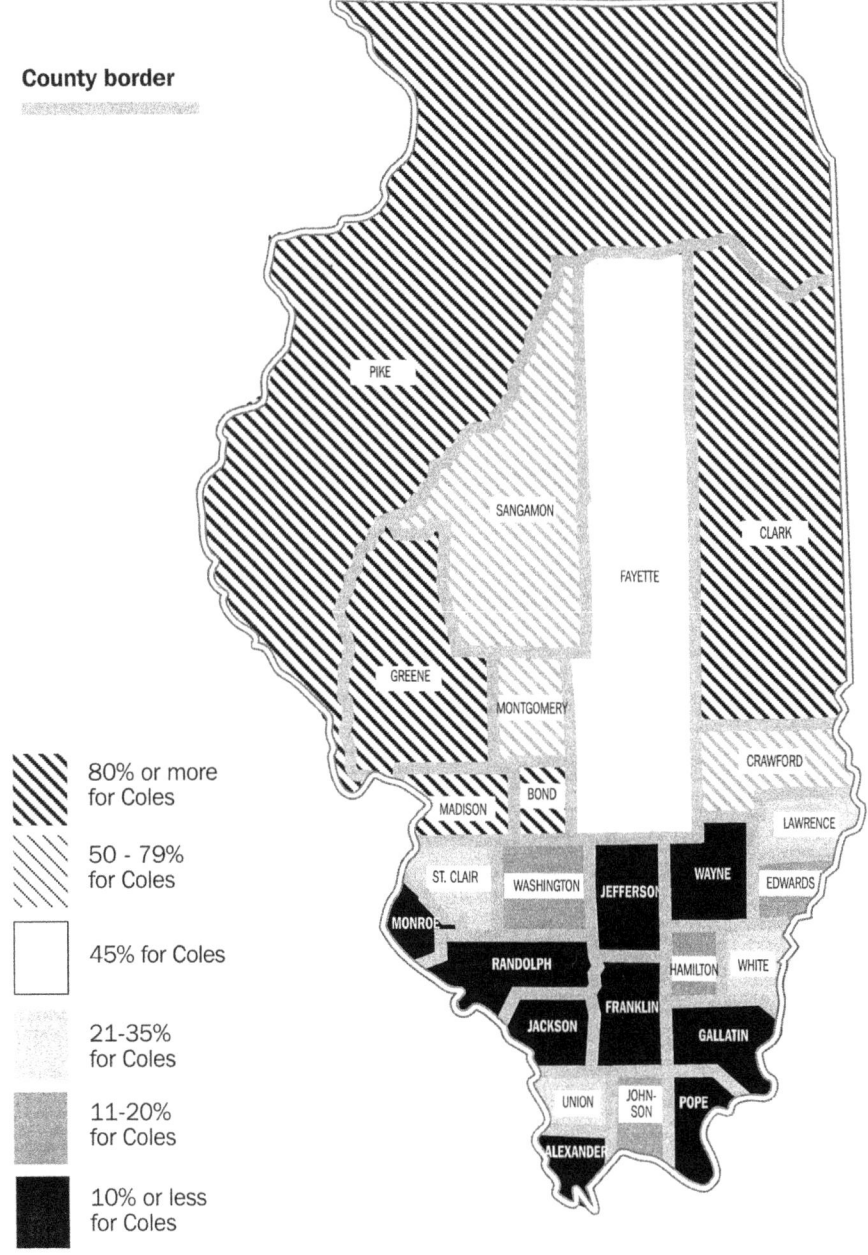

The election of 1822 (courtesy John Ailor).

and carried the fast-growing counties of Bond, Clark, Greene and Pike with margins equal to or larger than that. He carried the other northern counties, with the exception of Fayette, where he received 45 percent of the vote, with margins in the 55 to 60 percent range. Phillips failed to win a majority in his home county of St. Clair, but carried most of the counties along the Mississippi River, including the old French heartland. Browne's margins in the Saline region and most of the counties along the Ohio River were nearly as large as Coles' in the north.* In the absence of much of an effort by either the Thomas or Edwards factions, the pattern seems to be as much a reflection of people voting for the man from their section as anything. But it seems likely that Coles' role as Land Office registrar, particularly as the finances of the new settlers were strained by the burden of trying to pay off debt with deeply discounted bank paper (banks, that is, that were organized by the political elite, discounts the elite insisted on at their stores and mills) played an important role.

Did the slavery issue? The county that depended most on slaves—Gallatin, home to the Saline—voted for Browne, as did the counties around it. Most of the older counties, the ones mainly settled by migrants from the South, went generally for the pro-slavery Phillips, though Coles pulled more than a quarter of votes cast in Union and White counties. Coles' home county, meanwhile, had plenty of slaves and would be slave-holders itself, but still voted overwhelming for the hometown boy—while St. Clair, with a similar mix of views, somewhat favored its own local candidate, Phillips, if not as strongly as Madison did Coles. In both counties, as in the counties farther south, it is worth remembering that most Southern emigrants to Illinois did not come with slaves; many came precisely because they did not want to live, or felt they could no longer afford to live, in slave country. Few could have paid the price to buy and own a slave; and if an

*For readers interested in Coles' margins and the numbers of votes cast for him:

Northern counties	votes	share	American Bottom	votes	share	Eastern counties	votes	share	Southern counties	votes	share
Bond	252	81%	Madison	613	81%	Edwards	61	14%	Alexander	0	0
Clark	65	83%	Monroe	23	8%	Hamilton	25	11%	Franklin	22	9%
Crawford	165	59%	St. Clair	176	25%	Lawrence	60	21%	Jackson	20	9%
Fayette	104	45%				Wayne	15	7%	Jefferson	14	8%
Greene	438	86%	**Saline area**						Johnson	21	15%
Montgomery	67	60%		votes	share				Randolph	15	3%
Pike	89	85%	Gallatin	32	6%				Union	105	28%
Sangamon	278	55%	Pope	14	4%				Washington	43	16%
			White	137	26%						

Calculated from Theodore C. Pease, ed., Illinois Election Returns, 1818–1848 (Springfield: Illinois State Historical Library, 1923), 14–8.

5—A new home, a new challenge

indenture seemed an economic alternative to hiring hands, there were few enough free blacks around to sign up for one: indentures had to be purchased from the wealthy men who already held the bonds. Aspiring to own a slave was so far beyond the possible that it seems most likely that the majority of farmers, even those who came from the Southern states, gave it little mind. And while a mutual distaste of Southerners for Yankees seems to have carried over when each migrated to Illinois, no one could have doubted Coles was a son of Virginia—he could barely forget it himself, after all, if Warren is to be believed.

Was Coles' style too much the aristocrat, too clearly a member of the elite?* If so, Illinoisans in different parts of the state reacted strikingly differently (and somehow managed to consider a state Supreme Court Chief Justice and wealthy, politically active lawyer to not be members of the state's highest social reaches; just as they would ignore Ninian Edwards' fine broadcloth coat, florid speechifying and slave-driven carriage when they elected him governor in 1826). In the end, perhaps it was simply that the argument that a "come-here" newcomer shouldn't be elected governor may have resonated more in the older counties than in the northern region, with so many new immigrants of its own. And if it did, it could be that that was a hint that merely holding office might not impress Illinoisans as much as it had, when it came to deciding whether a politician had earned their support. Perhaps it was more what you did—how you helped implement a Relief Act—or the stands you took, on banking, on the canal, or even slavery, for those for whom that was the issue, that really counted.[43]

Coles so little expected to succeed that he had left for Virginia before the final count: "Mr. Coles, despairing of his election, left this place on Monday last, for his 'home' in Virginia," Warren snidely noted, a few days after the voting and before all the ballots had been counted. "If elected he

---

*James Simeone, Democracy and Slavery in Frontier Illinois, 17-8, 26, asserts Coles' highhanded manner alienated him from what he calls "The White Folks," the settlers and small farmers, mainly from the South, who made up the bulk of Illinois' electorate, but his brief discussion of the 1822 race of governor, p. 95, focuses on the implosion of the Ninian Edwards machine and says little about how or why Coles won. Kurt Leichtele, "Coles: An Agrarian," 121-144, suggests Edwards himself half-wanted to run and that his months of indecision discouraged stronger candidates. Coles' strong stand for an Illinois River–Lake Michigan Canal, which would be opposed by many in the southern counties as an expenditure of tax dollars with no benefit to them, was likely the decisive factor, Leichtele concludes. Suzanne Cooper Guasco's thoughtful review, "Confronting Democracy: Edward Coles and the Cultivation of Authority in the Young Nation" (Ph.D. diss., College of William and Mary, 2004), 200-2, makes the point Simeone might have about the impact of Coles' supposedly aristocratic style in the gubernatorial election, but notes that this was a charge that could be levied against his opponents as well; Coles' antislavery stand was critical to his effort to differentiate himself, and may well have worked, she argues. With what at least one newspaper writer called "a voice like a tornado," though, Coles might not have come across as quite the snooty Virginian that Simeone, in particular, posits.

will return in November and this state will be his place of residence for the ensuing four years." But as the votes were tallied, and it became clear that Coles would win, Warren muttered darkly about plots to promote Treasury Secretary Crawford or Congressman Daniel Cook, and blasted the *Intelligencer* for an editorial congratulating Coles on his election. "We do believe the circumstances of his election is degrading to the character of the state. The President can no longer hesitate, when he may wish to get rid of a useless lackey, to appoint him to a fiat office in Illinois," Warren wrote, gracious as ever. *Intelligencer* editor William Brown, though "concerned to find ... that we should have wounded the feelings of our 'typographical' friend at Edwardsville," replied that "in truth, we should have been better satisfied in the election of another candidate ... our 'adhesion,' therefore, as the Spectator is pleased to call it, was but an expression of our belief that in the choice of Mr. Coles the state would have nothing to regret." Brown then went on to point out that, as Cook and Crawford were political opponents, Warren's fears of intrigue made little sense. "To use a housewifely adage, the proof of the pudding is in the eating of it."[44]

Cook, in any event, won his re-election handily, with 56 percent of the vote; for all of Missouri's anger over his opposition to its bid for statehood, Illinoisans didn't seem to mind. On the other hand, pro-slavery Adolphus Hubbard won the lieutenant governorship, from which office over the next few years he would conspire with Coles' opponents to unseat him. It would turn out that roughly two-thirds of the men elected to the state Senate and House favored rethinking Illinois' half-hearted prohibition of slavery.

Coles didn't care. As if oblivious to the narrowness of his victory and his lack of allies in the legislature, he remained away from Illinois for weeks, visiting family and friends back in Virginia and in Philadelphia—and thinking hard, no doubt, about the import of his narrow victory, one he had not expected. His mentor, Madison, sending him a pedometer and the gently-jesting advice to "to walk in a straight path with measured steps," with the help of that step-counting, distance-measuring device.[45] Perhaps that gift, and the recollection of the many aggravations of lobbying a hostile legislature, as the wartime Congress had been, led Coles to consider how he would deal with state legislators he knew he'd have to fight; perhaps the little clock-like instrument reminded him of how slowly his heroes, Madison, Jefferson, had moved to secure the Rights of Man for every man, even (so Coles was convinced) for slaves. Perhaps, on the verge now of turning 36, he thought he might be running short of time to accomplish what he really wanted. In any event, he made it back to the tiny new capital, Vandalia, deep in the woods of southern Illinois, just in time for the December opening of the legislative session. There, in the small frame Capitol, primitive and plain as a Quaker meeting house and still lacking one of the two fireplaces a crooked contractor had promised to install, all but one of the 18 state Senators and the 36 state representatives crammed themselves into the 30 foot by 30 foot House chamber to hear what their governor had to say. And there, he flung out his challenge to the legislature and to the state.[46]

"On this first occasion of meeting you," he said, "it affords me great pleasure to be able to congratulate you on the high degree of prosperity which, notwithstanding some unpleasant features, the face of our country, both national and local continues to present. Let us never forget how much of this prosperity we owe to the blessings of a government founded on the unalienable and indefeasible rights of man."[47] These formal words likely would have struck an odd note with at least some of the legislators, squirming on the hard wooden seats of the low-ceiling chamber, thinking as they must have been of the neighbors paid with worthless paper for hard-won harvests. Some, too, would have wondered at this now-old-fashioned-sounding echo from the Declaration: for who fretted about the rights of man these days, four decades after the nation's independence had been won, and why now, as a state legislature convened for another session?

As the legislators wriggled and wondered and listened, Coles moved to his first major charge to the legislators: saying that the intelligent and virtuous men who lived under such a political system as Illinois,' to say nothing of the men who exercised power in that system, would surely be concerned to educate the generations to come. As the legislators had never been particularly interested in spending money on schools, their new governor's charge would have made them feel even more wary. Surely, too, the new governor blithely continued, such a people would see the importance of improving the channels of commerce that linked them to the rest of the nation. A canal from the Illinois River to Lake Michigan, improvements to the national road leading east to Wheeling, Va. (now West Virginia), were vital investments for the future of the state, he said. The state-owned salt works, and the vast tracts of Military Tract bounty lands held by people out of state, were potentially huge sources of revenue to fund these investments, he added. The men from the southern counties grew more concerned. So did many of the legislators who acted as agents for the out-of-state speculators, or who had been speculating in Military Tract lands themselves. Coles, having briefly raised the issue of how to pay, but leaving the details nerve-wrackingly vague, returned once more to discourse on the benefits of the canal.[48]

Then, abruptly: "The Ordinance, established by Congress for the government of the North-Western Territory, declares that neither slavery nor involuntary servitude shall exist in the country. Yet notwithstanding this, slavery still exists in the State."[49]

It was true, Coles added, that the French settlers were promised their rights and property would not be imperiled after the United States took over the Illinois country, but nobody could believe that was intended to forever bar Illinois from eliminating slavery, while "none should deny that after a lapse of near forty years she can do so without being subject to reproach, unless it be from having tolerated it so long."[50]

Now, said Coles, "Conceiving it not less due our principles than to the rights of those held in bondage, that they should be restored to their liberty, I earnestly recommend to the legislature that just and equitable provisions be made for the abrogation of slavery in the State."[51]

CHAPTER 6

The coup

Principles and rights were one thing, the presumption of the upstart governor quite another. Coles' bold call to free the slaves stunned the powerful men who had been quietly pushing for slavery; now, as the legislators organized themselves for the session, the little capital deep in the woods was abuzz; in its half dozen boarding houses, politicians and hangers-on would seethe and drink and plot. Coles had picked a fight, on purpose, that they simply had not expected of him. Still, shocked though they had been by Coles' speech, his opponents quickly regrouped to plot their counterattack; in the days that followed, the leaders of the state Senate would talk and lobby and count heads—and grow more and more certain they could carry off their plan to rewrite the constitution to allow slavery, and thereby remake the state. The 1822 election gave the pro-slave men 12 of the upper chamber's 18 seats; or, at least, they would have that when the curmudgeonly John Grammar, from far-southern Union County, finally deigned to show up and take his seat that he had so far, inexplicably, declined to claim. Once Grammar made it to the capital, the pro-slave men knew they would have two-thirds of the votes in the state Senate, and be able to demand constitutional change. The mechanism would be a resolution authorizing a referendum; it would be the voters themselves who, under the current constitution, had the power to call for a new convention. For now, the senators were content to ignore Coles and simply continue their call for a new convention, a convention they expected would legalize slavery, though their tactics shifted to this extent: "Constitution, not Slavery," would be their rallying cry.[1]

State Senator Theophilus W. Smith, already emerging as a leader of the pro-convention group, and "'up to the eyes' in every political intrigue of the day," now took on the task of replying to the governor's speech, on behalf of a five-member special committee of the Senate, slave-holders all. He dashed off the curt response that "there is no other means left by which to accomplish the object of the governor's message, than to call a Convention to alter the Constitution." In Smith, Coles would have his most formidable opponent. (Never a retiring man, Smith would later confront Ninian Edwards with a loaded pistol, and have his jaw broken moments later when the much-larger Edwards slapped the gun out of his hands.) The feisty little state senator "got his political education in Tammany Hall, and must have been an adept in the trickery for which that institution was famed," Judge Joseph Gillespie recalled. "Everything done in our political affairs that was rash, reckless and unprecedented, was laid to Judge Smith's charge." An Edwardsville man, he knew Coles, of course, but their relationship was likely badly strained: Smith was the man who had offered Coles' freed ex-slaves Robert Crawford and Thomas Cobb the job they had had so much hope for, during their third year in Illinois, the one making bricks at $20 a month—but he had refused to pay them in hard cash as promised, or as they thought he promised, offering only state paper, worth a third its face value. Though "very much out of temper" and complaining they had been deceived and cheated, Crawford and Cobb could do little about the powerful Smith, as the state's Black Code barred them from even testifying in court against him.[2]

Even as Smith wrote, skirmishing started. In the first days of the session, the Senate brushed aside a proposal by the fiery Baptist preacher Daniel Parker, who represented the eastern counties of Edgar, Clark and Crawford (and would later expound the "two seed doctrine" that would define an important branch of Primitive Baptist theology in the decades to come), to begin each day's session with a prayer; putting him in his place because the earnest pastor also had proposed giving the state more authority to oversee the terms of indentures and more power to protect freedmen from kidnapping.[3]

In the state House of Representatives, the pro-slavery, pro-convention party would be on less certain ground, for while they thought they had the two-thirds margin they would need to carry the resolution for a convention referendum, they weren't completely sure. Nervously, the pro-convention speaker, William Alexander, named a committee to draft a response to the governor. The chairman was the elderly Risdon Moore, of St. Clair County, a devout convert to Methodism who had bound under "voluntary" Illinois indentures the 18 slaves he brought with him from Georgia when he first moved west—and yet had run as an anti-slavery delegate to the 1818 convention. The two other committee members were men from generally pro-slavery counties, John Emmitt of far-southern White County, and Dr. Conrad Will, the Jackson County physician and merchant who had run his own small salt works and who was lobbying Coles, unsuccessfully as it would turn out, to be named superintendent of the larger

6—The coup

State Senator Theophilus W. Smith, a key leader in the campaign for a new convention to rewrite Illinois' Constitution to allow slavery (courtesy Abraham Lincoln Presidential Library).

U.S. Saline. Will had won a reputation as a clever operator when he once declared he would pay a bounty for every eagle killed, with the proof to be their gizzards—an organ, disappointed hunters soon found, that eagles do not have.[4]

As they waited for the committee, and started counting heads in the lower House, pro-convention leaders Alexander Field and Emmanuel West remembered the lesson from the last Territorial Assembly session, when in 1818 some of the anti-slavery delegates trapped themselves into arguing against statehood. It was the kind of debating tactic that always suited Field, a forceful young lawyer who had recently moved to Union County (and who would later move to New Orleans, where he would defiantly declare himself a Unionist despite repeated death threats). West, a Delaware man who loved to play politics so much that he would let his farm fail for lack of attention, had arrived in Illinois with his two slaves just in time to see opponents of slavery stumble into opposing statehood, and thought he could now set a similar snare. With "few superiors in conversation ... absolutely charming in that line," West had been elected as one of three state representatives from Madison County, Coles' home county and an anti-slave stronghold despite the relatively large number of slave-holders who settled there, too. Looking around at his neighbors, West was convinced that western Illinois' opposition to slavery was neither deeply felt nor universal.[5]

It would be an entirely different kind of politician who would challenge them. He was George Churchill, the awkward old bachelor from Madison County, "badly formed and unprepossessing ... sallow, his eye lusterless and expression dull." Churchill was nevertheless a popular man with his neighbors, an odd character who did not want elected office and who had run for the legislature because of his ferocious opposition to slavery, the same reason he had campaigned to be a delegate to the 1818 convention. Now, starting the first of what would be seven terms on the Illinois state House and state Senate, Churchill was determined to continue his war on slavery. Four days after Coles' speech, he rose to present a petition to the state House from several Madison County freedmen, men whom kidnappers had tried to smuggle into slave territory for sale and who were now seeking the right to vote, believing that full citizenship would give them protection that the laws of Illinois could not. Astonishingly, this man who "entered no rings or cliques" and "toiled like a dray-horse but never made a speech of more than five minutes' length" had won leave from the pro-slavery leaders of the House to offer this petition, seeking to extend rights to men whom those same legislative leaders believed ought to be slaves. Or perhaps not so astonishingly after all: for, it would turn out, the petition itself had been written by one of Churchill's political opponents, and the aim was to trick him into pushing for something—voting rights for freedmen—that was still unpalatable to many Illinoisans. If he balked, he risked being painted by his enemies as "the friend of kidnappers, or ... so illiberal and vindictive that we would not present a memorial written by a gentleman who opposed his election."[6]

His effort failed. Reassured, Field, West and Speaker of the House William Alexander wouldn't even allow the venerable Jacob Ogle, one of the first American settlers in Illinois, to offer a similar petition on the following day.[7]

But whether the consensus to keep freedmen from voting would become a consensus for allowing slavery was still unclear. Risdon Moore's committee did not fall in line; for while Dr. Will, as expected, argued for a convention, the second southern man on the committee, Emmitt, agreed with Moore that the Northwest Ordinance trumped all and that slaves, once in Illinois, were free, with their freedom a right that was beyond the power of the state to take:

> If upon the common law principle, that liberty depends not upon the complexion, Lord Mansfield, one of the greatest judges that ever dignified a British bench ... felt himself compelled to discharge the slave from the service of his master, far stronger must be on us the operation of the WRITTEN LAW in forcing us to the same result ... he who was once a

slave was already free—free from the very instant the master evinced his determination of becoming a resident of the Territory, if not indeed from the very moment the slave was made to set his foot upon the shore.[8]

Moore and Emmitt did not stop there: The indenture system, they continued, was a sham, for men and women could not bind themselves in the Illinois version without some form of legal consideration being paid and "your committee would vainly endeavor to persuade themselves of the existence of such a consideration in these indentures and they can consider the whole system as nothing less than an illegal and unjustifiable attempt to evade the provisions of the ordinance." The two legislators even wound up their report with a blast at the Black Code, complaining that its penalties were excessive and unjust, while "it is very questionable whether the General Assembly have a constitutional right to discriminate in the punishment of negroes and white men committing the same offences.... It would no doubt violate the constitution and every principle of legislation to punish a mechanic one way and a farmer another for the same offence. The impropriety, it strikes your committee, is equally great in either of these cases."[9]

To declare slavery a wrong so directly, to say so strongly that a Black Code was unjust, to argue that the law insisted on immediate emancipation, that liberation came with the simple act of stepping onto the soil of Illinois, was, like Coles' own inaugural speech, to take a radical stance. Their opponents would have a surprisingly difficult time responding, as if they had been taken aback both by the boldness of Coles' inauguration speech and by Moore and Emmitt's report. Even the saddler-turned agitator Benjamin Lundy (who had moved his newspaper, the *Genius of Universal Emancipation,* to Tennessee the year before precisely so he could challenge slavery from deep inside slave country) would have in these years a careful sense of how an abolitionist's call of conscience could disconcert and quickly warm to anger American politicians of the 19th century—he would warn a British sympathizer five years after the Illinoisans took their stand that he should go slow with a call for immediate emancipation because it was so "far in advance of American opinion." In contrast to the stance Coles, Moore and Emmitt took on emancipation and the Black Code, at this time the nation's leading anti-slavery organization, the Pennsylvania Abolition Society, still largely focused its efforts on helping freedmen and runaways in its own state fight in court for their freedom, as well as in helping Philadelphia's free black community build their own schools, establish their own churches and try to find work in an increasingly hostile city. While the Pennsylvanians turned inward, for having won their case for gradual emancipation in their commonwealth they felt it imprudent to push too hard in other states, other anti-slavery activists on both sides of the Atlantic tended in this period to turn their attention to the slave trade itself, which continued despite the fact that both the United States and Britain banned their citizens from participating; that this remained a serious concern even into the 1820s was likely underlined for them when in the summer of 1820 the U.S. Revenue Cutter *Dallas* seized the slave ship *Antelope* (with an American captain sailing under the Venezuelan flag) and her cargo of 281 Africans. After five days of argument before the U.S. Supreme Court in March 1825, Chief Justice John Marshall ruled that U.S. law deemed the slave trade to be piracy, but that since the United States couldn't write laws for other nations, the 39 Africans claimed by Spanish owners could be sold into slavery in the United States on their behalf. (Some of the Africans on the *Antelope* were claimed by Portuguese citizens, but the court felt their claims were obscure; most, presumably, were bound for places like Venezuela, the West Indies or the U.S. Gulf Coast, where, although their importation was banned, the *Antelope*'s owners nevertheless expected to find a ready market.) Frustrated that the most prominent anti-slavery Americans were no longer as focused on the condition of slaves in the Southern states, concerned that some were joining forces with "moderate" politicians from the South to push the American Colonization Society's idea that colonizing Liberia would be the best way to gradually liberate America's slaves, free blacks in Boston and Philadelphia were just beginning to think it was time to organize their own efforts to fight for freedom, with the Massachusetts General Colored Association forming itself in 1826 with a call for immediate emancipation and equality of the races. Their agitation, with such works as David Walker's *Appeal to the Colored Citizens of the World* in 1829, coming as the Second Great Awakening swept New England, rekindling religious feeling and teaching that it was an act of faith to fight for better conditions for men and women on Earth, would eventually spark the mass abolitionist movement that from the 1830s on would push the nation to understand it had to eliminate the scourge of slavery. But all this was, of course, years in the future. Though Coles, Moore and Emmitt understood what many of their fellow citizens, however humble in station, thought about slavery, the politically savvy men of the legislature and the factions did not.[10]

Unable to depend on their committee to deliver the expected riposte to Coles' call to abolish slavery, indenture and the Black Code, the somewhat baffled Field and West were now even less certain they could count on the 24 votes they would need to carry the call for a convention in the House. Will's call for a convention, like that of the Senate committee, was intended to undercut the anti-slavery men by painting them as opponents of the sovereignty of the voters, the same tactic that worked so well in 1818. By including Moore on a committee that they had expected would write a report rejecting Coles' proposals, the pro-slavery leaders in the House of Representatives expected they could overwhelm the handful of anti-slavery men in the legislature, convincing them that they could not win and should not spend their energy even trying. But now, as they started sounding out the rest of the House, they would find that many who were unwilling to fight about slavery were disinclined to fight for it. They would have to offer something to move these men. It would be time now for deal-making.

The biggest deal to make now involved the Lake Michigan canal. For many legislators from northern and western counties, the canal linking Lake Michigan with the Illinois River (which flowed south to the Mississippi) was, far more than slavery, the main issue of the session—canal trumped conscience for more than one northern man. It was in the eastern markets it would open, and the Yankee settlers it would bring, that these legislators saw Illinois' future wealth. The deal to be struck was obvious, and it was made. "The southerners offered to the northerners their support and votes in these terms: 'If you vote for our convention, we will vote for your canal.'"[11] By itself, though, the canal-for-convention swap would not lock up all the uncertain or undecided northern county men, Field and West feared. There would have to be other wheeling and dealing, over the division of rapidly growing counties, over the many offices in the legislature's power to grant. "It was well understood at Vandalia that there were two great objects to be accomplished by a new convention, which are these—the removal of [the statehouse from] Vandalia and the introduction of slavery," one Assembly-watcher wrote afterwards, adding: "Being so anxious for the convention we agreed to give them the canal."[12] "Log rolling, as it is aptly called, became the order of the day," Coles would complain. "No measure, however salutary, was allowed to pass unless its friends would consent to a vote for a convention." All in all, complained state Senator Thomas Sloo, "a very tedious and unpleasant session ... nothing but a continued scene of intrigue and electioneering."[13]

The backroom politicking was about to bring a bitter little squabble from Illinois' northern frontier to the fore, one that tells a lot about politics and how it was conducted by Illinois' professional politicians of the period. The election of 1822 had taken its strangest turn in the Military Tract, north and west of the Illinois River, a barely settled swath of prairie that had been reserved by the federal government for the veterans who had fought in the War of 1812. At the time, it was sketchily organized as the gigantic County of Pike. An ambitious, newly arrived lawyer from New York State named Nicholas Hansen had challenged the tough old frontier boss who had pretty much run Pike since he had drifted in as one of the first settlers on the Tract soon after the war with England. John Shaw, the "Black Prince," a hot-tempered former riverboat trader in Arkansas and Missouri, who owned a grist mill and tannery in Pike and dominated the sprawling, mostly unsettled county—Shaw "forged deeds even by the quire, doctored poll books ... so great was his influence, but at the same time so injurious to the settlers, that the public issue was gotten up in politics, of 'Shaw' and Anti-Shaw,'" early settlers recalled.[14]

Nor was Hansen above playing land games and politics. For the Military Tract was fertile ground—and not just for corn. Many of the ex-soldiers entitled to bounty lands found the prospect of a fast sale to a big speculator much more attractive than the thought of packing up family and household and making the hard trek west to clear a subsistence farm. St. Louis and Edwardsville merchants, as well as Illinois politicians of all stripes (including, of course, Coles), bought thousands of acres cheap, believing they'd soon be able to unload the land at a hefty mark-up. The taxes that non-residents owned, and sometimes paid, were a stream of cash that the state government and the men who ran it found irresistible, since those taxes were levied on men who did not vote by politicians elected by irascible, tax-hating Illinoisans who did.

The tight circle of "Yorkers," including Hansen, who had migrated to the Military Tract from New York, saw other possibilities as well, as did the Black Prince himself. The state of Illinois was to share some of the non-residents' taxes with county governments established, or soon to be established, in the military bounty lands. Since the business of those county governments was little more than the collection of fees for the recording of land sales, there was potential for much lucrative business to be done. In the scramble for this boodle, the Yorkers had already struck a telling blow the year before when, in January 1821, the legislature had split Madison County in two, designating the Military Tract and the Indian lands of northernmost Illinois as Pike County. Hansen had ridden down to Vandalia to lobby for the appointment of his friend, Daniel D. Smith, as recorder of deeds for Pike, working connections in the Thomas faction with success. And Smith, the infuriated Shaw would charge, was "as opposite and opposed to virtue, gratitude or generosity as the east is to the west," but nevertheless not so immune to the concept that "when HE was so fortunate himself as to get transferred from a state of starvation in Madison County to a good, fat office in Pike ... he was under the greatest obligation to get Hansen into some lucrative OFFICE." The office Smith had his eye on was Judge of Probate. "Mr. Hansen obtains the appointment and enters the county as a judge," Shaw complained. "The little business to be done in that office here, occupies but very little time, compared with the salary and charges—though these were trifling compared to the heavy debts they were able to discharge, the balance of his time is occupied in recording deeds at the office of his old friend the RECORDER."[15]

One coup of lobbying in the state Senate did not, of course, mean jobs for life. Security came with control of a county's seats in the legislature, and Hansen and Smith knew they had to bid for that. Quickly joining forces with County Clerk James Whitney, the Alton merchant Leonard Ross and his brother O.M. Ross, who was preoccupied at the time with promoting a settlement at the Pike County hamlet of Atlas, Hansen began organizing to take Pike's House seat in the 1822 election. "Accordingly, they made every exertion to secure all the justices of the peace ... to induce them to conduct the election just as THEY would direct," Shaw would write. The Yorkers won control of the county commissioners' court in 1821 and quickly divided Pike into three voting precincts, including the one at O.M. Ross' settlement, Atlas. That was a critical step, for the only polling spot in the Military Tract before the organization of Pike County had been at Shaw's tavern, in the Coles Grove settlement—in those days, owning a polling place gave advantages in an election that went far beyond the mere authority to count votes, since it necessarily included who would be allowed inside in order to vote. "It was clearly ascertained that I should have a large majority of the votes at Colesgrove and at Spoon River, and at the other precinct in Ross' settlement, Hansen would receive an almost unanimous vote, as every man who did not think in concert with Ross' views on the subject, was immediately coerced into a proper way of thinking," Shaw complained. Who would serve as election judge mattered in Pike County, particularly given Shaw's own reputation for inviting friends over from Missouri to drink and vote on Illinois election days. In the 1822 vote, Shaw's opponents in the county seat realized this sooner than did the Black Prince and dispatched an ally to Coles Grove to keep things honest. Once in the hamlet, the election judge insisted that voters declare their choice away from Shaw's tavern, and ordered the two official poll-watchers there to depart "on account of its not suiting the would-be election judge," Shaw sniffed. Shaw and the men who had gathered at his place to vote—"one half the citizens of Pike County," he claimed—simply went ahead and voted over the judge's objections. "Fellow citizens, let me ask you what would you have done in this case, when seventy or eighty of the most respectable people in this county saw a stripling man without any color of authority make choice of two young men who have neither property nor character, to judge of the most sacred rights of man? And this step take on purpose the render the poll illegal," Shaw continued.[16]

Shaw carried the Coles Grove poll by an unlikely and quite suspicious 83 to none; his votes there accounted for virtually all his support in the country, letting him handily triumph over Hansen's 54. "In the Kingdom of Pike, I presume they had a warm time," William P. McKee, who had been a clerk under Coles in the Edwardsville Land Office, wrote to his former boss a few days later, to let him know he had won a strong majority there, with 89 votes despite Hansen's loss—Hansen being, if not quite an ally, a man Coles was already hoping to win as a supporter (he had, back in 1819, at the Fourth of July dinner Coles attended in Edwardsville, given a toast that declared slave-holders' hearts were "scarred by avarice beyond the reach of human woes").[17] Hansen sued for the seat, accusing his opponent of winning with the votes of men from Missouri, as well as with the backing of residents of Madison and Greene Counties, Illinois. Even though he ran as a strong supporter of the Thomas faction, and even though his lawsuit came before Judge John Reynolds, a leader in the Edwards faction who would in a few weeks be lobbying the legislature to remove Thomas from his U.S. Senate seat, Hansen won his point. Perhaps it was Shaw's margin, or his reputation, or the odd pattern of votes in the three precincts that led the judge to question the credibility of the count. The House committee on elections, too, rebuffed Shaw, though there the consideration of such Thomas partisans as R.C. Ford, of Crawford County, may have been more to the point: "If Hansen were turned out Thomas would lose a vote," he grumbled to fellow legislator William Lowery. On January 9, Thomas won re-election to the U.S. Senate with 29 votes, including Hansen's.[18]

At this point, the legislative leaders who were pushing for a constitutional convention on slavery thought they had Hansen's vote locked up. He was a Thomas man, after all, and he had signaled quite clearly that he wanted things that it was in their power to give: he had suggested to them that his supporters needed the legislature to reserve $750 of non-residents' tax revenue to build roads in Pike County, as well as their desire to split off a new county, Fulton, to make sure Shaw could never again challenge their control of county offices and the fees they brought. The pro-convention leaders understood, agreed, and were content that they had a deal. In a test vote on January 27, Hansen was one of 22 votes for a convention, two short of the two-thirds required, except that one of the no votes was Thomas Rattan, a convention backer who voted with the losing side so he could reserve the right to call for a reconsideration of the vote later in the session. Field and West needed to nail down only one more supporter, and moved the Fulton County bill through that same day to make good on one of their promises to Hansen. Two days later, they shook loose from committee that bill that gave Hansen his $750 of non-residents' taxes.[19]

The last vote for a convention would be hard to find. The pro-convention leaders stepped up the pressure. They sent supporters—"couriers," they called them—racing out to seven critical counties, with the assignment of rounding up signed petitions calling for a convention. They hoped these "Instructions" might sway some of the men from southern counties who had opposed the convention, and wanted to be sure their own supporters did not bolt. They had limited success. John Emmitt, the legislator from far southern White County who had confounded the House leaders by backing Moore's anti-slavery declaration, and Thomas Mather, from the old French settlements of Randolph County, seem to have shrugged off whatever pressure the instructions from their home counties might have meant—Mather's constituents had re-elected him despite his well-known opposition to slavery.[20]

One reason the pro-slavery push had not been terribly effective was that the couriers, for all the fanfare of their urgent rides back to the voters, were not particularly the kind of men to convince ordinary citizens of anything; the legislators themselves had to remain in Vandalia, so, too, did the most influential lobby members, who, with such big issues as the canal still hanging fire, to say nothing of possible appointment to highly paid, undemanding state and county government jobs, did not have the time to spare to hit the hustings. In any event, the couriers didn't actually convince all that many to sign the Instructions: only 130 or so from Greene and Morgan did, "after the most indefatigable efforts" of the man the pro-convention men dispatched there. That man was John Shaw.[21]

The conventionists may have turned to Shaw because they needed all the help they could get, and he was hanging around Vandalia, still trying to unseat Hansen and stop his plan to carve up Pike County. But they may have had other reasons, too, to start talking to Shaw, and to start taking his campaign against Hansen more and more seriously—for in the taverns and boarding houses, there were lots of mutterings about Pike County's legislator. The most alarming to the pro-slavery men were that he had been seen with Coles—"in this very contact," one anonymous legislator commented later, "is to be found, in great measure, the excitement produced by the convention," for if Hansen hadn't changed his vote the convention proposal "would have been quietly submitted and quietly settled."[22]

The capital would soon feel as if things were even more out of control. The evening after the first test vote in the House failed, on Jan. 28, fire destroyed the state bank building, a block away from the statehouse, on 4th Street, by the town green. No one knew how the fire broke out, since cashier James Kelly had carefully checked the fireplace, unused since the morning, before locking up for the day to take his supper. Shortly afterwards, at about six in the evening, a passer-by spotted smoke, and raced to a nearby boarding house to spread the alarm; there, pro-convention leader Theophilus W. Smith quickly organized a bucket brigade. But within an hour, the building was a ruin, and although some papers from the upstairs offices of the Auditor of Public Accounts and Secretary of State survived, the bank's records were all destroyed. With the showdown over the convention looming, the canal not yet approved, and so many easy-money loans to the politically-connected bank directors and their friends outstanding, it was easy to be suspicious. Everyone in tiny Vandalia had seen the wheeling and dealing for votes.[23]

But Field and West simply couldn't tell whether they had nailed down their twenty-four votes or not. Field, finally, had an idea: if, instead of two thirds of each house, he could argue that two-thirds of the combined votes of both House and Senate might suffice to pass the convention resolution, he thought he could carry the day. The Senate was ready: John Grammar, the old slave-owner from Union County, had at last arrived. Two months after the start of the session, the pro-slavery leaders had their twelfth Senate vote in that angry old man—who had earlier made clear his views with the declaration that "fittner men mout hev been found to defend the masters agin the sneakin' ways of the infernal abolitioners, but havin' rights on my side, I don't fear.... Don't everyone know, or leastwise had ought to know, that the congress that sot at Post Vinsan [the Indiana Territory capital Vincennes] garnisheed to the old French inhabitants the right to their niggers, and haint I got as much rights as any Frenchman in this State?"[24]

The twelve Senate votes and twenty-three in the House—including Hansen—represented precisely two-thirds of the combined total of fifty-four. The Senate approved Field's proposal to count that way; a few days later, on February 10, after rejecting William Kinkade's protest that the count would make a mockery of the state constitution, the senators moved on to consider their long-delayed resolution to call for a convention. Kinkade stood again, shouting now that the issue must still be debated, that the majority was secretly trying to force slavery on Illinois. His fellow senators soon lost patience, as he repeatedly tried to make his point. Finally, he was gagged and forced into his seat. The Senate passed the resolution, by a vote of 12–6.[25]

Field could not convince the House to go along with his new two-thirds rule, a change that itself needed a two-thirds margin but that won only twenty yeas to sixteen nays, as a handful of pro-convention legislators balked and decided they could not stomach their leader's ramrod tactics. He had promises to back his call for a convention, and even a majority for the parliamentary maneuvering it may take to bring the issue up for another vote, but Field's control over his allies was far from firm.

Still, Field thought he might not need the new vote count rule anyway. He had won, finally, his twenty-fourth vote, the large-hearted if erratic William McFatridge, by an argument no one ever knew, though some suspected it involved moving the seat of McFatridge's home county, Johnson, in farthest southern Illinois—a move that in the event never did happen. Others might well have thought the old farmer's change of heart came in an even easier way for the convivial Field and West, since McFatridge was fonder of whisky than political life strictly required: "Mr. Speaker, Mr. Speaker," he once declaimed, somewhat the worse for wear, as the House prepared to close down for the evening. "You may adjourn the house and be hanged, but old Billy McFatridge will remain in session until sundown, and look after the interests of his constituents, while you are cavorting at Copp's grocery and getting drunk on the hard earnings of the people." When Thomas Rattan stood to make his long-planned motion for reconsideration of the convention, Field and West were sure they had it all sewed up.[26]

They did not.

"To their utter astonishment, [Hansen], who had always since the commencement of the session expressed his sentiments in favor of the measure, voted against it," a correspondent wrote to the *Edwardsville Spectator*.[27]

Hansen had switched, and Field had failed. Rep. J.G. Daimwood, from the Saline region, immediately moved for another reconsideration, but since he was a convention backer, who was part of the majority, even though his side had failed, Speaker Alexander ruled him out of order. The Speaker backed the conventionists, but would not break the rules for them.[28]

Field immediately moved that the whole house vote on the Speaker's decision, but that motion failed, 16–19, as several of his backers, including McFatridge and pro-convention leader James Turney, refused to go along with such a blatant attack on the legislature's rules. But though Turney could not back Field's challenge to the Speaker, he still had the presence of mind to quickly move another vote, this time that the resolution be reported to the state Senate with a request that the upper house send it back with the ayes and nays tabulated and attached. Turney's motion passed, 21–15, with the anti-convention leaders seeing no harm in it, now that they knew there was neither a two-thirds majority in the House nor enough support for Field's new method of counting to bull the convention resolution through.[29]

"The whole place was in an uproar," the *Spectator's* correspondent wrote, and Hansen's shocker was what everyone was talking about. "In the course of the evening, it was rumored that the Executive had bought him off, with the promise to give him the lucrative appointment of Recorder of Fulton County." The talk of bribery, carefully circulated in the taverns and boarding houses up and down Main Street and along Gallatin, inflamed the many political hangers-on who had flocked to the capital from all over Illinois—and at 12½ cents for a half-pint of whisky or twenty-five cents for that much peach brandy, gin or a cherry bounce, tempers flared easily. For the men who had by that point adopted the slogan "The Convention or Death," the fight was barely begin.[30]

"A little after dark, as by instinct, the citizens, legislators, strangers and almost all denominations flocked to the state house," the *Spectator*'s correspondent wrote. "Several of those who are here called lobby members, mounted the rostrum, in turn, and delivered, it is said, by far the best speeches upon the liberties of the people and the rights of a majority when obtained without fraud or deception, that have been delivered here this winter." The speech-making continued for an hour or two, before the crowd broke up and people began drifting back to their lodgings. "Everything appeared to be perfectly calm for an hour," the *Spectator* correspondent continued. "I had gone to bed, and was started by the strong shrill cry of O Yes, O Yes, O Yes, and instantly the cry of Hansen's effigy, Hansen's effigy, Hansen's effigy and fire, fire, fire, was reiterated throughout the town, and instantly drew to the spot nearly all that were able to reach there—the effigy in the meantime blazing beautifully."[31]

Some of the rousted townspeople and legislators, having seen what the commotion was, decided to return to their beds. Those who stayed began marching around the burning straw man, "as there had by this time arrived some musical instruments, such as the drum, the fife, the horns (God knows how many) triangles, tin pans &c &c." But the fun didn't last much longer after the music started, for the effigy's maker had put a pound of gunpowder in the lower part of the straw man, which soon exploded, scattering bits of flaming straw and clothing all around.[32]

The mob, about 200 in all, then marched to the boarding house of antislavery leader George Churchill, where, when the call was made to give three groans for the Madison County representative, "I am told by a spectator that three groans more solemn could not possibly have been given," the *Spectator*'s correspondent wrote. "After a solemn pause of a few minutes, the word was given three cheers for a convention, which was immediately complied with."[33]

The following morning, when the House reconvened, convention backer R.C. Ford rose on a motion of reconsideration—but not, this time, of the convention resolution vote; instead, Ford wanted his colleagues in the House to reconsider their December vote confirming Hansen as the winner of the Pike County election. Ford, who had, as George Churchill would sarcastically remind legislators, previously declared "that there was not least doubt of Mr. Hansen's right to the seat, and that it was cleanest case he had ever seen," now told the House that he had since seen new evidence to change his view, conveniently long after Hansen had voted for the way Ford wished in the U.S. Senate election. Four pro-convention legislators, William Alexander of Monroe County, Alexander Phillips, James Davenport and Thomas Rattan, rose to support Ford. Turney, whose quick thinking the evening before had kept the resolution for the convention barely alive, now presented an affidavit from one Levi Roberts, who stated that, in his opinion, Shaw had received a majority of 29 votes in Pike County: in other words, that all 83 votes Shaw collected at his own polling place, in his unanimous sweep there, were legitimate, that none were, as alleged, really from men who had come over from Missouri for the day and the drinks and to vote. Roberts made his affidavit on January 28, a half year after the election but the day after the House's first test vote on the convention question showed pro-slavery leaders they still hadn't secured the votes they needed. Already worried they might lose Hansen to Coles' wooing, Field and West clearly had arranged for the affidavit as a kind of insurance policy. Now, they would cash it in.[34]

Convention supporter John McFerron rose now to say he had originally backed Hansen despite "grave doubts" because he "then felt friendly towards him and was unwilling to hurt his feelings"; he was now, however, convinced that Hansen was entitled to his seat and would vote accordingly. Field then stood to make the case against Hansen: Simply, that the polling place where Shaw swept the count was a proper poll and that to insist the votes be cast at the official polling place and inspected by election judges selected by the county commissioners were technicalities that denied eighty or more men the right to vote, "a right which, when we cease to enjoy, Mr. F. said, he wished to cease to be a member of this society ... it has been with astonishment and surprise (Field continued) that he had heard gentlemen pronounce in this House, that we, when adjudicating on questions of this kind, cannot depart from the strict letter of the law, but are bound to observe all its niceties." Brushing aside Thomas Mather's concern that "If a member of the house is to be deprived of his seat on the basis of such testimony, whose seat, let me ask, would be secure?" the House voted to oust Hansen. Of the pro-convention legislators only Samuel Alexander of Pope County, Raphael Widen of Randolph County, and Zadock Casey, who represented Jefferson, Marion and Hamilton counties, broke with Field. Ten pro-convention legislators, including West, changed their original votes for Hansen to say he should now be removed. John Emmitt, facing a recall petition of his own that same day, which he successfully fended off, said he would not change his original vote against Hansen, even though it weakened his own side in the bigger battle over the convention.[35]

With Shaw now in the Pike County seat, the House then voted to overturn Speaker Alexander's ruling refusing a reconsideration of the convention vote. Three pro-convention legislators—McFatridge, McFerron and Turney—overcame their initial reservations and switched their earlier votes supporting the Speaker. Immediately afterwards, the Senate's canal bill was presented and passed by the House, "and nearly every friend to the convention supported it, had it not been for this, it would have had no possible chance for passing." Coles' wooing of Hansen was for naught. "The measure would not be carried but by resorting to the most unprecedented and unwarranted measures," he fumed in a letter to Madison.[36]

The conventionists gathered again that evening for a charivari, this time in triumph. With "drums, fiddles, bugles, tin horns and old daddy Wills's hounds" they paraded through the torch-lit streets of Vandalia, to the chant "Convention or Death," a "great carousal," as Thomas Ford later remembered. "They formed themselves into a noisy, disorderly and tumultuous procession headed by Judge Phillips [the pro-slavery candidate for governor Coles had defeated], Judge Smith, Judge Thomas Reynolds, later governor of Missouri, and [state senator] Kinney, followed by a majority of the legislature and the hangers-on and rabble about the seat of government: and they marched, with the blowing of tin horns and the beating of drums and tin pans, to the residence of Governor Coles and to the boarding houses of their principal opponents, towards whom they manifested their contempt and displeasure by a confused medley of groans, wailings and lamentations. Their object was to intimidate and crush all opposition at once."[37]

Many citizens, though, were simply repelled. "The most of them were Kentuckians and Tennesseans 'half horse and half alligators' the most contemptible of beings, the refuse of mankind," Horatio Newhall wrote to his family back in Massachusetts. Others thought the conventionists comical:

> Soon was each good convention fellow
> If not quite drunk—at least right mellow,
> And most internally intent
> On having fun and devilment...
> 'Huzza for the convention—boys
> Bring out whete'er will make a noise
> Let's march through all the streets in town
> And turn Vandalia upside down,'

one anti-convention man satirized them afterwards. The wild scenes on the streets of Vandalia celebrated a legislative coup, but its coming as they did immediately after Hansen was thrown out of the House for voting the wrong way, they would remind many Illinoisans of a different kind of coup altogether—and that would spell trouble for the conventionists, more than they may have realized in the first flush of their victory. "This proceeding in the General Assembly looked revolutionary and was condemned by all honest reflecting men," recalled John Reynolds, who was then, in fact, a backer of the call for a convention. "The night after the passage of the resolution there was a wild and indecorous procession by torchlight and liquor, that was also unpopular."[38]

Three days later, the pro-convention leaders took a more sober tack. They convened a "very large and respectable" public meeting in the state House of Representatives chamber, in the evening, after the legislators had adjourned, naming a committee of seven men to draft an appeal to the public at large. The committee was led by West, Field, Theophilus W. Smith, now recovered from the charivari, and William Kinney, a hard-shell Baptist preacher who held the state Senate seat for St. Clair County, with "absolute dominion over his flock ... a very bold man, and would grapple with any foe," as Judge Gillespie would remember: "His educational advantages had been so much so that he employed the little i as a personal pronoun, and when he was rallied about it, said that Gov. Edwards had used up all the big i's, and left nothing for him but the little ones." Kinney, who once declared he only represented the people and not any "man of colour," would be one of the most aggressive campaigners for the convention.[39]

The following Monday, February 18, the seven called a public meeting, and proclaimed there that the right to reconsider and revise a state's basic law, its constitution, was the most basic right of all: "We hold it to be a self-evident proposition that good governments, admit of changes in their superstructure, whilst the foundations remain unchanged," they said, arguing that there was, in particular, a crying need to reform the courts of Illinois. "Will the opponents to a convention, have the obstinacy to deny the existence, as well as the necessity of reformation in these particulars, or are they prepared to assert that the people are their own worst enemies?" the conventionists' declaration continued. "Have they not seen them, moving like the terrible powers of a tornado, sweeping in their course all before them? Have they not seen them infuriated by oppression, groaning under the weight of their miseries and misfortunes, break the adamantine bands, which bound them to the thorn of power and superstition, hurling alike the throne, the scepter, and its possessor to the earth?"[40]

But they said not a word about slavery.

The anti-convention men would. As the legislative session drew to its close, 15 senators and representatives, led by Risdon Moore and William Kinkade, joined in a memorial of their own, declaring; "We believe the people will do right; but we fear a convention may do wrong.... Slavery is unjust, because it is a gross usurpation over a part of our fellow beings for our interest and convenience, not their's," the memorial proclaimed. That raw taking of another's time and sweat, "whose prohibition is written by the finger of GOD upon all his works" was, the memorial continued, "unjust because it is appropriating the fruits of their labor to feed our mouths. Unjust, because it is sinking them in mental degradation, to support us in indolence and ease. Unjust because it is extinguishing in their bosoms, the love of country."[41]

The words are very like Coles', though he did not sign. He sat with the many of the signers the very night the pro-slavery men took to the streets of Vandalia to jeer him and to bellow their demand "Convention or Death." Somehow, despite the frenzy outside, Coles or an ally penned words that speak of the sufferings of men; they speak of patriotism, they speak of sin (though in the cool dispassionate way an ex–College of William and Mary student of the Enlightenment would). They are words of a man of privilege who had been shocked to understand the real source of his wealth and of his years of comfort. They were the words that would cast the struggle to come in Illinois in clear moral terms, and would be echoed on the pages of the newspapers, in the pamphlets, in arguments in the groceries and churchyards of Illinois during the long months that followed. "What a strange spectacle would be presented to the civilized world," the memorial continued, "to see the people of Illinois, yet innocent of this great national sin, and in the full enjoyment of all the blessings of free government, sitting down in solemn convention to deliberate and determine whether they should introduce among them a portion of their fellow beings, to be cut off from those blessings, to be loaded with the chain of bondage, and rendered unable to leave any other legacy to their posterity, than the inheritance of their own servitude. The wise and good of all nations would blush at our political depravity. Our professions of republicanism and equal freedom would incur the derision of despots and the scorn and reproach of tyrants. We should write the epitaph of free government upon its tombstone!"[41]

Chapter 7

To the people

The session staggered to a bitter, spiteful close. Contempt for the governor they had bested, along with a swaggering self-confidence after their Pike County coup, made the convention advocates bold; sure that they could fend off any challenge from the fussy, formal Virginian they still could not quite believe had become their governor. There would be, to put a point on it, no more memorials from legislators respectfully requesting Coles' attention to this or that, as the Senate now brusquely informed him that "the Governor is required to lay before" them the names of nominees for recorder in the new counties of Fulton and Morgan.[1]

This break from the usual legislative niceties, "novel and unprecedented" in Coles' words, prompted exactly the kind of elaborate dissertation that made him such an easy man for his opponents to mock, in their carefully cultivated homespun style. "With every disposition to comply," he icily replied, "not only with whatever the Senate has a right to require, but with every reasonable request be made express, I feel myself constrained, under my impression of the relative constitutional powers of the Senate and the Executive, to decline complying with the requisition." It was, he continued, the job of the governor to nominate people, and the Senate's to advise and consent, or not, to the nomination. To the men who hoped to sell the notion of a new constitution to the people, as the ultimate expression of the people's sovereign rights, the awkward aristocrat dared to lecture that "The power of the Senate being thus confined to approving or rejecting nominations, it is not known by what authority it derives the right to require of the Governor all the recommendations of the persons named, much less those of all the others who have been recommended; a precedent for which, it is believed, cannot be found in the proceedings of the Federal Government, or the Government of any of the States."[2]

The Senators, now, were furious. They summarily rejected Coles' nominee for Fulton County Recorder, John G. Lofton. "In these times of party heat," a still-angry Coles wrote to Lofton after that vote, "when the friends of freedom are oppressed, denounced and proscribed by the friends of Slavery—in such a time, I say, as this, I felicitated myself in having been able to select an individual so perfectly fitted in qualification, and so perfectly unexceptional in character that I had not supposed that the blackest demon of faction could have raised his head against him, but in this I was mistaken." As Coles "had been induced to nominate you purely for my regard for you ... the regret I feel at your rejection would be greatly increased if I should find that you were mortified at it, and it would be especially painful to me if I should have done what may prove displeasing to you."³

Apparently content with having given this slap to Coles by rejecting his friend, the Senate then adjourned without acting one way or another on his subsequent nomination of a local Fulton County lawyer. The legislators had other scores to repay, though. The tricky footwork that frogwalked Nicholas Hansen out of the House had offended William H. Brown, the editor of the *Illinois Intelligencer*. An anti-slavery man who had held his tongue out of deference to his pro-convention partner, Brown felt Hansen's expulsion left him no choice but to object: "Whether this be law-making or law-breaking, I leave to the people to decide," he wrote. "Shall a Convention succeed by such means? Surely the great solicitude of its success cannot proceed merely from a wish to amend a harmless constitution.... A deeper object is in view—the introduction of slavery to Illinois." The cost of Brown's anger was the lucrative government printing contract Brown's silent partner, William Berry, state representative for the counties of Fayette and Montgomery, had helped nail down. The legislature quickly passed a resolution designating a new government printer to replace the Brown & Berry partnership with an until then nonexistent entity called Blackwell & Berry, with pro-slavery lawyer Robert Blackwell, a former partner of Brown's, stepping in the fill the angry editor's place. Without the contract, Brown had no business. He was out. Coles had lost a key ally, and would, for months, have to struggle to reach the people despite a universally hostile press.⁴

But Brown got in one last blast. The legislature, he wrote, "has been charged by thoughtless and inconsiderate persons, of a want of veneration to that instrument which some think secures to us our property, lives and liberty." Not so, he said, sarcasm dripping from his pen. The naming of the new printer "not only confutes this idea, but shows that the members composing this body are even very scrupulous of living up to its very letter.... Not having been bred myself to the 'trade, art and mystery' of this profession," Brown said, using the words of the state law governing the printing contract, just as if his readers would not know he had had been running a paper longer than any other editor in the state, "the firm of

Brown & Berry were defeated."⁵ It was, of course, just a story of the capital. Few outside Vandalia, and not many in the tiny town, shared Brown's indignation, for now. But he was to be a bellwether.

Tiny Vandalia, isolated in the mud and mess of the dying winter, with the pro-slavery, "conventionist" (as they were soon termed) legislators packing every rooming house, the hangers-on of the lobby ready to buy them a drink or dinner, was afire for the convention and confident that the rest of the state would endorse the idea in the referendum, which would be held in 18 months' time, in tandem with the August 1824 congressional election. The anti-convention men "declared themselves in a language too strong to be misconceived, above the people who sent them, and not 'accountable' to them," said an angry "Plain Citizen," who demanded of one legislator whom he would not name but who was probably anti-conventionst George Churchill, "whether he really believes that compared to himself, three hundred and sixty respectable citizens of his county are mere Jack-Asses, and not to be trusted with their own interests."⁶

The atmosphere quickly grew still more fevered, the rhetoric still more grandiose. "The Convention question must succeed, and whatever means may be necessary to effect it, however out of the way, will be justified by the result," wrote "AB." At a dinner near the end of the session, Joseph Pogue offered a heavy-handed toast to "Ye sable sons of and daughters of Africa—may Illinois soon see her prairies brightened by your countenances," while S. Whiteside sarcastically toasted "executive influence, paralyzed by the sovereignty of the people," and lawyer William Gilham proffered a Biblical warning to the state representatives who voted against the convention: "The fifteen legislative protestors, Mene Mene Tekel Upharsen." "Never did I see or hear in American of party spirit going to such lengths, as well officially as privately, as it did here," Coles wrote to his old friend, the Philadelphia banker Nicholas Biddle, shortly after the legislature adjourned. "It seems to me that Slavery is so poisonous as to produce a kind of delirium in those minds who are excited by it."⁷

But Vandalia, triumphant and fervid, was not all of Illinois. Huddled over their closely parsed *Intelligencers*, *Spectators* and *Gazettes*, with a few weeks still before the spring plowing and sowing would compel all their energy, Illinoisans were disconcerted by the maneuvers over Hansen's seat and reports of the mob. Their growing sense of unease was not quieted by the proclamations of the pro-convention party, nor were they particularly amused by the sarcasm and sharpness of the pro-slavery men's attacks on the governor and his allies. "The advocates of a convention claim that two-thirds of the general assembly" wanted a convention, "A Farmer" wrote to the *Spectator*. "How that majority was obtained, that majority can perhaps best tell, if they will." But A Farmer was suspicious, and convinced there was more to the push for a convention than what the conventionists were saying, for: "Is it probable that all the unusual means that have been employed to influence legislative and public opinion on this subject, have been resorted to, to change mere details in the organic structure of our constitutional edifice, to paint and plaster it, and that no design is entertained of new moulding the edifice itself?"[8] Like A Farmer, "Citizen of Madison County" also felt the conventionists were wild, and out of control: "Had you been admitted into the nightly rendezvous of these persons, and witnessed their midnight orgies, you would frequently have heard them boast of their success in deceiving particular individuals," he said. "You would have shuddered at the indifference and sang froid with which they recounted the falsehoods and misrepresentations made use of to procure their success." The Citizen was upset by the way the conventionists rounded on Coles and Churchill, though, after watching the conventionists' gatherings, "you would not have been surprised at the ferocity displayed by these men towards a representative who refused to be their dupe ... but who being beyond their reach, they vented all the spite upon a quantity of harmless hay and unoffending old clothes!" The pro-convention men did not sense this unease in the western and northern counties. They were content to stay in the capital a few more days and roar in their triumph. Coles and his allies were not.[9]

Still aglow with the excitement of battle ("I assure you, I never before felt so deep an interest in any political question," wrote the man who helped a president hold his Congress in line for war, though he also allowed he was taken aback that the pro-slavery men "were very anxious to impress it upon us ... that we had made ourselves very obnoxious to the people"), Coles hastened home to Madison County—as best he could, that is, for heavy spring rain had turned the National Road into a mess of thick, gooey mud that at times he had to walk his horse around—in order to begin organizing his campaign against the convention. It was the fight, if he had only known it, that he had been seeking for years, a battle, as he would come to see it, for the soul of his country.[10]

His neighbors in Edwardsville urged him on: "as soon as I arrived in this place, a deputation of behalf of the Citizens of this town and County" called on him to hold a public dinner, the typical start towards organizing a campaign. "Freemen delight in giving applause to faithful servants," declared Henry Starr, the master of ceremonies at the March 5 event. Toasting "Liberty," he added: "While we enjoy her blessings, may we not be willing to withhold it from others." William Ottwell said Coles' "firmness in the hour of trial, and his adherence to the cause of freedom" had proved him "worthy of the confidence of a *free* people." Coles called the "between 40 & 50" people there to action: "The crisis: it is big with the fate of Illinois, and requires every friend of freedom to rally under the banners of the constitution."[11]

From there, Coles headed south, to St. Clair County, home of William Kinney, a conventionist leader in the state Senate, as well as anti-convention stalwarts Risdon Moore and Jacob Ogle, and a vital battleground. "Such a large party dined with me," he reported, "the room could not contain them all."[12] There, he most likely huddled with the Rev. James Mason Peck, the well-liked Methodist circuit rider who ranged over much of western Illinois, preaching and organizing the churches to which an isolated, lonely people flocked. Peck, in any event, agreed to Coles' request that he help organize anti-convention groups, recruiting the energetic Belleville lawyers David Blackwell and John Messinger, as well as the long-established farmer and preacher James Lemen (he of the straw-stuffed-plowing collar fame), and launching the "St. Clair Society to prevent the further introduction of Slavery in the State of Illinois" within the month. In Bond County, anti-slavery citizens gathered that to honor state Rep. Jonathan Pugh's vote against the convention, and resolved that they would never back a convention man for any public office. By the end of the year there would be 14 county groups.[13]

Back in Edwardsville, Coles and his "Land Office clique"—the office's clerk, William McKee, along with Judge Samuel Lockwood and Rev. Thomas Lippincott—contacted allies across the state, scrambling to organize anti-convention groups in as many counties as possible. (McKee and Lippincott, along with Coles' friends William Ottwell and David Prickett, for instance, would ride down to Monroe County, for its first public meeting on May 31).[14] "My present office increases the obligation I am under as a good citizen to exert myself to enlighten the minds of Fellow-Citizens," Coles would explain. "I conceive myself bound, both as a Citizen and an Officer, to do all in my power to prevent [slavery's] introduction into this state." He pledged his $1,000-a-year salary as governor to the fight.[15]

But Coles knew he and the Land Office clique would have to hammer out a strategy that would do much more than satisfy abolitionists, like himself or the prominent Quaker abolitionist Roberts Vaux. They would attack, head-on, the pro-slavery argument that a change in the state constitution would encourage settlement and create a market for settlers' newly cleared land, allowing them to cash out, pay off the installments they owed, and start again, with uncleared land for which the 1820 Act had slashed the price. They knew they would have to contend with ferocious racial prejudice—as Lippincott would note, there were plenty of Southern-born

Illinoisans with "many prejudices imbibed in infancy" who "hold negroes in the utmost contempt" and "look on *negers*, as they call them ... as an inferior race." The argument that formally allowing slavery would mean more blacks in Illinois was a potent, if ugly one, that even Coles would eventually add to his arsenal. Ultimately, though, they would argue that a real republican could not be a slave-holder, and that a republican society could not coexist with slavery.[16]

From the beginning, Coles told his friends now, even with his inaugural speech itself, he had wanted to draw Illinois' advocates for slavery out from the cover they had assumed: that they were simple frontier democrats calling only for a constitution less autocratic than the one many of the very same men had rammed through the first convention, just five years earlier. "Knowing that many who professed to be so hostile to the further introduction of Slavery would advocate" a new constitutional convention, "and believing it would have a salutary effect to furnish them an opportunity of evincing the sincerity of their professions ... I called the attention of the Legislature in a speech I delivered on being sworn into office ... to the existence of Slavery in the State ... and recommended that just and equitable provision be made for its abrogation," Coles wrote to his old Philadelphia friend, Nicholas Biddle. "As I anticipated, this part of my speech created a considerable excitement with those who were openly or secretly in favor of making Illinois a slave-holding, rather than making it really, as well as nominally, a free State—those who wished to fill it rather than empty it of slaves."[17]

Now, he told Biddle, he needed help, especially with four newspapers backing the convention and Hooper Warren's *Edwardsville Spectator* still as focused on attacking him as on the battle against the convention. What was needed, Coles said, was to go around the newspapers; he asked for pamphlets on the evils of slavery, and especially on the heavy economic toll he had always felt it levied. He could, he was confident, address the issue of where real republicans stood on slavery—it was Coles, after all, who knew Jefferson, Madison and Monroe. But the emerging argument that Illinois was harmed when slaveholders bypassed it for Missouri was a potent one, especially to settlers worried they could not cobble together the cash they needed to hang on to their land, and Coles in these early days of preparing a campaign against the convention thought it less useful to appeal to passion than to pocketbooks to make his case. He scrambled, too, for allies. "The great inducement with us both to emigrate to this state was the firm belief that we should not be disturbed by the clanking of the fetters of slavery, tyranny would not be given a legal sanction, nor afforded the food on which it could prey," he wrote to Richard Flower, leader of the

7—To the people

Left: Nicholas Biddle, the old friend from Philadelphia to whom Coles turned for help soon after the campaign against slavery started (Library of Congress). Right: Daniel Pope Cook joined with Coles in the early days of the anti-convention campaign (courtesy Abraham Lincoln Presidential Library).

English Settlement in Edwards County, in the Wabash River valley. Why not, he asked, start a newspaper in Albion, where there were "many persons who wield chaste and powerful pens" and who had to money to launch a paper? "Pardon me for asking it as a favor to me personally, and as a sacrifice to the furtherance of the best and most virtuous of causes, that all personal, section, national, county or town feelings, and all other unkind feelings, let them originate from what cause they made, shall be buried, at least while the great question is pending." Coles, pointedly, said he would sent the same message to his old friend Morris Birkbeck, with whom Flower was then feuding.[18]

Even as the conventionist leader Seth Crocker toasted his opponents: "May they ride a porcupine saddle, on a hard trotting horse, a long journey without money or friends," the anti-slave men worked quietly away. By May, there were anti-convention organizations in Bond, Monroe, St. Clair and White counties. "Among the curiosities of the time was the presence in [the St. Clair County] meeting of *thirty* preachers of the gospel, Methodists and Baptists," the circuit rider Rev. James Mason Peck recalled.

That association's recording secretary, Dr. Charles Woodward, "had occasion to travel into nearly every county in the State during the pendency of the question ... without being known as a partisan, he could easily find out who could be depended upon," Peck would remember years later. "And it is a single fact that not an instance ever came to the knowledge of the committee, of any one betraying his trust."[19] By the end of the summer, anti-convention groups had been organized in Coles' home county of Madison, the most populous in the state, as well as in the rapidly filling counties of Sangamon, Greene, Morgan and Pike. Angered by what they had read of the mob in Vandalia, and the removal of Nicholas Hansen, Illinoisans rallied to the anti-convention cause: "We will not support anyone for any office who walked in that nocturnal procession at Vandalia, the night Hansen's effigy was burnt," the Society to Oppose the Introduction of Slavery into Illinois vowed. "In less than six months, fourteen societies had been organized in as many counties," the Rev. Peck recalled. "Each society had its confidential correspondents in each precinct, and every succeeding month, accurate knowledge was obtained at the office in Belleville, of the state and progress of the question. An all-pervading influence was felt in every settlement." "The free party have been as industrious as possible," one settler wrote back to his family in the east. "A pretty considerable change has taken place in public sentiment ... if the vote should be taken now, a majority of 2000 would oppose a convention"[20]

The Fourth of July would see Coles and his allies campaigning at community dinners across the northern part of the state. In Greene County, citizens at the dinner in the county seat of Carrollton said Coles was "honored by *the people* of Illinois for his virtues and his political integrity" (at least, according to the report in ever-hostile Hooper Warren's *Edwardsville Spectator*). In Sangamon County, Coles and Congressman Daniel P. Cook, accompanying him to argue against the convention, were hailed for "their firm, independent and uniform *republican* conduct," while Morgan County celebrants toasted him, adding: "May his example and firmness be received as an incontrovertible evidence of his attachment to the principles of equal rights, and inspire confidence in his administration." There were similar meetings in Edgar and Fulton counties in the north, in Monroe County, down along the Mississippi River, and in Lawrence County, on the Wabash River, next to Indiana. Not simple toasts, these, but declarations of political positions; carefully scripted, meant to be reprinted in the paper, and to frame, for any who had not been following, what the controversy was and who its actors were.[21]

Coles' opponents, sure though they were that their years of politicking in Illinois gave them an overwhelming advantage in any contest with a man like the governor, were beginning to be alarmed. "The Governor is actively engaged in combining into a phalanx, the leaders of our holy religion to oppose the Convention and the pulpit is to be converted into a political forum," complained conventionist leader Theophilus W. Smith. The support of the preachers shifted the debate, at least metaphysically, into an arena where the anti-convention forces might make ground, pro-convention leaders feared. In the pro-convention *Intelligencer*, one conventionist complained he could "of late, scarcely step into a churchyard without beholding a newspaper or handbill spread before the eyes of the congregation, and those who are not employed in this way stand in little groups discussing with great warmth the question of a convention."[22] And "Not A Methodist" said that although he would have expected parishioners' anger over anti-slave sermons meant pastors in his part of the state "would take the hint and not quit the rock of ages for the quicksands of the moment," a recent visit to a camp meeting revival had taught him better. Though a strong backer of a convention, Not A Methodist said he "did not put so much as one newspaper in my pocket neither for nor against a convention, neither was it my intention to say one word on the subject." But when he arrived at the gathering, the first preacher he heard, using as his text Paul's Epistle to the Hebrews, "stepped into the political canoe, snatched up a slaveholder, and paddled off up the Styx to the sulphury regions of hell, where he took care to secure him in eternal damnation for no other cause but his holding of slaves." Not A Methodist stormed out, but he added that he had later heard that another pastor also preached mainly politics that Sunday evening, "and told his brethren if they would be faithful and true, slavery would never come into the state of Illinois."[23] The convention men had to struggle hard to undercut this, in their view, most unfair challenge. Sarcasm and an appeal to the racist views many Illinoisans held were their main rhetorical devices: "If you had the piety and filial affection, which you talk about," wrote "A Yankee" from Bond County, "I should think you ought to have no objections to the introduction of slavery into this state; it would not add one more to the number, but would give you charitable men an opportunity to administer relief to the poor and degraded race of Africans."[24]

Still, with their opponents on the anti-convention side led only by a man they dismissed as a priggish, prissy Virginia aristocrat, the pro-convention men were not worrying much at this point—they were, after all, contending for votes in a community whose rush to statehood four years before had been largely fueled by resentment that outsiders might tell it how to run its affairs. There were potent resentments for the pro-convention side to tap, its leaders knew. "Sir, if I were to judge from your letter," "Yankee" wrote that summer, "you are a Yankee or a York state man, and a office hunter, perhaps holds one now, and is afraid if Illinois should shape her policy in the vortext of that faction you are supporting." Governor-to-be John Reynolds, who had at first said he did not much like the convention bill, soon changed his mind and declared himself a backer, "and the only reason he offers for this change is this: if slavery is not introduced, the Yankees will rule the state."[25] Faction and power were what the fight was really about, the pro-slavery men argued. Democracy was the issue, they insisted, in the manifesto they published in early March; democracy was what the people wanted. The Council of Revision was an aristocratic hangover, they said; so too was the idea that people should have to wait every other year to vote. The courts were a mess, the terms of office of state officials too imprecisely limited. There were plenty of issues: if in White County, in eastern Illinois, convention backers said their aim was to allow slavery, they also proposed moving the state capital to the county seat, Carmi. In Randolph County, when the pro-convention men drummed up signatures for their petitions, they told French-speaking farmers who couldn't read the papers that the idea was to reduce taxes. "In Madison county," complained Coles, "the people were told the objects were to remove the seat of government to Alton" and that it was "absurd and deceptive" to say the aim was to allow slavery, "well knowing that the people of Madison were opposed."[26] But above all, the pro-convention men argued, the preachers and the governor were trying, insultingly, to assert a moral superiority to push a political program that would hold Illinois back and that would oppress the ordinary citizens of the state. "I ask where is the great danger of referring this question to the people?" an angry "Plain Citizen" wrote from Vandalia. "Remember the question is not as the gentlemen in the minority would make us believe, Convention and Slavery, No Convention and Freedom—but the simple unvarnished question, shall we have a convention." And if, "Plain Citizen" continued, the people decide the constitution does need change, and if then "this word Slavery, so terrible to the political hopes of some gentlemen should be raised—it would also be referred to the people, the legitimate source of all power—and on this subject also shall the voice of the people prevail."[27]

But the anti-convention men had a populist appeal, too. "The planters are great men, and will ride about, mighty grand, with their umbrellas over their head, when I and my boys are working ... in the hot sun. Neighbors indeed! they would have all their own way and rule over us like little kings ... but if we lacked to raise a building—or a dollar—the d—l a bit would they help *us*," Morris Birkbeck, writing as "Jonathan Freeman," noted. They were men who acted much with an arrogant disregard for the real wishes of the people, as the past legislative session had made clear, he said. "The interests of the public have been bought and sold in the face of day; the law of elections, and the established rules of legislative proceedings, have been set at nought," Birkbeck wrote, in a widely circulated pamphlet. "Such a sense of base intrigue was never before exhibited under a representative government."[28] It was a potent argument, then as now, to attack an entrenched political elite's wealth and cozy self-isolation in the halls (built of logs though they might be) of government; Illinoisans, stuck on their small farms, worried that their crops might fail, frustrated that the money they might earn lost value almost the instant it was in their hands, resented the wealth of their political leaders.

The conventionists' attempts to whip up sectional resentment against Yankees prompted resentment in turn, especially as families from New England and New York began filling the northern counties. Coles and his allies were not shy about keeping the antagonisms alive: "Emigrants from the east will bring us money and industry—the very things we want," wrote Coles, as "Aristides," in the *Intelligencer*. "Emigrants from the south will bring us idleness, vanity, luxury and the slow but fatal disease of slavery—the very things we do not want." Aggrieved by the wealth of others, repelled by the idea that human beings might be owned, these new Illinoisans were voters Coles understood he had to win. Already, Coles told them, the pro-slavery men in the legislature were trying to take rights from newer citizens, since the legislative districts to be used in electing delegates to the convention under-represented the northern frontier counties. "A large majority of the population of Illinois would have a frightful minority of representation in the convention ... they know well that if the people once consent to a convention, there will afterwards be no necessity for asking their consent to anything. They know that the people's opposition to a convention, at the next election, is the people's armour; and if they can steal that armour the conquest will be easy. The minority will then rule the majority. The love of power will make them hold fast to it."[29]

But other Illinoisans also resented the wealth of slave-owners; many of the Southern men who had come to the frontier knew and loathed what slavery did to the men who owned men, how it transformed them from neighbors to grandees; it "begets in its possessor a haughty, insolent, oppressive, overbearing temper dangerous to liberty," commented on anti-convention man." "Many of us have been long accustomed to living in slave states, and we know the poor people in those states suffer," another told a public meeting in Lawrence County, in the eastern part of the state. "Haughty slaveholders," he added, let "the poor white man ... become the companion of slaves" while they "sit in the shade and drink their grog."[30]

Coles tried to underline the connection between slavery and anti-republican arrogance, and to suggest a parallel to the link between slavery and tyranny he had seen so many years before in Bishop Madison's classroom. A slave-owner, Coles declared (again writing as Aristides), "is the chief of a petty principality, but little dependent on his neighbors. The lash goads from his slaves all that he deems necessary to his perverted appetites; and he cares for no more." Such a man, said Coles, is no one a frontier settler would want living down the road: "To improve the condition of his poor neighbors is a thought that but rarely enters his head. His vanity, his ambition are concerned to keep them in their degraded condition."[31]

Taking rights from some could clear a way for taking rights from the rest, the anti-slavery men argued. "We are a society of free men: our fundamental laws know no such being as a slave. In this State, every inhabitant is free by right, derived from a power paramount to all majorities. Freedom is the basis of our social compact," wrote Coles' friend and ally Morris Birkbeck. "If the majority have the power of affixing the brand of slavery on one portion of the community, what is the limit of this power? What portion is safe? What security remains for you or for me, if we chance to be in the minority?... Difference of color makes no difference in the nature of oppression, in the crime of inflicting it; and that only is a free country where every man in it protected from oppression."[32]

Try as they might to play the democrats, said Coles, "the veil has become so thin" that his opponents could no longer mask themselves as republicans; they were instead, he continued, clearly exposed as advocates of a "political *heresy,* that ... *republicans have an undoubted right to enslave a portion of their fellow man.*" Putting words in the conventionists' mouths, feeling they had played into his hands by pushing the nomination of John Reynolds, a pro-slavery ally of Sen. Jesse Thomas, to be a state legislator from St. Clair County, Coles said they were men who held "'*the swinish multitude*' must have no hand in making the nomination: that power belongs to the *nobles*—the *patricians*—the *lords*—the *big men.*"[33]

The implication that it was they who were the opponents of democracy stung the pro-slavery men. "It appears to me, that nothing can be more illiberal, intolerant and reprehensible than to denounce indiscriminately all who are in favor of a convention," complained "A Conventionist." "This, the constant practice of non-conventionists, is in direct opposition to the principles for which the whole party professes to contend, namely liberty." Upset that Coles and his allies were still resisting them, after their victory in Vandalia, the pro-convention men lashed out, heatedly arguing that their opponents were ignorant and hypocritical when contending it was the convention side that was the side of privilege and undemocratic goals. A sarcastic letter to the *Intelligencer*, for instance, proposed to quote a conversation between two anti-convention squatters (who apparently managed to carefully and precisely enunciate all their misspellings to that they could be committed to paper):

> We are working very heard and strugling to make money a nuff on our Improvements ... and if we turn fools and vote for a convention we wil Be a voting they morsell of Bread out of our own mouths ... they Big men than wont thank us for it for no dought they will pore in hear with theire great Droves of niggors and of course they must have Land to Live on and for the Black Buggers to make pone a pon and then away goes our Improvements for these niggor holders will By our houses over our heads and turn us and all our wives and children out of dorse ... so I will go the hole a ganst them wicked fellows that is so Red Hot for a convention.[34]

The pro-convention men, at least those few still candid enough to admit that opening the door to slavery was in fact their intent, had to address Coles' moral challenge and so also argued that theirs was a humanitarian position. To do this, picking up an argument from the struggle over Missouri's statehood, they claimed that a revision of Illinois' constitution would eventually lead to a general emancipation of slaves across the country. "You cannot deny, sir that the more slaves are dispersed throughout the government, the more their situation is improved," wrote "A Yankee," of Bond County. "This being the case why should the prairies of Illinois be excluded from the benefit of their services?" Roger, of White County, noted that "indeed, an unlimited slavery is something to be dreaded," but added that this was not what the pro-convention men wanted: "It is notorious that only a qualified slavery is wished to be introduced into this State, in order to establish a system of gradual emancipation for the relief of the suffering Africans.... It is so far from taking away the dearest rights of man, that it would give liberty and happiness to thousands who must groan in wretchedness to the day of their death." To the anti-convention side, added Roger, "'Iron-hearted monster' is term that is applicable to yourselves, as long as you wish to prevent a goodly number from enjoying happiness and plenty in this state."[35]

The reply of the anti-slavery men was simple: "Some pretend to say, he eats, he wears, he fares as we do, and has less to perplex him, and is consequently happier than if he was free," wrote James Good, a Madison County farmer. "But if those who think so should change conditions with the negro, then they may be believed. If liberty was worth the blood of thousands, why withhold it from negroes?"[36]

To that question, the anti-convention men would argue, there was no good answer. Slavery was cruel, and would be no less cruel in Illinois than by the feverish bottomlands and bayous of the lower Mississippi. Its dispersal would not bring its end, and to argue that point, or to contend it encouraged the conversion of blacks to Christianity, as many pro-convention leaders argued, was disingenuous. The only motivation for holding slaves was greed, and grandiosity, and a desire to lord it over others: "It is the love of money ease and wealth that is the cause of their sufferings," wrote Josias Wright of Madison County.[37]

Still, among some of anti-convention men, feelings towards the slaves took a decidedly less benevolent turn. Unlike Coles, they could not find in within themselves to like a black man. These men argued, as did "Brutus" in a letter to the *Intelligencer,* that "the rapid increase of the blacks" likely to result from allowing slavery in Illinois "would be sowing the seeds of a moral pestilence which no human power could afterwards exterminate." Although Coles would find such rhetoric repulsive, he agreed that violence, too, came with slavery—and not just the lash of whips. "Slavery is admitted to be a national and state evil of no ordinary magnitude—an evil under which many of our sister states have long groaned, and from which they are destined to suffer rebellions that will waste their blood, and endanger their existence," Coles, writing as "Aristides," argued. "On what principle is it, that we are to justify the planting of so dangerous a foe in our own bosom?"[38]

The key to winning, and retaining, the support of those Illinoisans who did not like blacks, or who simply feared them—the majority in those days when most Americans were blithely, thoughtlessly racist—was still to make an economic case, Coles' experience in those first few months of campaigning confirmed. "What is the only strong inducement held out to the voters for slavery?" wrote "A Shoal Creek Farmer" to the *Edwardsville Spectator* that summer. "Inquire of every candid advocate for the measure ... he will tell you, it is pecuniary interest—a relief from his distress, his embarrassments." Though Coles, almost uniquely for the times, called his former slaves his friends, he knew that to utter the very word to a freedman would choke most Illinoisans: They might be willing to let other men live in freedom, but they were uninterested in letting free black men and women live near them. Coles thought one way to win support was to show that the cost of letting enslaved people live nearby was even higher than an offense to prejudice. He pushed leaders of the increasingly unfocused abolitionist movement for help arguing an economic case. Although Coles had written to Roberts Vaux asking for help within just a few days of the legislature's vote for the convention referendum, and although within a few weeks a stack of pamphlets assembled by the earnest Philadelphian had arrived in Illinois, they were not quite what Coles felt he needed now. One, for instance, attempted to show slave labor was not profitable, another outlined the "cruelties of the slave trade" and the third was written "to show that the interminable bondage of any portion of the human race is, on the part of the oppressors, a great violation of natural and Divine justice and utterly inconsistent with the doctrines of our Holy Redeemer." Illinoisans needed to hear something different, Coles felt. "We want facts to ... show that slavery would operate to the injury of the poor or laboring classes," he politely wrote back to Vaux. "Strange as it may appear it is nevertheless true, that there are many persons who are in principle opposed to slavery who will yet vote for making this a slave-holding State, under the belief that by so doing they will be enabled to make an immediate and advantageous sale of their lands." Coles was convinced, and he believed his own experiences in Virginia and Illinois proved, that there was a strong economic argument to be made against slavery.[39]

It was not an obvious one to Illinois land speculators, wondering why their holdings had yet to appreciate in value. "Give us plenty of negroes," conventionist Thomas Burgess proposed at a rally in Lebanon. "Wealthy and intelligent farmers moving to Missouri, seeing our excellent soil, regretted they could not stop with their slaves in Illinois, which fired our people for

Emigrants on the trail west to Illinois. Fears that settlers would bypass Illinois because of a ban on slavery became one of the convention party's most potent arguments (Northern Illinois University Library).

slavery," governor-to-be John Reynolds recalled. The primitive roads through Illinois were jammed with the long lines of slaves trudging west, and the men who drove them on never failed to tell the Illinoisans they met that "if they could only hold their slaves, they would settle amongst us." Judge Joseph Gillespie would later say, recalling one barefoot old man, rifle slung over his shoulder, "his old woman mounted on an old gray horse, the bones of which were ready to cut the skin," who when asked why not stop in Illinois "spoke up in an angry mood and said 'Well, sir, your sile is mighty fartile, but a man can't own niggers here, God darn you.'" Slavery would transform Illinois, the pro-convention men said, and many voters, watching people they thought might buy their land bypass them to head for slave lands in Missouri, found the argument made some sense. Even squatters, who never bothered to buy the land they farmed, stood to gain, since Illinois law allowed them to sell the improvements they had made, the clearings, the fences, the cabins, even if they could not sell the land. "The distresses of the country are increasing, the means of alleviating them is unheeded ... inquire of every advocate for the measure and he will tell you, it is pecuniary in interest," "Farmer" of Bond County wrote.[40]

Coles was dismissive of such argument. As "Aristides" yet again he sarcastically asked: "The government has millions of acres to sell in Illinois, at one dollar and twenty five cents an acre. Is it likely that the slave-holder will leave these, and pay a high price for yours?" And, though Illinois settlers were desperate for hands to help with the heavy labor of clearing trees or breaking root-bound prairie land or draining sloughs, slaves were an unlikely source of help. "Could those men," Coles argued, "who are too poor to buy a quarter section of land, or who require an eight year credit to pay for quarter section, buy slaves? Surely not. But we are told that slavery will increase the price of land. Is this true? Where does land command the highest price? In the free states, according to all experience." Worse still, said Morris Birkbeck, writing as "Jonathan Freeman," if some men had slaves, that would mean the wages that many hard-pressed settlers relied on earning, doing farm work for their neighbors, would be depressed. Ask any man who moved from a slave state why he left, Birkbeck continued, "and he will tell you it was because it was impossible for free men to thrive by honest labor among slave holders and slaves."[41]

The cash crisis of the western frontier helped the anti-slave campaigners underline their economic points, while Coles had gained much credibility because of his outspoken opposition to the shenanigans at the State Bank of Illinois by the men who were now his political opponents (William Kinney was director of the Edwardsville branch, William M. Alexander and William McFatridge were borrowers who never paid off their debts;

conventionist leaders Michael Jones and John McLean, meanwhile, had been directors of the failed Bank of Illinois, while Benjamin Stephenson was a director, along with Ninian Edwards, of the Bank of Edwardsville).[42] Anti-slavery politicians brushed off as laughable the half-hearted efforts by their main opponent to say a convention would allow a rewriting of the constitution to prevent the issue of paper money that had impoverished so many settlers. "State paper was created by the same party which is now striving to call a convention for the admission of slavery," "A Farmer" contended.[43] Coles pushed his economic case hard. "There is always more productive laborers in a free, than slave state," he said, writing as "Aristides." "The labor of a free man is always more productive than the labor of the slave. The white laborer has an interest in his toil and in his reward.... In the slave states, the case is different. The wealthy monopolize large tracts of country, and only cultivate so much as will pamper their price, luxury, and vice, and barely subsist their wretched negroes—the remainder lies waste." In contrast to those profligates, Coles continued, "the great body of emigrants from slave and free states will consist of poor people, who will have ventured into this wild, to gather a little of this world's goods." For emigrants from free states, and Southerners who don't have slaves, "what little property the non-slaveholding emigrant owns, will be converted into cash and that little will come with him into this country," Coles argued, while the "wealth that a slaveowner can save from the wreck of his fortune will consist of slaves."[44] By being able to link settlers' worries about cash, with their disdain for others' idleness, and their anger over their own fading prospects, Coles had created a potent message, and one that could resound with Illinoisans, as Daniel 'Rarified' Smith's bitter toast at the Fourth of July dinner at Alton suggests: "The Legislature and rag currency of Illinois/ Both a disgrace to the state/ And both sixty six and two thirds percent below par. May the former be purified and the latter burnt."[45]

With his battle joined, his allies organized and his arguments starting to be aired in Illinois newspapers, Coles gradually grew more confident. "The advocates of a convention have been losing ground," he wrote to Nicholas Biddle, back in Philadelphia. It was a wonderful summer, the summer of 1823, he would always remember. There was none of the brooding and illness that had marked so much of his time in Washington, none of the boredom and isolation of his first years in Edwardsville. "This has been the most cool and agreeable, and by far the most healthful summer I have ever seen in this country," he told Biddle. "This spring was too wet and we were apprehensive of an unfavorable summer both for health and for vegetables but we have been most agreeably disappointed. My health was never better." One of his closest allies, the preacher John Mason Peck, would remember of that time that "the anti-convention part had the whole state under their control, and the question virtually decided, before their opponents got up a public organization at Vandalia." But it would be a false calm.[46]

By the fall, the pro-slavery men would recognize that the raucous demonstrations against Coles and his allies in Vandalia during the legislative session had damaged their cause more deeply than they had understood, and that the deal-making that had won them their victory there were troubling many voters. "This outrage," John Reynolds declared, "was the death blow to the convention." But, misled by their command of the state's newspapers—four of the five weeklies published in Illinois at the time backed the convention, while the fifth, Hooper Warren's *Spectator*, spent almost as much time sniping at Coles as it did challenging his opponents—the conventionists did not realize for many months exactly how badly organized they were or how quickly they were losing ground. They had set up only two county organizations outside Vandalia, while Coles and Peck had established a statewide network within weeks of the legislature's adjournment. "If there is not a majority opposed to the measure, there is at least a large minority," one conventionist, "A Voter" commented.[47]

But as the summer faded into fall, Coles' uneasiness grew. While his opponents may have still seemed unorganized, at least as compared with his own efforts among the anti-slavery men, Coles was sure they had not given up. He was tired of being sniped at, and had spent all of his salary as Governor in the campaign against the convention, and was worrying that a pleasant summer did not necessarily mean a profitable harvest come the fall. "I have found the honor, duties and emoluments of the office of Governor less gratifying than I had expected," he complained to a favorite niece. "The state of party feelings & party contention, are alone enough to render the office disagreeable, but the want of competent means to live comfortably greatly increases it." Were it not, he added, that "my desires are so moderate and my republican simplicity so great ... I should be driven into a vortex of debt as well as melancholy." Now, with the year drawing to a close, he had to return to the capital. All his opponents were already gathering there for the start of the state Supreme Court term and for the huge auction the state treasurer had just announced to sell approximately 7,000 tracts of land the counties had taken from out-of-state speculators for non-payment of taxes. The little town of Vandalia was filled with politicians and land buyers and lawyers again. All had business to do, of course. But the crowded taverns, the rude dining rooms, were abuzz again with talk about the convention and the battles to come. "For the last four weeks, there has been a great crowd of persons here ... an excellent opportunity of collecting the sense of the people," Coles wrote to his new Pennsylvanian friend, Roberts Vaux, that December. "I am happy in assuring you, from the best information I have been able to collect from all parts of the State, I am more confirmed in my belief that a majority of the people will be opposed to calling a convention."[48]

Possibly, now, the pro-slavery men saw the same thing. On December 3rd, Samuel McRoberts, a choleric judge from Madison County who was soon to play a large role in Coles' personal affairs, joined with General Willis Hargrave to call a meeting to propose creating a central committee of 18 pro-convention leaders from around the state. The aim was to set up five-man committees in each county; in turn, these were to form three-man groups of "guards and pickets, corps of advance and reserve" in each precinct.[49] These new signs of life alarmed Coles, who told Vaux he was worried by "the extraordinary efforts that have been made here in the last three or four weeks." The convention side's leaders were beginning to act "with the utmost concert and effect," he continued; the result was to "convince the friends of freedom that their opponents are yet in the field." To his friend Morris Birkbeck, Coles grumbled that "when bad men conspire, good men should be watchful."[50]

Then, on December 9, the State House burned down.

How it happened, no one could ever say. It was a shabby, sloppily-constructed building, but it should not have burned. The legislature had not yet convened, the fireplaces were unlit. No one should have been inside with lamp or candle. Some suspected it was set; if so, the question of who it might benefit seemed clear—especially since one party had already won such a name for itself by burning effigies. "This accident will operate in favor of a convention," Coles noted. "Many profess to be opposed to slavery but in favor of a convention to remove the seat of government. There is now, if course, less inducement for keeping it here."[51]) Possibly to cool the speculation they were to blame, pro-slavery leaders quickly organized a fund to pay for a replacement; Coles declined to contribute. "I had the misfortune to lose by fire two-thirds of all the buildings and enclosures on my farm, together with about 200 apple trees and as many peach trees," Coles explained. Robert and Kate Crawford lost their home in the blaze, as well.* "Soon after, the State House having been consumed by fire, a project was set on foot to rebuild it by subscription. Not liking the plan and

---

*James Simeone, Democracy and Slavery, 3, helps launch his picture of a state in flames with righteous anger over the actions of an elitist and isolated Coles, by asserting flatly that arsonists burned his farm, citing this letter, which does not make that accusation. Suzanne Cooper Guasco's "Confronting Democracy," 241, says Coles suspected his political opponents set side to his farm, discounting the idea of a natural prairie fire, and citing a Jan. 21, 1824, letter from Coles to Roberts Vaux saying it was intended "to break down my pecuniary resources"—but Coles in that letter was referring to a lawsuit filed against him earlier that month, alleging that he violated state law by not posting bonds for the slaves he freed, and suing him for $2,000, as discussed in the next chapter.

arrangements, I declined subscribing and proposed others ... this however was immediately laid hold of by some of the factious Conventionists ... they busied themselves in misrepresenting to the multitude my reasons and motives for not subscribing my name to their paper, and with the aid of large portions of whisky, contrived to get up a real Vandal mob, who vented their spleen against me, in the most noisy and riotous manner, nearly all night."[52]

The crowd gathered in the early evening gloom, and paraded around and around the streets by the public square for hours, growing angrier and noisier all along. "About two in the morning," wrote the *Spectator*'s correspondent, "I was again awakened by the appalling cry of fire! And from the light that was thrown into the window of my chamber, I concluded that there was a serious danger." But this time, "instead of a building on fire, I saw a man of straw, which the mob called the Governor!—and which was burnt, amid the groans of the mob, and the cry State House or death!"[53]

CHAPTER 8

Hard road to victory

The riot in Vandalia, along with many "other instances of defamation and persecution" late in the year 1823, "create in my bosom opposite feelings: one of pain, the other of pleasure," a somber Coles wrote to his friend Morris Birkbeck. "Pain to see my fellow man so ill-natured and vindictive merely because I am a friend to my species, and am opposed to one portion oppressing another—pleasure that I could be in a situation which enables me to render services to a just and good cause." His fighting spirit was high, though, Coles continued. A family friend, Walter Gilmore, wrote reassuringly to Coles' older sister Mary Carter, who passed on the gist to her mother: Edward "has not lost his popularity ... the Mob was composed of the lowest grade.... [I] assure you from him that no importance ought to be attached to it." For a man who had been burnt in effigy by a drunken mob, Coles seemed to be taking things awfully calmly, all in all. "I am thankful to Providence," he told Birkbeck, "for placing me in the van of this eventful contest, and giving me the temper, zeal and resolution which I trust will enable me to bear with proper fortitude the peltings which are inseparable from it."[1]

For the contest had turned even more personal. On January 7, the Circuit Court in Madison County issued a summons to Coles, to answer a charge that he owed the county $2,000 for bonds that a neighbor (and political opponent) said he should have posted for the freedmen who had come with him to settle in Illinois back in 1819. A law passed barely a month before Coles came to Madison County required a $1,000 bond for every slave liberated in the state, for the purported aim of ensuring that they did not become wards of the county. It was the Illinois version of legislation then coming into force across the South and in some of the border states intended to discourage manumission. In any event, the Illinois law set a penalty for failing to post a bond at $200 for each freedman, a sum that exceeded the cost of an 80-acre farm and one far beyond what most new settlers could easily afford, even men with the resources Coles had. With his purchase of Prairieland, he'd spent a little more than $13,500 on land in Missouri and Illinois and $700 more moving his former slaves out west and setting up his farm—the fees for posting thousands of surety dollars or the $2,000 in penalties for failing to do so would have just about tapped him out. "What is truly farcical in this suit is, that a poor worthless fellow, who has no property, and of course pays no tax, has been selected to initiate it, from the fear he had of being taxed to support the negroes I emancipated, when they, who are all young and healthy, are so prosperous as to possess comfortable livings and some of them pay as much as four dollars a year tax (the highest rate) on their property."[2]

At first, though, Coles paid his fee for the bond requested as if the case were an ordinary dispute—less than ordinary, perhaps, since the alleged violation had existed for years and his lawyers were confident it had no merit. The message implicit in its timing, so soon after the devastating fire, so soon after his opponents had scored their points off him for not contributing to the fund to rebuilding the State House, completely missed him. Then, a few days after he had been served, "an old and intimate friend, a clergyman in the neighborhood" came by the see the governor, at the request of one of the county commissioners, Hail Mason, to ask Coles to withdraw the bond he had posted. The lawsuit, the preacher said, "was a mere party proceeding, intended to persecute and harass, without any expectation of ever succeeding in making me pay the penalty." Mason, who was appalled by the lawsuit, was sure the matter would simply go away once the issue of the convention had been resolved. Coles and his lawyers thought much the same, and tried to brush the suit off, saying simply that he was not guilty of violating the law, which had not even been published, and so could not have taken effect, until five months after the freedmen had arrived in Illinois. On top of that, the lawyers argued, Coles had freed his slaves outside of Illinois, and the law applied only to those who had been emancipated in the state.[3]

But the suit was meant to sting, and did. Never quite really the wealthy dilettante some had painted (and some still do), Coles' finances were already strained: he faced big bills to rebuild his farm; the destruction of his orchards meant a significant loss of income for a farm that was barely breaking even. He had pledged his salary to the anti-slavery fight. "The friends of a Convention appear to become more and more bitter and virulent in their enmity to me, and seem determined not only to injure my standing with the people, but to break down my pecuniary resources," Coles complained to Birkbeck. "I should indeed, my friend, be unfortunate were I now compelled to pay $200 for each of my negroes, big and little, dead and living (for the suit goes to this)." He was still trying to rebuild the Crawfords' house, his farm buildings and fences, and the cost was not trivial. Moreover, it wasn't just the money that hurt: "Now, for the first time in my life, to be sued for what I thought was generous and praiseworthy conduct, creates strange feelings." But despite the attack, he vowed, "no dread of personal consequences will ever abate my efforts." To his niece Sarah Carter, however, he admitted it had been "a very lonely and disagreeable winter.... There may be honor but there is not pleasure in being Governor to such a people in such a crisis."[4]

For the moment, and mistakenly, Coles felt he had addressed the mess. In any event, he had little time or energy to spare to fret about it—for the fight over the convention was clearly about to grow much more intense. The pro-slavery men, having poked at him with the lawsuit, were starting to push harder on other fronts. In January, they tried to elect William Jones, a Baptist preacher, to the Commissioners' Court for Madison County, without mentioning that he, unusually for a clergyman of his church, was one of their supporters. In the county seat, *Edwardsville Spectator* editor Hooper Warren accused them of trying to use Jones' election to boast, falsely, that Madison was strong for a convention. Blasting the trick in print, he was able to forestall the coup.[5]

But the pro-convention men grew more and more confident, more and more combative. Casting themselves as underdogs, they complained again that the preachers and the rich were trying to shut them up. "When he ventures to speak in favor of a convention, he is to be branded with the epithets of corrupt, oppressive, dishonest, inhuman and unjust," one pro-convention writer noted in the *Illinois Intelligencer*. Other letter-writers would echo this feeling in Illinois newspapers in the months that followed.[6]

In camp meeting, in church, in the backwoods groceries, wherever people gathered, feelings ran high. "The convention question gave rise to two years of the most furious and boisterous excitement and contest that was ever visited on Illinois," the future governor John Reynolds would remember. "Men, women and children entered the arena of party warfare and strife, and the families and neighborhoods were so divided, and furious and bitter against one another, that it seemed a regular civil war might be next." War, Reynolds continued, was far from being too strong a word for what was happening: "Many personal combats were indulged in on the question and the whole country seemed, at times, to be ready and willing to resort to physical force to decide the issue."[7] "Old friendships were sundered, families divided and neighborhood arrayed in opposition to each other," William Brown remembered. "Pistols and dirks were in great demand ... even the gentler sex came within the vortex of this whirlwind of passion; and many were the angry disputations of those whose cares and interests were usually confined to their household duties." One farm wife complained to the *Illinois Republican* that her husband was spending half his days in political cabals, and would "neglect his ordinary business ... impoverish his family and break his wife's heart by unkind words and ill looks in his zeal for politics."[8]

Out of the pro-convention men's December caucuses in Vandalia that Coles watched so closely came a return to the strategy of downplaying slavery. Even before the caucus, in White County, in far southern Illinois, a public meeting of Fox River valley residents declared that, in their view, the convention question had nothing to do with slavery, agreeing as well to form a committee "to communicate with other groups like themselves in other towns and counties throughout the state." In Vandalia, taking a lead from the White County group, a key central committee resolution outlined the carefully refined appeal that "the people have a right to alter and amend their social compact whenever they shall find the same oppressive or inefficient." In the next month, the pro-convention party's central committee would go on to resolve that slavery was not their "moving consideration" but that abolition of the Council of Revision, eliminating the county Commissioners' Courts, and replacing biennial elections with annual ones were. "Massachusetts may have her convention, New York has had her convention, all the states have had, or may have, their new conventions, but poor degraded Illinois must be denied the dearest privilege of a sovereign, independent state," "Republican" complained in the *Intelligencer*. The newly energized convention party men contended their opponents were engaged in a "mere struggle for power," one obscured by "the hue and cry of Slavery! Slavery! Slavery!" Opposition to slavery, the pro-convention men argued, should not mean opposition to the convention; indeed, they started noting, if anti-slave men objected to the indenture system then current, they should be supporting a constitutional reform. "If the constitution is defective, it should be amended regardless of any scare crows which have been brought to bear against it," wrote William Berry, nearly a year after his anti-slavery partner Brown was forced out of the editorial seat at the *Illinois Intelligencer*. "If the people of Illinois are opposed to a change in our constitution so as to admit slavery in this state, we are certain they can prevent it, although a convention be called."[9]

Still, the pro-convention leaders couldn't leave the slavery issue alone. Illinoisans had taken for themselves the keys to power, Col. William Alexander told a mass meeting in Monroe County, but "immediately after the keys were surrendered, those agents who were opposed to the people getting them, climbed up and wrote in large letters over the door 'Beware how you enter, Slavery dwells here.'"[10]

The idea that the call for a convention was only about cleaning up undemocratic features of the 1818 constitution was not an easy sell to many Illinoisans, however. The pro-convention men made poor democrats, for all their attacks on Coles as a snob and aristocrat, it seemed. As "A Farmer," for instance, noted, "it is a remarkable fact that nearly all the defective parts of our state constitution, which are so much complained of by the conventionists, are the work of the distinguished individuals of the convention party," adding that "the Council of the revision was the production of Mr. Kane" while the commissioners court was the work of Joseph Kitchell, "another thorough-going conventionist."[11]

In March, the pro-slavery men tried yet another tack. Coles was the leader of the anti-convention movement, Coles had forced the issue, Coles had insisted, and kept insisting, that the issue was slavery. Coles was in the way; surely, they thought, they could clear the path by appealing to his ambition and getting him out of Illinois. That winter, Ninian Edwards had decided to resign his U.S. Senate seat and accept appointment as U.S. minister to Mexico. Illinois' ambitious lieutenant governor, the pro-convention stalwart Adolphus Frederick Hubbard, visiting Washington at that time, thought he saw his chance. He hastened back to Illinois with Edwards' notice of resignation and went directly to see Coles. "He told me Mr. Cook and Mr. Edwards had induced him to come on, under the belief that I would either resign my office and accept a seat in the Senate from him or confer it on him," an astonished Coles recalled.[12] The two were not intimate, and Coles had only contempt for a man who had made his name in part with an often-quoted speech in the legislature on a proposed wolf bounty. ("Mr. Speaker," the irrepressible Hubbard had said, "I remember that once on a time as Judge Brown and I were riding across Bonpas prairie," the judge called out "Hubbard! Look! There goes a wolf. And I looked and I looked and I said Judge, where?... Mr. Speaker, if I did not see a wolf this time, I think I never saw one. But I have heard much and read more about this animal ... when all nature reposes in silent oblivion, and then commits the most terrible devastations upon the rising generation of hogs and sheep."[13]) As tempting as it must have been to send such a thoughtful speaker to Senate, "it was with some difficulty," noted Coles drily, "that I could restrain my indignation at the idea of thus sneaking into the Senate, or of sending to it such a simpleton as my Lieutenant."[14]

Still, for many of Coles' allies, it seemed as if their campaign had started drifting. "Let us shake off this alarming apathy," an anti-slavery caucus in Belleville resolved. "The convention party is making every effort to effect their views; and if we sleep on our posts, they will carry the day." But Coles wasn't sitting idly. A long-secret plan, aimed at winning a powerful new voice for the anti-slavery cause, was about to unfold. For, despite the careful organization, despite the sermons in the pulpits, despite the pamphlets from his Quaker friends, with four of the five papers in the state urging a convention, it had been difficult for Coles to reach many of the voters who would ultimately decide the issue. "The only press whose editor is in favor of freedom, although a pretty smart editor, has rendered himself unpopular with many by his foolish and passionate attacks upon many of the prominent men on his side of the question," Coles complained, referring to his old enemy, Hooper Warren.[15] The editor, meanwhile, had for months been aggravating other supporters and simultaneously entertaining his pro-convention opponents: "The inconsistencies, the gross misrepresentations and the unblushing effrontery with which the most groundless assertions are made ... I would invite the attention to that particular paper and ask whether that cause must not be a very bad one which has to be supported by such means," "A Plain Citizen" wrote early in the convention campaign.[16] With Warren's relentless disdain for him, Coles knew that his efforts circulating the pamphlets his Quaker friends had sent, despite the organized letter-writing to pro-convention papers, were not enough. He knew, and had known from the start, that he would need a press of his own.

And he had been working on that almost from the start. As William Brown and William Berry, proprietors of the *Illinois Intelligencer*, took their dispute over the convention issue public after the House finally pushed its resolution through, the governor began to muse about the advantages of having a trustworthy anti-slavery newspaper in the battle to come. Despite Warren's fervent opposition to slavery, Coles was even then far from sure the disgruntled editor could set aside his personal enmity, an antipathy that would baffle him for the rest of his life. (He'd be proved right, of course.) With his $1,000-a-year salary as governor pledged to the campaign, another $1,000 in state bills that a group of anti-convention legislators had pledged from their own salaries, Coles thought he could buy a newspaper, and from early on, had his eye on the *Intelligencer* itself. What he had in mind, he would explain to his ally, the Rev. John Mason Peck, was complicated, and started with the appointment of a new secretary of state. Judge Samuel Lockwood, part of the Land Office clique of anti-slavery Edwardsville men, had resigned that sinecure. Coles needed a lawyer, and wanted an anti-convention man, to fill the slot, intending, as Peck recalled, that "as a matter then strictly confidential, he must be able on a certain contingency to conduct the editorial department of a newspaper." Coles then planned, "through a friendly agency," to buy a stake in the *Intelligencer*, "a paper that by an outrage on the part of the majority of the legislature, had been taken from the control of William H. Brown, Esq., and made the leading organ

8—Hard road to victory 145

Hooper Warren's print shop in Edwardsville. Warren's intense dislike for Coles colored the *Edwardsville Spectator*'s coverage, frustrating the anti-slavery campaign, despite Warren's personal opposition to slavery (Library of Congress).

of the convention party." Peck thought he knew just the man to step in, the lawyer David Blackwell, a friend who happened to be the brother of the man who stepped in as Berry's new partner to take control of the *Intelligencer* and its state printing contract, a contract specifically reserved, by an act of the legislature, to the printing firm Blackwell & Berry. "The Governor sprang to his feet, and exclaimed 'He is the very man; why did I not think of him,'" the ever-innocent Rev. Peck would remember. Coles, who had surely been thinking of precisely this friend of Peck's, had little trouble convincing the pastor to hasten to Belleville, "soon as daylight appeared," to recruit Blackwell. "Like other lawyers in that moneyless era, he was in straightened circumstances, and the Secretary-ship was a real God-send to supply the wants of a young family," Peck remembered. It took twelve months for Coles and Blackwell to finally acquire their interest, and when Blackwell & Berry, with a new, and anti-slavery, Blackwell involved, announced the paper's opposition to the convention, in May 1824, three months before the referendum vote, "a bomb-shell falling from the sky and exploding in camp, where no enemy was thought to be near, could not have produced greater consternation," Peck would happily boast. With the change at the *Intelligencer*, "there was a great fever for the 'anti's,'" Reynolds agreed.[17]

Coles, writing now as "One of Many," came out swinging. Reminding readers that the pro-slavery men in the state Senate had gagged William Kinkade, while the leaders of the House of Representatives had frogmarched Nicholas Hansen from his seat when he voted against them, Coles asked, in his initial blast, "would it be wise or prudent to intrust all our great sovereign rights into the hands of men whose conduct is this dark and mysterious?" This was not the way the honest men of the frontier liked their politics to played, he said, adding: "I wish now merely to remind you of their intrigues, and of the unprecedented and unwarrantable means they resorted to, to effect their end—the adoption of the resolution recommending a convention—and then ask you if you are willing to trust such men to make a constitution." The pro-convention leaders, Coles argued, were not telling people the truth about their goals; they were asking for a trust they had not earned, "singing the Syren song of peoples rights; the people are sovereign; the people cannot err," while in fact asking that the people of Illinois "give their approbation to the call of a convention, without knowing its object, merely upon the recommendation of their Representatives." He dismissed the idea that the whole point of a convention was to resolve questions, such as slavery, on which Illinoisans might disagree: "This is what is called policy. But it is not the kind of policy recommended by the father of his country. He differed from the advocates of a convention; he declared 'honesty to be the best policy.'"[18]

In the weeks that followed, Coles kept hammering home his point that the pro-convention leaders were slavery men, and that slavery would harm, not help, the economy of Illinois. He argued against the idea that "diffusing" slavery would lessen its sting and eventually allow it to wither away—an argument that had emerged in Illinois and one which would be floated regularly in the years to come by national politicians urging the expansion of slavery across the Mississippi River; "these beautiful and fertile prairies" were not a place for "the descendants of Africa, who are not only unlike us in person, but are to be a degraded race of slaves," a nasty pander to the usual racial prejudice of the times.[19] He argued that were Illinois to become a slave state, slave-holders would, at last, attain the majority they had so long sought in the U.S. Senate, despite the decades of compromise invested in trying to maintain a balance between the sections. Slavery would flourish here, continuing to subvert the United States' role as a beacon of liberty for the entire world.[20] But there was new emphasis on another note, one that was central to Coles and that, he now argued, was even more important than the economic question. The issue of slavery was an issue of what the people of Illinois believed about justice and about what was right, he said. "We are literally the offspring of freedom, and inherited from a virtuous parent an exemption from the curse of slavery," he wrote. "If we are to have it, the illicit and unnatural fiend will be a bantling of our own begetting.... If Illinois should become a slave holding state, will it not be always held up as an example to justify the continuance of slavery, wherever it may exist."[21]

With Coles, Blackwell and Brown enthusiastically banging away on the evils of slavery in their own, and widely circulated, paper, pro-convention leaders could no longer try to simply finesse the issue and hope it would go away. And faced with this challenge, where they found their response was by turning to the unthinking but virulent racism of the day, the distaste, hatred and fear of blacks that was only barely balanced by frontier settlers' firm belief that individual rights were meant for all Americans, in the words of preachers that God was God for all humankind. One pro-convention man, supposedly just a poor farmer, declared that "a white man could not stand to work here—that the negroes were made for slaves, that white people ought not to be obliged to work," the letter-writer Spartacus recounted in the *Intelligencer.*[22] There was good money to be had in slavery, others argued: "[E]xtend the right of bringing indentured servants into the state, and a new spring would be given to emigration, which would soon people our woods and prairies," wrote one. "The emigration to Missouri, through this county, is not less now.... we have it from a very respectable gentleman, who keeps a public house, on the Vincennes Trace, that about two hundred wagons, with families, have passed that road, this fall, on their way to the same country."[23] As emigrants passed through a still-economically-depressed Illinois on their way to Missouri, some settlers found it harder to think of other peoples' rights than their own; Spartacus' neighbor, for instance, "with furious gestures with the glass which he held in his hand," held forth at length and "swore he had as good a right to have slaves as the people of Missouri or any other state."[24] Pro-convention appeals were often even cruder: "When we have such men as Jonathan Freeman, alias the gentleman who resides at Wanborough, declaring at the seat of government that he would be perfectly willing to dandle a black grandchild on his knee ... is it not certain that it has excited a confidence among free blacks of other States to migrate to this, where they are promised such a warm reception?" wrote one angry pro-convention man.[25] For many, inevitably, it would all come down to race. One flier, in the form of a sample ballot, spelt out the argument for a convention simply: "For a new constitution. For article prohibiting backs. For exclusion of negroes and mulattoes. No right of suffrage or office for negroes or mulattoes. For laws excluding negroes and mulattoes from coming into and voting in this state."[26]

It was the issue Coles could not touch—the closest he could come, in his "One of Many" letters published in the spring and summer of 1824, was to argue again that slavery required force to maintain itself, force that sooner or later inclined to tyranny, tyranny that inevitably affected all men, not just those with black skins.[27]

But as ordinary Illinoisans continued hissing and scrapping with one another over slavery, a few pro-convention leaders like Elias Kent Kane were starting to be concerned that the fight for a convention might cost them victory in fights that mattered more to them: the ones for political offices. The August election would give Kane and his backers in the Thomas faction one more shot at the anti-slave congressman, Daniel Cook, who by this point had married Ninian Edwards' daughter and was reconciled with the grandiose former Senator—and it was Cook's connection with Edwards far more than his opposition to slavery that preoccupied the Thomas men. At the same time, the popular former governor, Shadrach Bond, who was close to Thomas if not formally a member of his faction, had already declared for the seat in Congress. Raising the stakes still more, 1824 was a presidential election year, and faction leaders were eager to be seen as early backers of the eventual victor; Bond, like Cook (and Coles, for that matter), was a supporter of the peculiar old Georgian Treasury Secretary, William Crawford, preferring an orthodox Jeffersonian to candidates who might have at least a chance of election. If Bond, loosely tied to Thomas, were to win, there could be consequences Thomas and Kane might not want to live with—and Bond "had this advantage ... in that, by a judicious bestowment of his patronage, he had created many political friends, who were bound to do battle in his behalf, and expend their energies, influence and time in securing his election."[28]

Bond danced around on the convention question; Cook, too, said little, for all his stern and stalwart opposition to slavery in Missouri during the congressional debates on that territory's admission to the Union. In the legislative contests, too, it was tough to pin down some of the candidates. A voter in Gallatin County wrote to ask that would-be legislators "publically declare your views and sentiments on the questions which now agitate the publick mind, particularly that of the Convention."[29] But legislative candidates, by and large, resisted the temptation. Most of the representatives and senators who had voted for the convention resolution were running for re-election, and they were growing alarmed by the numbers of their constituents who opposed slavery. "Is it possible," asked Coles, "they can entertain so despicable an opinion of the understanding of the people, as to suppose they can thus treat them with contempt ... and then can lull them into acquiescence, and gain their object, by singing the siren song of the peoples rights?" The conventionists would say anything to anyone, except to admit to an anti-slave man they favored slavery. "Thus if you should be in favor of removing the seat of government to Alton, or to Carmi, to Edwardsville or to Palestine, Kaskaskia, Covington or Carlyle, the friends of each in turn is assured that his particular wish will be effected by having a convention," Coles wrote, as "One of Many," making the case he thought would resonate most with a people, still unsettled by the riot and mayhem in Vandalia, who increasingly mistrusted what their long-established political leaders had been telling them. "If you have no other objection to the constitution but the commissioners court and the council of revision, then these are the only alterations that will be made to it," Coles continued. "If one is opposed to the extension of Slavery, he will be told that it is not contemplated ... if on the other hand he should be in favor of making this a slave holding state, he is assured that that is the great and chief object in view."[30]

The appeal to Illinoisans' democratic rights to write, and re-write, their own constitution was falling short in the face of Coles' counterattack. As the anti-slave campaign stepped up its attacks on the motives of their opponents, more and more settlers began to feel the pro-convention men's words rang hollow. The republican rhetoric from men who connived at faction politics and who were numbered among the richest in an otherwise very poor state sat ill with many voters. "We now have no proud nabobs, to turn up their noses at their poorer neighbors—no haughty masters of a hundred slaves to display their superiority ... but introduce slavery and the case will be different," "Mechanic" wrote to the *Spectator*.[31] "Over every district, and through every plantation, must resound the lash of the slave driver and the yells of its victims, to satisfy their unnatural, their infernal appetite!—Yet they call themselves Republicans,—with liberty on their tongues and tyranny in their hearts!—One hand displaying the Declaration of Equal Rights—the other clenching the Code of Slavery with a monstrous avidity," Morris Birkbeck, writing as Jonathan Freeman, argued.[32]

For all the pro-convention party leaders might try to divert attention from slavery, Coles' and Birkbeck's letters to the papers, the pamphlets that Coles paid for, and the paper that he bought, all made clear that it was the very root of the battle. The politics of faction, of section, of resentment were all fought, and fought hard. The question—the everlasting question—of majority rule and its limits, the pride of citizens in the sovereignty of their new state, the fundamental belief that the people had the right to write the rules by which they were governed, all seemed to pale beside the still greater issue of slavery, the issue that would inexorably drive the nation to a bloody, bitter war in a generation. Paled, perhaps, because the people of Illinois understood Coles' argument that democracy depended on rights for all people, not just "White Folks." Paled, perhaps, because they understood the real import of the challenge he threw down to the General Assembly when he took his oath of office. "Some people tell us, that is a political evil and does not belong to our mission" to speak out against slavery, the preacher Benjamin Ogle, brother of state Representative Jacob Ogle, who had voted against the convention. "But we would ask, is it not a moral issue?"[33]

It seemed to be. On August 2, Illinoisans trooped to the taverns and courthouses where their county Commissioners Courts had set up polls, past the fence posts and tree trunks bedecked with fliers, some still arguing angrily over the great question, others, somber and serious, going quietly to vote. It was a steamy summer day. More than 11,600 showed up and cast ballots (35 percent more than had voted in the 1822 gubernatorial race). "The election was a hot time. The weather was warm enough, being early August, and the people were heated with excitement," Rev. Thomas Lippincott remembered. "Yet it is believed that as few excesses occurred on that day as on any general election since."[34]

Morris Birkbeck, the English liberal, founder of the Albion settlement in eastern Illinois, was a stalwart opponent of slavery. Line print from frontispiece of *History of the English Settlement in Edwards County, Illinois;* 1882; artist George Flower (Chicago Historical Society [ICH:-09524]).

The vote was 4,972 for a convention, 6,610 against. Coles and the anti-conventionists picked up several counties he couldn't carry in the 1822 race, including, in the far southern part of the state, Union County (home to the popular pro-slavery state Senator Grammer); he nearly won Johnson County, across the Ohio River from slave-holding Kentucky, eking out a 74–74 tie. Coles won Lawrence and Edwards counties in the east for the anti-slavery cause, as well as populous St. Clair and Monroe counties, which, located across the Mississippi River from Missouri as they were, had attracted pro-slavery campaigners from that state. He carried the mainly Southern migrants who had settled in Washington and newly-formed Marion County, as well. In Randolph County, where most of the slave-holding French settlers lived, Coles and the anti-convention campaigners won 44 percent of the vote (he had eked out 3 percent in the 1822 election). The anti-convention campaign made big gains from Coles' single-digit votes in 1822 with voters in the southern and eastern counties of Alexander, Hamilton, Jefferson and White.[35]*

Oddly, for all the furor of the 18 months just past, many voters supposedly didn't cast ballots on the convention issue, even if they did vote in the race for the state's sole seat in the U.S. House of Representatives, re-electing Daniel Cook in a landslide, with 7,592 votes. Odd, too, that nearly half the difference in votes cast for Congress than on the convention issue came in just one county, far southern Pope, where Cook won 195 more votes than the anti-convention campaign did, enough votes to have swung that county against the convention. The same pattern, on a much smaller scale, emerged in Alexander, the southernmost county, wedged between slaveholding Kentucky and Missouri. Though Johnson

*For readers interested in the convention vote:

Northern counties			American Bottom			Saline area			Southern counties		
	pro	con		pro	con		pro	con		pro	con
Bond	63	240	Madison	351	563	Gallatin	597	133	Alexander	75	51
Clark	31	116	Monroe	141	196	Pope	273	124	Franklin	170	113
Crawford	134	262	St. Clair	408	506	White	355	326	Jackson	180	93
Edgar	3	234							Jefferson	99	43
Fayette	125	121				**Eastern counties**			Johnson	74	74
Fulton	5	60					pro	con	Marion	45	52
Greene	164	379				Edwards	9	391	Randolph	357	284
Montgomery	79	90				Hamilton	173	85	Union	213	214
Morgan	42	432				Lawrence	158	261	Washington	112	173
Pike	19	165				Wayne	189	111			
Sangamon	153	722									

from Theodore C. Pease, ed., Illinois Election Returns, 1818–1848 (Springfield: Illinois State Historical Library, 1923), 27-9.

1824 Election

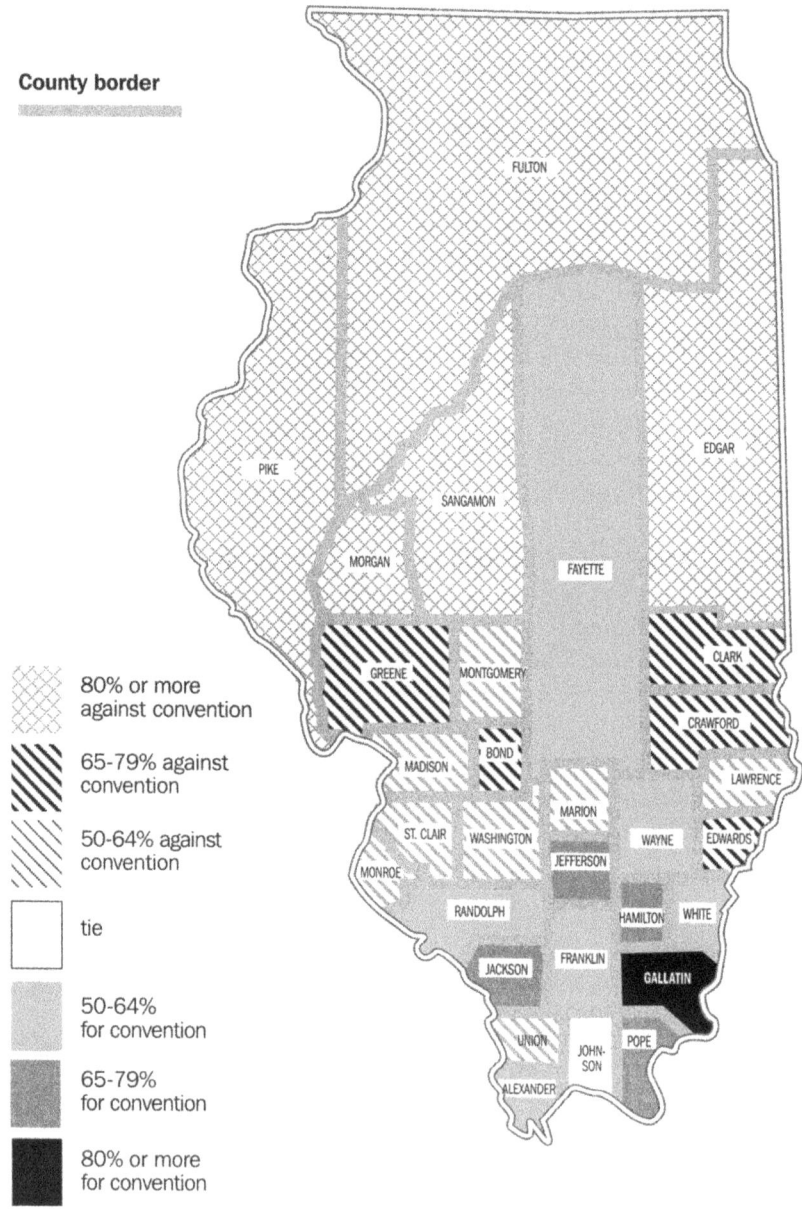

The referendum vote of 1824 (courtesy John Ailor).

County split 74 votes to 74 on the convention question, it gave Cook a 20-vote margin. In Gallatin, Cook won 153 more votes than the anti-convention question did, though the split there would not have been enough to carry the home county of the U.S. Saline for the anti-slavery cause. Other southern counties—where the pro-convention party leaders had counted on Southern emigrants to vote for slavery—seemed more ambivalent on the convention question; besides the straight-down-the-middle split in Johnson, a majority in Union County, just across the Mississippi river from Missouri, opposed the convention while nearly half of voters in White County also voted against a convention. Cook also outpolled the anti-convention question in what had become the biggest county, St. Clair, where the county clerk was a convention man, and initially refused to send his vote count on to Vandalia—until, that is, a rifle-toting crowd assembled at the courthouse to insist. The incident raises the intriguing question of whether or not the big discrepancies in votes cast in Pope, Gallatin, Alexander, Madison and St. Clair signify some anti-convention votes were simply not counted. Coles and allies, as victors, would have felt no need to raise an objection, of course, since they won. The pro-convention leaders, presumably, would have no interest in complaining about a count that made their loss larger. Still, it seems odd that, despite 18 months of intensive campaigning, hundreds of voters felt the question was not important enough to cast a ballot on. In any event, however, the count in the southern counties makes it clear that many of the Southern emigrants who had settled near the Ohio and Mississippi rivers were not as monolithically in favor of slavery as the pro-convention campaigners had believed.[36]

The vote counts, and the odd pattern of supposedly uncast votes in the southern counties,* suggests it may be overly simplistic to say that being originally from the South, or living near a slave-holding state, would move voters to support the pro-slavery conventionists. Perhaps they were swayed by the economic arguments Coles so carefully assembled or the suggestion that formally allowing slavery would mean more of the slaves they despised, whether for reasons of economic competition or simple racial prejudice. For many devout Baptists, Methodists and Quakers who had come to Illinois from

---

*The lower vote for the convention, and the unusual pattern of Cook votes and anti-convention votes in the southern counties, seems to have attracted little attention or comment, either then or in more recent histories. Since polling place judges were appointees of the county commissioners, most of whom needed the support of Illinois' faction leaders and lieutenants, especially in the pro-slavery legislature, it seems possible that many of these men might well have managed to miss convention votes if they were going against their cause. On the other hand, no complaints about miscounts emerged in newspapers after the election.

the South, men like James Lemen or Braxton Parrish, it is worth remembering that they considered religious teaching to be clear; there seems little doubt that the efforts of Rev. John Mason Peck and his allies in the clergy swayed many. Voters were, no doubt, upset by the back-room conspiring of the legislators, deeply offended by the Hansen incident, concerned that the powerful had taken power from the people, despite the pro-convention campaigners' rhetoric that it was they who sought to restore it, through the means of a revised constitution. For some, perhaps, what may have been decisive was Coles' basic view that the words of the Founding Fathers left no room for doubt on the question of slavery.

The northern counties, in contrast, were overwhelmingly opposed to the convention.* In fast-growing Sangamon, where the tree-fringed prairie was rapidly filling with settlers from New England, New York and Ohio, the vote was nearly five to one against the convention. (The anti-convention party widened Coles' margin here by nearly 30 percentage points.) The new frontier counties of Edgar, Fulton and Morgan cast more than 90 percent of their votes against the convention. In Pike, Black Prince John Shaw notwithstanding, the vote against the convention was nearly 90 percent. Coles' home county, Madison, with 45 slave-owning households reported in the 1820 Census, voted by a roughly 60–40 margin against changing the constitution. It would be to the north, of course, where Illinois' future growth would be and in these counties that the political climate for decades to come would be set.

"Our Governor is a plain good sort of man, but many of our most influential public officials are dear lovers of Slavery and would gladly introduce into this state the same system which prevails in the South," was how one of those northern county settlers summed it up. In swinging seven counties that had rejected him as governor, in helping wrack up 30

---

*Historians generally see the results of the 1824 vote as confirming a North-South split that some argue has characterized the politics and culture of Illinois to the present time; see for example Leichtle "Coles: An Agrarian," 187–8, and Guasco, "Confronting Democracy," 263–265. Simeone in Democracy and Slavery sees the results of the vote as a rejection of elitism—with Coles himself as the exemplar—and argues that the difficult economic times Illinoisans faced after the Panic of 1819 provoked a revolt by voters. This revolt, apparently (if not entirely logically), found expression by supporting the positions of a governor whom Simeone says Illinoisans disdained. Theodore C. Pease, Frontier State, 90, says the Thomas and Edwards factions' internal inability to agree on a stand left the field open, with Coles and Birkbeck's pamphleteering and newspaper letters proving decisive; Washburne, Sketch of Edward Coles, 142, e.g., credits Coles' leadership and writings as decisive in winning the anti-convention cause. Ford, History of Illinois, 53, may have it the most right, having lived through the times and being a particularly perceptive political analyst himself. He simply states: "The question was thoroughly discussed. The people took an undivided and absorbing interest in it; they were made to understand it completely ... after one of the most bitter, prolonged, and memorable contests which ever convulsed the politics of this State, the question of making Illinois a slave state was put to rest, as it is hoped, forever."

percent to 50 percent margins for his cause in other counties where he had seen only a few dozen supporters in 1822, one thing seems clear, though: Coles, for all his supposedly aristocratic elitism, somehow managed to connect with voters in the two years in which they had had a chance to get to know him.[37]

It was a triumph for Coles. "Happy for your commonwealth! Creditable for our country! Slavery will not be permitted to overrun Illinois!" his friend, Roberts Vaux, would write. "The result of conflict is truly joyous; you have said to the moral plague, 'Thus far, but no farther, shalt thou come.'"[38]

CHAPTER 9

A kind of rejection

With relief, Illinois slipped back to the easy routines of late summer. Like an August thunderstorm, the angers and anxieties of the convention battle swept over the state, and moved on. "The defeated party submitted quietly, the triumphant party rejoiced without any noise or show.... The only demonstration I remember was a day of Thanksgiving held by a few of those who had been actively engaged," the Rev. Thomas Lippincott remembered. "Departed this life on Monday," Hooper Warren editorialized, "That celebrated character, known by the name Gothewhole Convention.... On the occasion of his interment there was none of that music, pomp, and display of fireworks, which were witnessed upon his entry into life at Vandalia.... His only child was daughter, Discordia, and it affords me great pleasure to announce that she died last Saturday evening, just after the mail came in, of despair."[1]

Still, the convention storm and the apprehensions it stirred would not be entirely forgotten—or forgiven. "His tongue was very muscular and subtile," Warren's "obituary" on the convention mused, "the facility with which he twist it ... was most apparent when he was tippling in groceries and grog shops—a vice to which he was much addicted.... As evidence of his mental poverty, he was not able to comprehend some of the most obvious truths—such as that all men are born free and equal."[2]

Ill will remained on the other side, too—at least for some. It would mean Coles would have little time for congratulation in the weeks after the battle. In September came the trial in the suit against him for failing to post bond for the freedmen who had come with him to Illinois. Coles was sure this almost-forgotten irritation would disappear; his case, he thought, was simple and the resolution of it obvious: He had freed his slaves before arriving in Illinois, while the law talked of men and women freed in the state. Though he had recorded the emancipation papers in Illinois, a necessity to protect the newly-liberated slaves given the way slave-takers ranged through the state, the manumission occurred hundreds of miles to the east. On top of that, the law requiring bonds be posted had not yet taken effect, because it was not published until several months after the freedmen had settled in Pin Oak Township. Two of the ex-slaves for whom bonds were demanded, Ralph Crawford and Tom Cobb, were dead. None of his former slaves were a burden on the county, fear of which was the purported reason for demanding bonds; they were instead taxpayers. Robert and Kate Crawford, married now, had started renting Prairieland—black farmers working a 400-acre spread must have galled some of Coles' more strident opponents—for a modest rent of 30 bushels of corn a year.[3]

But the judge, the pro-convention zealot Samuel McRoberts, "a violent advocate of a convention; an enthusiast for slavery," disagreed with Coles' arguments on points of law and ruled that all of Coles' testimony was illegal. He would not let Daniel Cook or Emanuel West testify for Coles, unimpressed by Cook's position as the state's sole Congressman or West's prominent role as a leader of the pro-slavery party. The jury, whose foreman was one of the plaintiffs in the lawsuit, decided that the recorded certifications of emancipation showed that Coles had freed his slaves in Illinois, and therefore owed the cash-short county the $2,000 fine called for by law for failing to post the bond. The sum was huge, and, Coles feared, beyond what he could raise. "I had hoped," Coles wrote to his friend Morris Birkbeck, "after the great and decided majority which was given at the late election against a Convention, my political enemies would have ceased to persecute me, But in this I was mistaken. It would seem I must be sacrificed. Nothing short of my entire ruin will satisfy my enemies, and they seem determined to effect it without regard to the means."[4]

Coles appealed, arguing that the court had refused to let him make his case. His witnesses, Cook and West, could have explained the reason why Coles had recorded the certificates of emancipation which were the only evidence against him. Coles had acted on the advice of both men when he wrote the certificates—including his note that "I do not believe that any man can have a right of property in his fellow man, but to the contrary that all mankind are endowed by nature with equal rights"—in the hope of protecting his former slaves in their new home.[5]

Offended by the vindictiveness and the unfair process in Madison County, and hoping to make a gesture of reconciliation, legislators that winter enacted a law releasing all penalties incurred under the bonding law. But Coles' opponents in Madison did not take the hint. His new trial had been carried over to the March term of the county court, and the irascible Samuel McRoberts would hear the request. McRoberts abruptly rejected Coles' request for a new hearing, observing for good measure that the legislature did not have the power to make a law forgiving the penalties, a view the state Supreme Court would, 14 long months later, find laughable as it overturned the Madison judge's decision.[6]

Coles' troubles continued. His candidate in the presidential election that autumn, Treasury Secretary William Crawford, fared poorly, despite Coles' efforts in alliance with his opponents from the just-concluded convention battle, Jesse Thomas and Thomas Sloo. The legislature, as he convened them for the extraordinary session that November to elect a new U.S. senator, ignored his repeated call to repeal the 1818 Black Code. He named Morris Birkbeck to take over as Secretary of State, after Blackwell won a seat in the legislature and had to resign the office. Birkbeck, surprised by the offer, accepted, "expressing gratification at such a flattering proof of my friendship and high opinion of him," but the state Senate "much to my regret, and to his mortification" rejected him, a last dig by the pro-slavery convention men at the men who had bested them. Coles also would be left out in the cold as Illinois politicians began to forge the new alliances that would shortly evolve into the state arms of the national party organizations that emerged in the wake of the controversial presidential election of 1824—though the anger over John Quincy Adams' victory over Andrew Jackson, won by a vote of the U.S. House of Representatives, would not have in any event stirred a man who had hated parties since his days as Madison's secretary, and who would never warm to Jackson.[7]

The new year brought no relief. In June, Birkbeck died: while returning to his farm from a visit to New Harmony, Indiana, he drowned trying to cross the rain-engorged Fox River. Back in Edwardsville, Judge McRoberts wrote a lengthy screed attacking Coles, seven columns' worth in the *Spectator*, "teeming with the most violent, vindictive and blackguard abuse of me," as Coles would describe it. Furious, Coles replied with an angry attack on McRobert's conduct as a judge and partisan in the convention battle. McRoberts replied by sending two lawyers to the Grand Jury saying Coles had libeled him. The jurors returned an indictment and McRoberts sued Coles for $5,000. By this point, Coles, disgusted and upset, had long since left for a trip back east.[8]

When he returned, after 10 weeks away, that October, he found his aggravating, clownish lieutenant governor, Adolphus Hubbard, happily playing governor and completely unwilling to yield back the powers he had temporarily assumed. Hubbard, arguing that Coles had in fact forfeited his office during his long absence from the state, tried to test his authority, and thereby confirm his position, by issuing a commission naming William L.D. Ewing as the state Paymaster General. When Secretary of State George Forquer refused to go along with this attempted coup, Ewing proceeded to the state Supreme Court seeking an order installing him in office, an order that would necessarily have to find that Hubbard was the legitimate governor of the state. The court unanimously rejected the argument, with a stern opinion written by a man who had been a pro-convention party leader, Theophilus W. Smith. Hubbard had no better luck in the legislature, where, Coles told his friend Roberts Vaux, "the current of public opinion ... was too strong in my factor to be resisted by any but the most desperate antagonist." Hubbard would have no better luck, nine months later, when he went before the people as a candidate for governor in the 1826 election. "Fellow citizens," he said at that time, "I offer myself as a candidate before you, for the office of Governor. I do not pretend to be equal to Julius Caesar, or Napoleon Bonaparte.... nevertheless I think I can govern you pretty well. I do not think it will require a very extraordinary smart man to govern you; for to tell you the truth, fellow citizens, I do not believe you will be very hard to govern no how."[9]

It was an appeal Illinoisans found less than irresistible. The ever-larger-than-life Ninian Edwards won that race, defeating both Hubbard and pro-convention leader Thomas Sloo, eking out a 447-vote margin over Sloo. (Coles could not succeed himself, under the 1818 state Constitution.) The old senator, who had failed in 1824 to win the legislature's support to return to the U.S. Senate, ran as a reformer, promising most especially to do something about the cash squeeze that had plagued Illinois, and all the western states, echoing Coles' attack on the state bank as a corrupt failure as well as his call for construction of a canal to Lake Michigan. Edwards' real platform, of course, was himself. The contest, as with almost all the others to that point in Illinois, except Coles' election and the convention battle, would look like the usual clash of Edwards versus Thomas—but the election of 1826 would be last trot around the track for the former senator and territorial governor. Edwards' 6,280 votes were no ringing endorsement; Sloo's weak run, meanwhile, may mean he was hurt by his prominence in the convention at least as much as by Edwards' unrelenting attack on the legislature over the state bank question.[10] New political feelings were stirring, new alliances were forming.

But they came slowly to Illinois. The man who would galvanize the west, General Andrew Jackson, could not best the patrician John Quincy Adams in the 1824 presidential election, failing in Illinois as he did in the Electoral College, even as the former leaders of the pro-convention movement each jockeyed to declare himself more Jacksonian than thou. Jackson swept the rest of the west and much of the South, winning 41 percent of the popular vote nationwide. That wasn't enough for an Electoral College majority, and the general lost when the House of Representatives elected Adams, with one of his votes being Illinois congressman Daniel

Cook's. It was a vote seen as violating a campaign pledge, since Cook had said he would cast his vote for the candidate that carried the majority of Illinois' new-formed election districts: although Adams won by a 140-vote margin statewide, Jackson had carried two of the three districts. "The people believed that Gen. Jackson had been cheated out of the election by bargain, intrigue and corruption ... they resented his defeat with generous indignation which consumed all opposition and which has continued to burn," Gov. Thomas Ford would write more than two decades later.[11]

Conventional wisdom now describes Cook's vote, and the reaction to it, as the end of the era of faction, of Thomas versus Edwards, in Illinois, and the start of something new: the kind of political party organization Coles so detested when he watched federalist and republican squabble in Congress while his president, Madison, was trying to win a war. But though Edwards' protege, and son-in-law, Cook was swept out of office in 1826, it is worth remembering that Edwards won his bid to be the state's third governor and that, while he himself was careful not to connect his platform with Coles,' many Illinoisans might well have remembered anyway—just as they remembered how Sloo and Hubbard pushed for the convention and for slavery in opposition to the outgoing governor. For all that Edwards "was drawn in a fine carriage driven by a negro," for all his "great pomp and ... diffuse and florid elegance,"[12] for all that Illinoisans knew his great wealth included human chattels, he had never quite been pinned down on the convention question. That ambiguity, as much as anything, may well have been enough to win Edwards his race, given his opponents' stances. The after-echoes of the 1824 convention battle were faint, but the hard-line pro-convention leader William Kinney's failure in his 1830 run for governor to the conventionist, but much more discreet, John Reynolds, as well as Judge McRoberts' unsuccessful bid to become the state's attorney general, suggest there were some, and that they did not favor the most strident conventionists. That few anti-conventionists had much of a political life in Illinois after 1824 may speak more to the limited nature of their ambitions than their popularity.[13] As a lame duck in 1826, in any event, Coles' views carried little weight; no one cared who Coles supported or what he had to say.

Still, they listened, more or less politely, to his farewell address to the legislature that December. After months of hearing Edwards excoriate the management of the state bank, Coles took a moment or two in this final speech to note simply that his efforts to inspect the bank's books and redeem its notes seemed to be having an effect and that with further cuts in expenses, the bank might yet become a solid institution. He urged legislators to tighten state laws on the enforcement of contracts, the replevin laws that made it so hard for creditors in Illinois to collect the monies they were owed—for, old Jeffersonian though he was, Coles' economics were becoming more and more those of the emerging Whig political party and the commercial and financial interests for which it spoke, and even farther removed from the easy-on-debtors political attitudes of his Virginia forbears. A revised digest of Illinois law, though requiring "considerable labor and the most studious and careful attention," ought to be a top priority of the new session, he added.[14]

And, as legislators cleaned up the state's laws, "I cannot but call your attention in an especial manner" to that part of them governing "that unfortunate class of our fellow beings the descendents of Africa," Coles continued, adding that he wanted to "earnestly recommend that they be amended and made less repugnant to our political institutions and local situation."[15]

He was not giving up, even though the rest of the state had decided it was time to move on. "On two former occasions," Coles doggedly continued, "under a strong sense of duty, I urged the gradual abolition of the remnant to slavery which still exists in violation of the fundamental laws of the State, and am amelioration of our code in relation to free Negroes." Painful though it might be to revisit the issue, in the wake of the convention furor, "I now emphatically renew, and earnestly press this recommendation," he said. Now Coles made reference, though only in the most oblique of ways, to his victory in the 1824 referendum: "If the legislature shall still think proper to decline abolishing slavery" despite the desires of "a people who love liberty, and have resolved that their land shall be the land of the free," it should nevertheless move to "adopt such measures as will ultimately put an end to slavery," Coles said. "Let us at least fix the time when servitude when servitude in Illinois shall cease."[16]

Illinois didn't want to hear this yet. Tired of the fight, reassured that Illinois would never be a slave state, though there were still people held in bondage, the anti-convention organization quietly dissolved. Pro-convention men, with the occasional angry exception of men like Samuel McRoberts, accepted that they had lost and, watching as the northern prairie lands filled with northern men and their families, understood that there would be little point to reopening the debate. There was no more in the papers about slavery—except, that is, for the occasional advertisements for help tracing runaways from across the Ohio and Mississippi Rivers. Although in late 1824 the legislature, in a conciliatory gesture, passed special legislation to relieve Coles of his legal miseries in Madison County, marking a first—albeit very small—step towards clarifying the mechanics of how to free a slave in Illinois, the state's laws governing slaves and freed blacks remained harsh. In 1826, despite Coles' call for moderating the Black Code, the legislature tightened it to say slaves who had escaped and were recaptured would have extra time added to their indentures. A year later, the same legislators would enact a law barring blacks from being witnesses in court cases against any white. Two years after that, the legislature would bar slaves from suing in court for their freedom, while in December 1828, the state Supreme Court would rule, in the case of *Nance v. Howard*, that indentured servants "are goods and chattel and can be sold." That same year, in the case of *Phoebe v. Jay*, the anti-convention leader Samuel Lockwood, who had been a close ally of Coles and who was now sitting as a justice of the state Supreme Court, held that the slave Phoebe, indentured in 1814 for a term of 40 years to one Joseph Jay, could be owned by his son, William, since all of Joseph Jay's property had been willed to him upon his father's death. Lockwood was presented with an issue that Illinois judges had long hoped to dodge: whether the old territorial law allowing such indentures was void because the Northwest Ordinance barred involuntary servitude, as Coles had been arguing for years. Lockwood said that was exactly so. But, the judge continued, the 1818 Constitution's language on indentures superceded the Ordinance as the basic law of Illinois. The citizens of Illinois and the U.S. Congress had accepted that situation when Illinois became a state, which meant an indenture, if not a slave, was property, and that the indenture could be willed and was a matter for the executor of a will to dispose of. "I conceive that it would be an insult to common sense to contend that the negro, under the circumstances in which he is placed, had any free agency," Lockwood ruled. "The only choice given him was a choice of evils. On either hand, servitude was to be his lot." As it would have been the lot of a young woman named Venus in 1831, except that a Shawneetown merchant named Emanuel Ensinger and his neighbors were outraged that the inheritor of her indenture (an indenture signed 21 years before, when she was just 13 years old) had hauled her off the New Orleans where she was sold as a slave. Born a slave in South Carolina, Venus had been taken to Illinois, sold twice while living in the supposedly free soil territory and state, before being taken down the river for the last sale. Ensinger and his fellow citizens eventually won a Louisiana court order declaring her to be free. It'd be years yet, despite Coles' plea, before an Illinois court would make a similarly clear ruling.[17]

The commerce in slaves would continue into the 1840s. Despite the laws forbidding the kidnapping of freedmen that Coles had urged, Missouri bounty hunters continued to range through Illinois, seeking fugitives and snatching freedmen when they couldn't find the slaves they sought. Mugging a young man in a river town and hustling him aboard a steamboat bound for Memphis or New Orleans could easily net such slave-takers a few hundred dollars. The state and its officials cared little. But as the years passed, ordinary Illinoisans grew more and more outraged by the sleazy business. When a Mr. Burlingame, a farmer in St. Clair County, learned the Missouri slave-hunter Mose Twist was ferreting around in the hamlet of Sparta, he stormed into town, found Twist and angrily informed him that the slave he sought "is at my house. You come there at your peril." Twist did not go. Perhaps he had heard of what happened to the two bounty hunters who had tried to tackle John Walker, who also had found refuge in Sparta, slipping into Illinois without his Tennessee freedom papers in his pocket and eventually finding work as a hired hand to the farmer Archibald Hood. When the slave-takers came, Hood and his sons held the one and let Walker fight the other for his freedom; Walker beat the man to a pulp and proceeded with the Hoods to a nearby tavern to celebrate.[18]

It would not be until 1836 that the courts would start to carve away at the Black Code and indenture laws, with one case holding that blacks could not be held in bondage if they had not been registered as indentured servants within 30 days of arriving in Illinois, and with another that held that the children of indentured servants were free, with the parents' masters having no claim at all upon their services. Finally, in 1843, Judge J.D. Caton, of the Circuit Court in Bureau County, threw out a charge against Owen Lovejoy for harboring the black woman named Nancy, declaring flatly that "the right to property in a slave is not one of those natural rights which necessarily and spontaneously result from the organization of society, like the right to property in animals, in fruit of agriculture, minerals and the like ... by the constitution of this state, slavery cannot exist here." Coles would have been proud. As he would have been vindicated when the court continued that "If, therefore, a master voluntarily bring his slave within this state, he becomes from that moment free, and if he escape from his master while in this State, it is not an escape from slavery but it is going where a free man has a right to come." Finally, in 1845, the state Supreme Court would make that ruling the law of Illinois when it ruled that Joseph Jarrot, who had been owned as a slave because his mother, Pelagie, was a slave since her purchase in 1798, when she was four years old, was in fact a free man, simply by virtue of living in Illinois.[19]

So, in the end, it would take Illinoisans two decades to accept Coles' challenge to them. For the state, as for the nation at large, opposition to slavery would be slow to develop. A distaste for those who, like Coles, insisted it was evil would persist for decades to come—in 1837, for instance, the Illinois legislature approved resolutions condemning abolitionists, and even the six dissenting state representatives (including a young Abraham Lincoln) who objected on the grounds that it was slavery that was the true injustice, would feel it necessary to note that the "promulgation of abolition doctrines tends rather to increase than abate the evils." Through the summer of that year, mobs in Alton threatened to tar and feather the abolitionist editor Elijah Lovejoy, whose editorials in the *Alton Observer* flatly declared slavery an evil and a sin. In August, a mob destroyed Lovejoy's printing press. In September, when Lovejoy's new press arrived, another mob grabbed it from a warehouse and dumped it into the Mississippi. Lovejoy ordered yet another press from the east, and asked some of his supporters to stand armed guard over it. On November 8, a mob gathered outside the warehouse once again. As they began battering the warehouse house, Lovejoy's supporters started shooting; a young carpenter, newly arrived in Alton, was shot and fatally injured. The mob backed off briefly, but soon returned, shouting that they planned to kill every abolitionist in Alton. As some screamed "Fire the house!," "Burn 'em out," others found a ladder and propped it against the stone wall of the warehouse, apparently planning to set fire to the roof. Lovejoy and four others ran out from the relative safety of the warehouse to fire a volley they hoped would scare the fire-setters off; they went back inside to reload, but Lovejoy came out once more to see if the mob was preparing to try again to fire the roof. In the bright moonlight, he was an easy target. He was shot, five times, and died on the spot.[20]

For most Illinoisans, though, slavery and abolition were issues that aroused limited passions. In the aftermath of the convention battle, Warren's *Spectator* folded. Peck and Parker were soon immersed in the affairs of their churches, Birkbeck was dead. As for Coles, though a July 4 toast to him, at Vandalia's celebrations, drew nine cheers, and though his friend Nicholas Hansen would assure him "No man refuses Edward Coles the character of an honest man and consistent politician ... to be short, the want of you is felt," he would return to Edwardsville with few political prospects. A new county, carved from Clark and Edgar, in the eastern part of the state, would be named for him in 1830; while a letter to the *Illinois Intelligencer* praised him for having "with a steady hand pursued the noblest tenor of his way, regardless of bar-room clamors and the malignant denunciations of aspirants." His friend William B. Archer would try to inspire a comeback, writing to a political ally that "Coles is rising rapidly and deservedly. He is a man of business and could be elected again, no man in the state could beat him." Coles was, Archer added, "by far the most honest man in the state."[21] But his quiet feeler in the 1828 legislature for election as U.S. Senator came to nought. He tried again, in 1832, writing to Madison that he had "been very unexpectedly prevailed on to become a candidate" for Congress, adding that while "my frequent & long absences from the state will operate against me but my friends are nevertheless sanguine of my success."[22] So was he. Calling himself "the People's Governor," he said that was "now once more called upon by many of the same high-minded people, without distinction of party, and who have no other motive than a desire to promote the public good, to leave the pursuits of private life" and run. He reminded voters that he had not only been their governor, but had been President Madison's private secretary, as well as serving as registrar of the Land Office. He had a record, he reminded them. "I trust," Coles added, "I have too long resided among you, been too much before the public, and am too well known to the people, to render it necessary for me, on this occasion to give an expose of my political principles and the course of conduct I should pursue if elected."[23]

But he hadn't really. It didn't help that he spent the winter of 1831–32 traveling in the east—or, for that matter, that he been spending months at a time on extended, leisurely trips to the east every year since the convention fight. When he was in Edwardsville, he had been far too quiet for a man with ambitions in politics. And while he promised his fellow citizens to "on all questions vote and act agreeable to their known wishes, and what I shall believe to be their true interests," he went on to promise "I will not be the creature of any party nor the humble follower of any man, but guided by republican principles, will endeavor to promote the best interests of the country." Eight years after Andrew Jackson's loss of the presidency to John Quincy Adams and four years after his eventual triumph, Coles sounded impossibly old-fashioned. Illinois, like the rest of the nation, wanted political parties, and had them. Coles ran third in a field of five, with just 3,304 votes. Incumbent Joseph Duncan won re-election with 12,769.[24]

That was the year that Robert and Kate Crawford struck off on their own: buying 40 acres of land near Edwardsville, followed four years later with the purchase of another 40—already improved land, with "twenty or thirty acres" fenced and in cultivation, as well as "good dwelling houses, stables, barns, fruit trees" that they bought at bargain prices. They paid $50 for each tract, cash on the barrel head, less than half the going rate for a private sale at the time, suggesting they were able to buy (Coles bought two nearby 40-acre tracts himself at the same time).[25] They continued to rent from Coles, as well; in the difficult years of the 1830s, the Crawfords would do better than many of the emigrants who had come to Illinois, farming 400 acres, "as large and well stocked ... and as neatly fixed as most" with "several horses, oxen, many cows, cattle, sheep, hogs." Over the years, Crawford would be known, affectionately, by his neighbors as "Uncle Bob," "the aristocrat," William Prickett recalled, "a preacher and a man of dignified carriage and manners," while Kate "upheld the dignified character of her husband."[26]

But, defeated, Coles had already headed east even as the Crawfords set down their roots in Pin Oak Township. Again, he headed to Philadelphia; already a place he found it difficult to leave, when it came time to head back to Illinois. His close friends Nicholas Biddle and Roberts Vaux were there. Through them he came to know many of the most prominent Philadelphians, a genteel, wealthy group, who made him welcome in the cosmopolitan city that was, at that point, still the nation's center of business and culture and that to Coles was feeling more and more like his real home. After his mother's death in 1826, he spent less time in Virginia, for relations with his brothers, except for Isaac, were strained by his staunch opposition to slavery. Though a diffident politician, Coles remained outspoken on slavery: "It is unnecessary for me to remind you," he lectured Thomas Jefferson Randolph, grandson of the late president, "that the relation of master to slave is unnatural, & and in the spirit of the age & in the nature of things cannot continue."[27] Fewer and fewer Virginians had patience for this view.

The Quakers of Philadelphia were much more congenial. On his visit in 1832, Coles met a young cousin of his friend Roberts Vaux named Sally Logan Roberts. The daughter of a wealthy ironmaster, supposedly descended from a Welsh Quaker with royal connections who had emigrated to Pennsylvania with William Penn in 1682, she was a beautiful young woman, much younger than the 46-year-old Coles, who quickly proposed and was as quickly accepted. He never returned to Illinois. On a long, slow trip to Virginia to show her off to his family, idly thinking of taking her west, Coles was disconcerted by reports of cholera outbreaks, and then delighted to learn he was soon to be father. He rented a house on upper Chestnut Street "in a pleasant part" of Philadelphia, so Sally's mother could help with the baby, paying, he grumbled, "more than I ought."[28] In a chatty letter to his old mentor, James Madison, he worried about his money and wondered "whether I should be happy with so little to do."[29]

The couple would have two sons and a daughter, and Coles found himself immersed in the social and intellectual circle of wealthy Quakers, largely formed around Dr. Caspar Wistar's discussion group and the American Philosophical Society.[30] With these social connections came financial connections, too. In 1835, Illinois Gov. Joseph Duncan, who had been one of the rising young men of the Illinois Jacksonian party that Elias Kent Kane had come to lead, but who had won election as a pro-business (that is, pro-canal) Whig, appointed Coles president of the Board of Commissioners for the Illinois and Michigan Canal that the state hoped to build. Coles worked hard to convince bankers in the east, and even in Europe, to finance the project. When he found they insisted on a full guarantee of repayment by the state, in case toll revenue fell short, he helped convince the legislature to enact that measure in its 1836 session.[31]

Coles happily settled into the life of a wealthy, if absentee, landowner and investor (just as Biddle had urged him to three decades earlier), with rents from his property in the booming city of St. Louis and income from selling off his tracts in western Illinois. His lots in St. Louis brought him $3,000 in his second year of marriage; the next year, after Sally's father died, her inheritance would bring nearly that much a year to the household. Committing himself to Philadelphia, he bought a house in Girard Street, and fretted about "the want of punctuality & bad treatment of the different mechanicks we have employed."[32]

His ties to Illinois grew more tenuous. His former slaves Robert and Kate Crawford rented land from him: a letter in 1837 gently asks if a $43 payment is all that is coming to him for the yield of the past two years— "I wish you would attend to it & do the best you can for me," he wrote, while noting that the land he gave them with their emancipation seem to be growing more valuable, adding that some land in the area was going for $1,500 per quarter section. It would remain an amicable partnership for many years to come, though his efforts to convince the Crawfords that they should consider emigrating to the new colony of Liberia, now, he was convinced, the best way to provide for the emancipation of America's slaves, would come to nought. He said he would "go with them, & ... assist them with any pecuniary requirements," but noted they were "so happy & content where they are, that they seem reluctant to change their situation."[33]

Coles, like many, had come to feel that the angry efforts of a new generation of abolitionists, men such as William Lloyd Garrison and Illinois' own Lovejoy, posed as serious a menace to the Union as did such bitter slave-holding sectionalists as John C. Calhoun, with their talk of nullification and their increasingly ferocious talk of violence and separation. There had to be a middle way, and, preoccupied as he had always been with what Jefferson and the Founders thought—or what he thought they thought—he felt he might have an answer. Brooding about his exchanges with Jefferson, so long ago; remembering the Sage of Monticello's glum views, even from his *Notes on Virginia* written so long before Coles' birth, the man who'd freed his slaves with a single phrase, on a flatboat on the Ohio River, began to think less drama and more caution might be the answer. Convinced, he said, in part by the "disadvantages and indignities" his freed slaves faced in Illinois and the long, slow process of finally

Sally Logan Roberts Coles (courtesy Winterthur Museum).

eliminating the bondage of indentures and the shame of the Black Code, and more importantly by what Jefferson had written, Coles had come to believe black and white could "never ... associate as equals, & live in harmony & social intercourse" as long as the one race had ever "been held in bondage & looked upon as a degraded race by the other," words closely echoing Jefferson's own views in *Notes on Virginia* and other writings.[34] It did not mean emancipation could not happen, but that freedom would have to come gradually, he argued. Sending freed slaves to the African colony of Liberia would ease the strain. In a public letter to former president James Monroe that he submitted to the *Richmond Enquirer*, Coles pseudonymously wrote that he "had not believed the most enthusiastic friend of emancipation ever entertained the idea of immediate liberation," belying his own action as a younger man. Jefferson himself, Coles wrote, had suggested linking gradual emancipation with colonization four decades earlier—a program which "would not cost the Commonwealth [of Virginia], or its *white* citizens, one dollar." He proposed that the children of the state's slaves be freed when they turned 21, which, he said, would allow enough time for slave-owners to recoup the costs they'd incurred when the slaves were children. After that, he said the newly freed slaves should work for their former masters, for pay, for a couple of years to earn the money to pay for emigrating to Liberia. Coles would stick to this hobbyhorse for years, urging it on Jefferson's grandson, Thomas Jefferson Randolph, when he took a seat in the Virginia House of Delegates. He lobbied the aging Madison, telling him he should rewrite his will. "It would be a blot & stigma on your otherwise spotless escutcheon, not to restore to your slaves that liberty and those rights for which you have been through your life so zealous & able a champion," Coles wrote. But since Madison also felt, as Coles had come to, that it would not be possible for his freed slaves to stay in Virginia, his will should provide for them to emigrate to Liberia; the way to do that, Coles suggested, was to continue to employ them until they earned the cost of traveling across the Atlantic. Doing so would, no doubt, inspire others to follow suit, allowing, at long last, Virginia to shake off the scourge of slavery, he argued. Madison never took up the challenge. When he died, in 1836, Dolley was unable to maintain their estate at Montpelier; Coles described a slave trader arriving at the farm, "a hawk among the chickens," as the ex-president's slaves ran, crying, to ask Dolley to save them, saying they had been promised they would never be sold.[35]

And yet he had no second thoughts about what he himself had done in freeing his own slaves. For all the zeal that he devoted to the idea of colonizing former slaves in Liberia, even offering to pay Robert Crawford to travel there and "write a full & faithful account ... for the information of his black brethren generally," neither Robert's refusal nor Coles' repeated requests could affect the warmth of feeling between the two, on either side. When the Crawfords, dictating through a letter-writer, thanked him for their freedom, as they had before and would again, he spoke his heart in reply. "My highly respected and much esteemed friends," he wrote, "I returned to you what was mine by the laws of man but yours by the inherent principles of right & the immutable laws of God." He had, he wrote, no regrets at all: "You both have well justified your hearts and mine in every respect."[36]

He would be much sharper with his manager, an Isaac Prickett, complaining that "your conduct while here in July not only surprised me, but gave me just cause to find fault with you ... though my child was ill and suffering very much, I called to see you at the Hotel almost every day while your remained, without having the good fortune to see you ... Is it possible, I exclaimed, he has left the City without letting me see him?" He spent years trying to collect a $1,000 note from neighbors A.J. and J. T. Lusk, a note co-signed by Prickett, and in 1842 complained that "I am at great loss to know what answer to make ... or how to express my surprise that you & my old friend Lusk should request me to take land in payment of your debt to me."[37]

Coles was land-rich but now beginning to feel cash-poor. In 1841, he tried hinting to an old acquaintance, President John Tyler, about the possibility of a government post. By 1842, he was worried enough to write, awkwardly, to a friend from his youth, Winfield Scott, seeking his help to secure a government job. Scott was chief of staff of the Army, and a Major

Roach was rumored to be on the verge of leaving his post as commissary general of purchases. Coles, deeply embarrassed at having to ask for help, suggested he might be a suitable successor. "This I would not make known in this way even confidentially to you my old friend were it not for the great reduction to my income & losses I have sustained by Bank and Rail Road stocks." His handwriting is cramped and ill-formed in this letter, his discomfort obvious: "I have such a repugnance to be considered an applicant for office that I will not write to any other person ... in this to me delicate business."[38]

Poor Coles. As awkward as ever, he had put his friend in an untenable position. Scott was barely on speaking terms with President Tyler, who suspected Scott and his enemies in the Senate were playing games with the purchasing commissary as they plotted to unseat Tyler from the White House in the next election. All of Washington was abuzz over the affair: "What upon earth could have led you to address me? ... had I possessed but one-tenth of the feeling I entertain for you, my oldest friend & and my dear old adjutant [Roach]—you would both be politically damned at the White House for the next three years."[39]

Hoping to help his friend, and, even more, to divert some of the President's suspicion, Scott forwarded Coles' letter with a note that "no doubt the letter ought to have a different address ... Gov. Coles can stand in no need of a recommendation to the President, as his virtues, claims & business abilities must be well known in that quarter."[40]

In an agony of humiliation, Coles hastily tried to take it all back. "EC presents his compliments to Gen. Scott & begs leave to make known to him that he has just written to the president to ask the favor of him to return to him his letter to Genl Scott, which the Genl had enclosed to the President. EC regrets having written this letter & wishes to destroy it, & and that its existence as well as its contents should be obliterated from Gen'l Scott's recollection."[41]

A few months later, Coles would be writing to try to repair what he feared was an estrangement with Martin Van Buren; a mutual friend had suggested to the former president that Coles' sister Rebecca had the sense that Van Buren had been cool to her during a visit to Philadelphia in 1841 and that that was due to Van Buren's anger with Coles. That, in turn, was supposedly caused by rumors Van Buren had heard that Coles had written something insulting in a note to Madison. Coles assured Van Buren he had done no such thing: "I never ... intended or calculated to wound your feelings or injure you in any way." Van Buren, in turn, dashed off a reply that he felt no coolness to Coles and asked him to express his regards to Coles' sister.[42]

They were depressing little codas to what many had expected would be a brilliant public career. Coles resumed the quiet life of a Philadelphia dilettante, raising his three children, occasionally visiting his family in Virginia, and mending fences with his brothers. By 1850, he reported his real estate holdings as being worth $20,000, little better, after all the years that had passed, than the value of the land and slaves he had inherited from his father. He also administered the estate his wife had inherited.[43]

The question of slavery, though, would not go away. He felt he still had something important to say: that his role in Illinois, not yet forgotten, had earned him the right to speak to an ever-more divided nation; feeling that he could bridge the divide as a man of the South, who had freed his slaves, and come North to settle in a city whose conservative, commercial leaders feared the turmoil they thought the burgeoning abolitionist movement could wreak. When Free Soil Party leader B.W. Richards offered Coles a flattering invitation to outline what the political giants of the nation's past had really felt about slavery, Coles jumped at the chance. The Founders, "all of them," opposed slavery, he told Richards, holding "that it was a great moral, social and political evil, and one they hoped would soon cease to exist." The new generation of Southern leaders, aggressively contending that slavery was "the cornerstone of our free institutions, without which they could not exist," were simply wrong; Jefferson, Madison and Monroe, though each had owned slaves and never freed them, all believed that all men were born equal and that human bondage could not coexist with a free society. But there was, Coles added, a painless way for the nation to resolve the dilemma slavery posed. If the people would simply agree to stop the expansion of slavery, as of course, he had done in Illinois, "time and the natural progress of events will eventually exterminate slavery from amongst us," Coles argued. It was, he believed, as did the conservative Northerners who formed the Free Soil Party, the only way to prevent the question from tearing the country in two.[44]

Coles weighed in again, with the rekindling of the debate over slavery in the west as California, whose Gold Rush settlers had approved a proposed state constitution banning slavery, petitioned for admission as a state. Southern politicians thought both California and the rest of the territory between it and Texas, which the United States had taken as the fruit of victory in the Mexican War, should be opened to slavery; Northerners objected; and Henry Clay, the senator and would-be president from Kentucky, suggested walking a careful line that would have excluded slaves in California but allowed it elsewhere, if whatever territories were formed there decided on that course. Coles dashed off a note to encourage the Kentuckian, enclosing a copy of an 1834 plea for national unity that

Madison had written for publication after his death. Clay wrote back, saying he would use the document, "should a suitable occasion offer."[45] Convinced his special connection with the nation's Founding Fathers gave him a special insight that could uncover a decisive argument from history for the restriction of slavery, Coles spent much of the 1850s trying to confirm his conviction that Madison had intended to free his slaves but that, in the end, Dolley had ignored the ex-President's wishes. He turned from parsing Madison's will and his widow's acts to write what he felt would be a definitive history of the document he had relied so heavily upon when he decided to free his slaves and take them to Illinois: the Northwest Ordinance. The first version, published in the *National Intelligencer* in January 1853, argued that Jefferson's original draft of the Ordinance had extended to all territories acquired by the federal government, whether the North West Territory ceded by Virginia, Connecticut and Massachusetts after the Revolutionary War, the Louisiana Purchase, the Oregon country or the former Mexican territories.[46] He spent the next two and a half years writing a more extended version, his History of the Northwest Ordinance, which argued that laxness in enforcing the clear intent of the Ordinance, as had occurred in Illinois, had permitted slavery to continue for decades after Jefferson intended. The cost of doing so was human suffering and political turmoil; just as happened when the Kansas-Nebraska Act of 1854 cleared the way for slavery in Kansas and produced "nothing but contention, riots, and threats, if not the awful realities of civil war." Read before the Historical Society of Pennsylvania in June 1856, the paper would never have the impact Coles had hoped for.[47]

Still, mouldering away in Philadelphia, he knew he had once done a great thing: "The abuse I endured, the labor I performed, and the anxiety I felt, weren't without their reward," he wrote. And that was, he added, "To have it concluded by opponents as well as supporters, that I was chiefly instrumental in preventing the call of a convention, and making Illinois a slave holding state."[48] That is the way, for a time, others would remember things: President-elect Abraham Lincoln, coming through Philadelphia on his way to Washington to take his oath of office, "expressed great delight to see him" when the elderly Coles was able to push his way through a crowd of cheering supporters at the Continental Hotel. Coles, said the president-elect, "was held in universal reverence throughout the state of Illinois."[49]

Yet it would pass. Americans are impatient when told they ought to do the right thing—when we think of temperance crusaders, we see faces as sharp and mean as the hatchets that they wielded, smashing our saloons; we snicker at the tightly-buttoned "good-government" municipal reformers of the early 20th century, mocking them as "goo-goos," preferring our

Frank Hagues, James Michael Curleys, Richard J. Daleys; we've grown cynical about the settlement house ladies who were heroines in our schooldays. We dislike privilege, as well; other people's, that is. Happy in our polling places to reject someone whose studied nasal drawl bespeaks a youth in private school, to believe another's carefully-cultivated "y'all" or football talk or earnest gaze is reassurance that he speaks for us, we think far more of image in our politics than what our politicians really say or stand for. When it comes to reputation, perhaps Coles never had a chance.

A child of wealth, but the youngest son of five, Coles was well-off, but not so much more so than the men with whom he contended for the people's support in Illinois. A protege of presidents, true; but others such, unlike Coles, could win no office at all—his brother Isaac, despite his connection with an even more highly regarded president than his younger brother, could never win election even in the state that revered his mentor Jefferson. Many have an opportunity to do great things; of those who try, most will fail whether through human frailty or sheer bad luck. Every run for office is a risk.

And elections turn on many things. Was it a friendly word to a settler, a hand with forms, a view on banks that won Coles his office? Inept political machines, about to die? A stand against slavery? All of these? Some? In 1824, was it the Yankee settlers in the north whose voices led Illinois to reject its leaders' bid to bring slavery there? Was it a fear that slavery would bring too many blacks, would cut the rate a hired hand could get? Was it the resentment of a Southern migrant towards the slave-holding grandee he had thought he left on the other side of the Appalachians? Was it the Southerners whose Bibles told them slavery was wrong? Who felt the basic premises of American democracy made slavery anathema?

When we look backwards far enough, we want to see a movement, a grand trend, a theme. Last year's election, we tell ourselves, was decided by a mix of things, an issue that caught fire, a bumbled debate, the way the people way downstate have always leaned. The election of 1822, the referendum of 1824, likely came out the way they did because of many things; not just a North-South split, not just a class of hard-pressed farmers finally taking charge; not just a moral view on slavery. And surely not, considering he led the cause that won in 1824, because Coles failed to connect with the people of frontier Illinois.

Important, too, is this: Because of Coles, because he stood before a hostile state legislature that December day in 1822 to declare that slavery could end, for real, in Illinois, the people of the state would have a chance to vote on the question. It had happened nowhere else. Not in Missouri, where a political establishment a lot like Illinois' pushed through a constitution enshrining slavery and then provoked a national crisis to make sure it got its way. Not in Ohio or in Indiana, where delegates to constitutional conventions were happy to take the Northwest Ordinance's ban on slaves as a given. Not in Vermont, where the men who wrote the 1777 Constitution carving their counties from New York decided there would be no slaves in the Green Mountains. Not in Massachusetts, where Chief Justice William Cushing told a jury, deliberating on whether one Quock Walker was a free man or slave, that while the King of England had allowed such things, as had the Province of Massachusetts, "a different idea has taken place with the people of America, more favorable to the natural rights of mankind." The verdict finding Walker was free would confirm that the 1780 Constitution's language on rights implied a ban on slavery.[50] The closest that anyone else ever came to voting, yes or no, on slavery was when, after two years of being solicited to approve constitutions allowing slavery, Kansans voted in 1859 for one that banned it. There were no pollsters in 1824 to tell us what the people felt. Perhaps the vote in Illinois is far more important than we might think.

As is the man who provoked it, who organized the opposition to the convention, whose writing shaped the argument, whose salary went to distribute the pamphlets and to buy the newspaper that got the word out.

The what-ifs of our history are ever-intriguing. What if, for instance, Coles and his allies, Peck and Parker, Warren and Brown, Birkbeck, Blackwell, Lockwood and all the others, had not managed to stop the push for a convention and the endorsement of full, unlimited, Southern-style slavery it would likely have brought? What if Illinois had not been a free soil state, had not, therefore, sent one of its adopted sons, the Kentucky-born Abraham Lincoln, to the White House and tens of thousands more to the battlefields of Shiloh and Vicksburg, Gettysburg, Atlanta and Appomattox? Just across the Mississippi River, in territory no more naturally suited to plantation agriculture, Missouri chafed at the lines that tied it to the Union throughout the Civil War; the battle to hold it for the national government was a long, slow drain on the Northern effort to command the great river valley. If Illinois, too, had found some of its citizens loved owning slaves more than they loved their country, would the victory in 1865 have looked as inevitable as now it seems? If the earnest, amateur politicians of the anti-convention effort had not so firmly trounced their conventionist foes, had not sounded, as they did so consistently, the cry of no slavery for Illinois, had they not insisted as clearly as the times allowed that slavery was a moral issue above all else and that holding men and women and children in bondage denied everything Americans said they believed about the rights of human beings, how much more painful would the struggle to come have been? If Coles had not deliberately provoked a confrontation over slavery, when no one else wanted to bring the matter before the people, if he had thought it sufficed merely to free the black men and women whom he had owned, and whom he called his friends, how much harder would have been the struggle others waged for their civil rights and the rights of any fellow citizens whose skins were different colors? Perhaps emancipation was inevitable, perhaps the role of Illinois as a keystone holding a new kind of nation's sections together was inevitable as well, mere questions of the imperatives of moral progress or demands of geography. But the fact is that an odd, supposed aristocrat from Virginia, an antebellum embodiment of the idealist and oft-mocked liberals of our own day, did make a stand, arguing, ultimately, that the civil rights of citizens—to go where they will, work as they can, live as they choose—are the foundation on which our nation was built, the classic and fundamental position of American liberalism. It is a modern view, as out of step with Coles' times as was his decision to liberate his own slaves. His retreat, later in life, to Jefferson's position that black and white must live apart only shows how hard we must still wrestle with the demons we unloaded along with the first slaves to stumble off a ship and into the stockaded little village of Jamestown in 1619. It is important most of all to remember, as we consider Coles' place in our history, that he did more than just force the confrontation over slavery. The fact is that he did carry his point. The fact is that it would cost him everything he might have hoped would come his way in politics.

As perhaps, in the end, it would cost him everything that really matters, more than three

Edward Coles, shortly before his death (courtesy Winterthur Museum).

decades after his fight for freedom in Illinois. For in the end, for the nation, unlike Illinois, the question of slavery would be decided by war: "There is little or no prospect of my ever being happy again," he wrote to his brother-in-law, after the attack on Fort Sumter and Virginia's secession.[51]) The issue that split the nation had split his own family as well. In 1859, Coles' beloved younger son, Roberts, decided to return to Virginia, to settle in the state that still, deep down, claimed his father's heart. He bought a farm, the Plantation Tract, in the northern portion of the enormous Enniscorthy holdings his grandfather had amassed. Two years later, when war came, Roberts did as many young Virginians would, and enlisted in what he saw as his state's cause, the cause that had fired his father with a passion to make men free—and that his son saw as his own inheritance. "I claim my share of the paternity in Enniscorthy," he wrote. "When Virginia was invaded and its existence threatened, I volunteered." In February 1862, watching a Union fleet of 65 vessels slowly steam up Pamlico Sound to the Confederate earthworks on Roanoke Island, N.C., where his regiment was dug in, he would he declare: "Now, I strike for Virginia."[52] In doing so, one of 1,500 against the Union force of more than 11,000, he would give his life.

Four years after that, in 1868, Coles himself would die, all but forgotten.

Notes

Preface

1. See, e.g., Robert P. Howard, *Illinois: A History of the Prairie State* (Grand Rapids, Mich.: William B. Eerdmans Publishing Co., 1986), 133.
2. Kurt Leichtle, "Edward Coles: An Agrarian on the Frontier" (Ph.D. diss., University of Illinois-Chicago Circle, 1982), 4.
3. Thomas Ford, *A History of Illinois from Its Commencement as a State in 1818 to 1847* (Urbana: University of Illinois, 1995), 3.
4. James Simeone, *Democracy and Slavery in Frontier Illinois: The Bottomland Republic* (DeKalb, Ill.: Northern Illinois University Press, 2000), 2–5, 16–18, 26, 66, 121–2, 130, 140–1, 202; argues the White Folks versus Big Folks case, casting Coles as the arrogant, elitist outsider.
5. See Leichtle, especially chapters 2 and 3. Leichtle focuses on Coles as the anachronistic Jeffersonian, who dithered over what to do about his slaves and missed his opportunities to become a significant political figure.
6. Robert M. Sutton, "Edward Coles and the Constitutional Crisis in Illinois, 1822–1824," *Illinois Historical Journal* 82 (1989): 33.
7. Theodore C. Pease, *The Frontier State 1818-1848* (Urbana: University of Illinois Press, 1987), 90; Ford, 45.
8. Judge Gillespie here is quoted in Elihu Washburne, *Sketch of Edward Coles* (Chicago: Jansen, McClurg & Co., 1881), 213.
9. Robert and Kate Crawford (by dictation) to Edward Coles, Oct. 23, 1840, Edward Coles Papers, Princeton University.

Chapter 1

1. Edward Coles to Rebecca Coles, April 24, 1819.
2. Ibid.
3. Edward Coles to James Madison, July 25, 1815; Wilbur T. Norton, *Edward Coles, Second Governor of Illinois* (Philadelphia: J.B. Lippincott & Co., 1911), 15.
4. Coles' ailments are outlined, among other places, in Edward Coles to James Madison, Sept. 22, 1812; Edward Coles to John Coles, Nov. 25, 1812; Edward Coles to James Madison, May 25, 1813; Edward Coles to Dolley Madison, May 22, 1813; Edward Coles to John Coles, Sept. 8, 1813. For a description, see Edward Coles, passport certificate, 1816.
5. Edward Coles to John Coles, July 28, 1815; Sept. 11, 1815.
6. Edward Coles to Rebecca Coles, April 24, 1819.
7. Washburne, *Sketch of Edward Coles*, 17.
8. Edward Coles, "History of the Northwest Ordinance," *Historical Society of Pennsylvania Press* (1856); see also Paul Finkelman, *Slavery and the Founders: Race and Liberty in the Age of Jefferson* (Armonk, NY: M.E. Sharpe, 1996); Peter S. Onuf, *Statehood and Union: A History of the Northwest Ordinance* (Bloomington, Ind.: Indiana University Press, 1987); Frederick D. Williams, *The Northwest Ordinance: Essays on Its Formation, Provision and Legacy* (E. Lansing, Mich.: Michigan State University Press, 1987).
9. David Brion Davis, *The Problem of Slavery in the Age of Revolution 1770-1823* (New York: Oxford University Press, 1999), 25–7, 80, 89, 197, 232, 251; John H. Russell, *The Free Negro in Virginia* (Baltimore: Johns Hopkins University Press, 1913), Chapter 4.
10. See, e.g., Davis, op. cit., pp. 255–6; Winthrop D. Jordan, *White over Black: American Attitudes Toward the Negro, 1550-1812* (Chapel Hill: University of North Carolina Press, 1968), 342, 347; Robert McColley, *Slavery and Jeffersonian Virginia* (Urbana: University of Illinois Press, 1964); Glover Moore, *The Missouri Controversy 1819-1821* (Lexington: University of Kentucky Press, 1953), 170–175.

11. Moore, op. cit., pp. 35-40.

12. Coles told the story of his liberation of his slaves in his 1844 handwritten "Autobiography" as well as his 1827 "Emancipation of the Slaves of Edward Coles," both of which are to be found in the Coles Collection of the Historical Society of Pennsylvania; the vivid picture he painted in Edward Coles to Rebecca Coles, April 29, 1819, is the source of information about the weather, the sacked pilot, Mr. Green, and the illness of his slaves; Washburne's Sketch of Edward Coles, 38, reports on the horse and buggy adventure of 1815; Coles in "Emancipation" and "Autobiography" reports Ralph Crawford had gone west with him on his earlier trips. .

13. Edward Coles to Rebecca Coles, April 29, 1819.

14. Coles, "Autobiography."

15. Edward Coles to Thomas Jefferson, July 31, 1814; Thomas Jefferson to Edward Coles, Aug. 2, 1814; Edward Coles to Thomas Jefferson, Sept. 26, 1814.

16. Elizabeth Langhorne, K. Edward Lay and William D. Rieley, A Virginia Family and Its Plantation Houses (Charlottesville: University Press of Virginia, 1987), 132–3; Coles, "Autobiography"; Edward Coles to John Coles, Dec. 17, 1810.

17. Coles, "Emancipation."

18. Coles' slaves are described in Complaint, County Commissioners of Madison County v. Edward Coles, Circuit Court, March term, 1824; Edward Coles to editor (Hooper Warren), Edwardsville Spectator, July 6, 1822, discusses Manuel; Edward Coles to Rebecca Coles, April 24, 1819.

19. Coles, "Emancipation."

20. Davis, The Problem of Slavery, especially 28–32, 197; also for the extent of anti-slavery feeling in the period, see Alice Dana Adams, The Neglected Period of Anti-Slavery in America, 1808-1831 (Boston: Ginn & Co, 1908); Martin Duberman, ed., The Antislavery Vanguard: New Essays on the Abolitionists (Princeton: Princeton University Press, 1965); Dwight Lowell Dumond, Antislavery: The Crusade for Freedom in America (Ann Arbor: University of Michigan Press, 1961); Larry E. Tise, Proslavery: A History of the Defense of Slavery in America, 1701-1840 (Athens: University of Georgia Press, 1974).

21. Coles, "Autobiography."

22. Ibid; for the Ohio laws see Leon F. Litwack, North of Slavery: The Negro in the Free States, 1790-1860 (Chicago: University of Chicago, 1961), 72–74.

23. Ibid.

24. Edwardsville Spectator, July 6, 1822; Hooper Warren, "Replication," Chicago Free West, May 10, 1855 and July 5, 1855, cited in Clarence W. Alvord, ed., "Gov. Edward Coles," Collections of the Illinois State Historical Library 15 (1920): 349, 361–2, recycles the rumors Coles didn't really free his slaves, and the hint he was the father of the youngest Crawford children. Simeone, Democracy and Slavery, 222, also questions whether Coles really freed his slaves. Warren's July 5 "Replication," Alvord, 363, is where the editor questions Coles' motives in freeing his slaves. Neither Warren nor Simeone note that Coles paid the former slaves he employed.

25. Edward Coles to Roberts Vaux, Jan. 24, 1824.

26. Gillespie, quoted in Washburne, Sketch of Edward Coles, 213. For representative current analyses see Leichtle, "Edward Coles: An Agrarian," 1–7; Simeone, Democracy and Slavery, 22, 26, 66, 222, 224, 249.

27. For the value of Rockfish, see Edward Coles to John Coles, Nov. 30, 1810; for Rockfish and its slaves, see Langhorne, Lay, and Rieley, A Virginia Family and Its Plantation Houses, 133, and John Coles, "Account Book for 1790"; for Illinois and Missouri land purchases, see Edward Coles, tally of land purchases dated April 15, 1818, as well as "Ledger: Land Transactions 1819–1869" in the Coles Collection at the Historical Society of Pennsylvania; Coles, "Emancipation," says he finally got the price he wanted for Rockfish before moving to Illinois, as does Leichtle, "Edward Coles: An Agrarian," 224.

28. Coles, "Sketch of Emancipation"; for Ralph Crawford's reaction, see Edward Coles to Rebecca Coles, April 24, 1819.

29. Leichtle, "Coles: An Agrarian," 122; Simeone, Democracy and Slavery, 100–102.

30. Coles, "Autobiography."

31. Coles, "Sketch of Emancipation."

32. Coles, "Sketch of Emancipation," discusses the difficult time the Crawfords and Cobb had at the brickyard and trying to start farming. For the conditions freed slaves faced in Virginia, see Russell, The Free Negro in Virginia, chapter 4; for Illinois, N. Dwight Harris, The History of Negro Servitude in Illinois and of the Slavery Agitation in That State, 1719-1864 (New York: Haskell House, 1969), 6–15; more generally see, e.g., Robert S. Starobin, Industrial Slavery in the Old South (New York: Oxford University Press, 1979), 88–9, 114–28; Willie Lee Rose, A Documentary History of Slavery in North America (Athens, Ga.: University of Georgia Press, 1999), 61–66, 176–97.

33. Coles, "Autobiography." The fate of the freedman can be traced in the County Commissioners' charges filed against him in March 1824, in the reasons for a new trial his attorneys

proffered in September, and in the bond he posted to the County Commissioners, January 31, 1825, Madison County Circuit Court records; while Coles' letter, *Edwardsville Spectator*, July 6, 1822, discusses Manuel and Sukey. For Cobb's death, Coles to John Mason Peck, April 30, 1855, printed in *Free West*, May 25, 1855, cited in Alvord, 353. For the Crawfords' renting of his farm, see Coles to Robert and Kate Crawford, Feb. 7, 1837; Coles to Isaac Prickett, June 24, 1843.

34. Coles to Robert and Kate Crawford, Feb. 7, 1837; Robert and Kate Crawford (by dictation) to Coles, Oct. 23, 1840.

35. Edward Coles to Rebecca Coles, April 24, 1819.

36. Ibid.

Chapter 2

1. Edward Coles to Richard Flower, April 23, 1823.

2. "Notes on Edward Coles," 1863, Historical Society of Pennsylvania Collection, by older son Edward Coles; Langhorne, Lay, and Rieley, *A Virginia Family*, 23, 26, 133.

3. "Notes on Edward Coles"; Langhorne, Lay, and Rieley, *A Virginia Family*, 6.

4. Langhorne, Lay, and Rieley, *A Virginia Family*, 6–7, 11–12.

5. Nicholas Biddle to Edward Coles, April 11, 1816; for Albemarle's early days, see John Gwalthney, *Twelve Virginia Counties: Where the Western Migration Began* (Richmond, Va.: Deitz Press, 1937), 331.

6. "Notes on Edward Coles," Langhorne, Lay, and Rieley, *A Virginia Family*, 18; Leichtle, "Edward Coles: An Agrarian," 9.

7. For the economic and agricultural situation of eighteenth-century Virginia, see T.H. Breen, *Tobacco Culture: The Mentality of the Great Tidewater Planters on the Eve of Revolution* (Princeton: Princeton University Press, 1985), 175–180; Virginius Dabney, *Virginia: The New Dominion* (Charlottesville: University Press of Virginia, 1983), 91–9, 122, 276; Rhys Isaac, *The Transformation of Virginia, 1740-1790* (Chapel Hill: University of North Carolina Press, 1999), 53–7, 93–4.

8. "Notes on Edward Coles"; the recollection of Coles and his manner of speech is from Joseph Gillespie, *Recollections of Early Illinois and her noted men*, Fergus Historical Series, no. 13 (Chicago: Fergus Printing Co., 1880), 13.

9. "Notes on Edward Coles." The college later moved to Prince Edward County, Va., where it remains, spelling its name now as Hampden-Sydney College.

10. Coles' complaints about the school are in Edward Coles to John Coles, Sept. 2, 1805; for an overview of the school's difficulties at the time, including Alexander's departure and Rice's hard line, see Howard Miller, *The Revolutionary College: American Presbyterian Higher Education, 1707-1837* (New York: New York University Press, 1976), 250, 267.

11. "Notes on Edward Coles" for the severity of his broken leg; Edward Coles to John Coles, Dec. 6, 1805 complains about Williamsburg; Edward Coles to John Coles, 21 Nov. 1806, is tempted to dance.

12. Eliza Coles to Edward Coles, April 1, 1807.

13. Coles, "Autobiography"; he describes his roommate William Tucker, a Bermudian, in Edward Coles to John Coles, Nov. 2, 1806.

14. Bishop Madison's sketch is based on his entry in the *Dictionary of National Biography* (New York: Charles Scribner's Sons, 1933), 182–4 (the Tyler quote is on 183), as well as Suzanne C. Guasco, "Confronting Democracy: Edward Coles and the Cultivation of Authority in the Young Nation" (Ph.D. diss., College of William and Mary, 2004), 29. See also Richard B. Davis, *The Intellectual Life of the South in Jefferson's Virginia, 1790-1830* (Knoxville: University of Tennessee Press, 1972), 53.

15. Isaac Coles to Henry St. G. Tucker, July 20, 1799.

16. James Madison, "An Address to the Members of the Protestant Episcopal Church in Virginia, 1799" (Worcester, Mass.: American Antiquarian Society, 1964), 19, 22.

17. Madison entry in *Dictionary of American Biography*; Coles' quote is from his "Autobiography."

18. Ralph Ketcham, *James Madison: A Biography* (Charlottesville: University Press of Virginia, 1990), 377, for Payne and his sale of slaves and later bankruptcy; Petition of James to the Virginia General Assembly, Nov. 30, 1786, Legislative Petitions, New Kent County, Virginia State Archives.

19. Thomas Jefferson, *Notes on Virginia* (Chapel Hill: University of North Carolina Press, 1982), 138.

20. For Gabriel's Rebellion, see Dabney, *Virginia*, 184–188; Douglas R. Egerton, *Gabriel's Rebellion: The Virginia Slave Conspiracies of 1800 and 1802* (Chapel Hill: University of North Carolina Press, 1993), and James Sidbury, *Ploughshares into Swords: Race, Rebellion, and Identity in Gabriel's Virginia, 1730-1810* (Cambridge: Cambridge University Press, 1997).

21. Benjamin DuVal et al. to the Virginia General Assembly, Dec. 20, 1804, Legislative Petitions, Virginia State Archives.

22. Coles, "Autobiography."
23. Ibid.
24. Ibid.
25. Ibid.
26. Ibid.
27. Dabney, *Virginia*, 180–2; Melvin P. Ely, *Israel on the Appomattox* (New York: Knopf, 2004), 2–4.
28. American Convention of Abolition Societies, Minutes and Proceedings, 1798, 11.
29. American Convention of Abolition Societies, Minutes and Proceedings, 1801, 30–33.
30. A. Glenn Crothers, "Quaker Merchants and Slavery in Early National Alexandria, Virginia, the Ordeal of William Hartshorne," *Journal of the Early Republic* 25 (2005): 47, 66–71.
31. John Coles to Edward Coles, June 10, 1807.
32. Coles, "Autobiography."
33. John Coles, will, Albemarle County Will Book, vol. 4, 298. The slaves' ages are calculated from "Charges of County Commissioners of Madison County against Edward Coles, March, 1824," reprinted in Alvord, "Gov. Edward Coles," 206.
34. Coles, "Sketch of Emancipation."
35. Edward Coles to Frederick Campbell, 1808.
36. Coles, "Sketch of Emancipation."
37. Petition of Samuel Templeman to the General Assembly, Dec. 21, 1809, Virginia Legislative Petitions.
38. Peter C. Mancell and Joshua L. Rosenblum, "Slave Prices and the Economy of the Lower South," http://www.eh.net/Clio/Conferences/ASSA/Jan_00/rosenbloom.shtml.
39. Rebecca Coles' undated "Memorandum" in the Coles Collection at the Historical Society of Pennsylvania for the 1809 trip; Coles, "Autobiography," mentions putting Rockfish up for sale and his discussions with his family.
40. Edward Coles to his friend Meade, Dec. 9, 1809.
41. Edward Coles to Frederick Hawkins, March 1, 1809.
42. Isaac Coles to James Madison, Dec. 29, 1809, Annals of Congress, 11th Congress, 2nd Session, 685, 705, 987–8.
43. Isaac Coles to Joseph Cabell, Jan. 29, 1811.
44. Isaac Coles to John Coles, Jan. 8, 1810.
45. Edward Coles to James Madison, Jan. 8, 1810.
46. Coles, "Autobiography."
47. Patrick Henry to John Coles, March 19, 1797.
48. Isaac Coles to John Coles, Jan. 8, 1810.

Chapter 3

1. Preston, quoted in Katharine S. Anthony, *Dolley Madison, Her Life and Times* (Garden City: Doubleday, 1949), 204.
2. Edward Coles to Rebecca Coles and his sisters, Feb. 4, 1810.
3. For Coles' role, see Ralph Louis Ketcham, *James Madison: A Biography* (Charlottesville: University Press of Virginia, 1990), 407, 477; Guasco, "Confronting Democracy," 77–8; Leichtle, "Coles: An Agrarian," 33–4; for the pre-war challenges facing Madison, see Ketcham, 491–9.
4. William Pinckney to Edward Coles, undated, seeking appointment of a political ally named Goldsborough; Richard Rush to Edward Coles, Nov. 25, 1811; Joseph Story to Edward Coles, Nov. 28, 1811.
5. Leichtle, "Coles: An Agrarian," 36.
6. Ford, *History of Illinois*, 30.
7. William Pinckney to Edward Coles, undated; Joseph Hawkins to Edward Coles, Feb. 10, 1813; Nicholas Biddle to Edward Coles, Nov. 6, 1813.
8. Edward Coles to John Coles, Nov. 30, 1810.
9. Robert Fulton to Edward Coles, Jan. 17, 1815.
10. Edward Coles to Dolley Madison, June 10, 1811; Edward Coles to James Madison, May 22, 1813.
11. Edward Coles to John Coles, Jan. 28, 1811.
12. Edward Coles to his family, Feb. 3, 1810.
13. Edward Coles to John Coles, Nov. 30, 1810.
14. Irving Brant, *James Madison, Commander in Chief, 1812–1836* 5 (Indianapolis: Bobbs-Merrill & Co., 1961), 122.
15. Edward Coles to John Coles, March 26, 1812; Edward Coles to John Coles, May 26, 1812.
16. Edward Coles to John Coles, Nov. 30, 1810.
17. Isaac Coles to Joseph Cabell, Dec. 9, 1809; Isaac Coles to Joseph Cabell, Nov. 5, 1816.
18. Edward Coles to John Coles, Jan. 14, 1811; Edward Coles to John Coles, May 6, 1812.
19. Office of the Chief of Military History, *American Military History* (Washington: U.S. Army, 1988), chapter 6; Ketcham, *Madison*, 337–368.
20. Edward Coles to James Madison, Sept. 22, 1812.
21. Edward Coles to John Coles, Nov. 25, 1812.
22. Edward Coles to John Coles, March 28, 1813.

23. Edward Coles to Dolley Madison, May 22, 1813.
24. Edward Coles to John Coles, Sept. 8, 1813.
25. Dolly Madison to Edward Coles, May 13, 1813; Edward Coles to Payne Todd, Jan. 3, 1815.
26. Edward Coles to John Coles, Dec. 16, 1811.
27. Edward Coles to Payne Todd, Jan. 1, 1815.
28. Edward Coles to Payne Todd, Jan. 31, 1815.
29. Ketcham, *Madison*, 548, 576–81; *American Military History*, chap. 6; Edward Coles to James Madison, Aug. 10, 1814.
30. Anthony, *Dolley Madison*, 205.
31. Edward Coles to Hugh Grigsby, Dec. 23, 1854.
32. Edward Coles, "Autobiography."
33. Edward Coles to Thomas Jefferson, July 31, 1814.
34. Thomas Jefferson to Edward Coles, Aug. 25, 1814.
35. Edward Coles to Henry S. Randall, May 11, 1857.
36. Warren, "Replication," *Free West*, May 10, 1855, recalls the incident; cited in Alvord, "Gov. Edward Coles," 347–8.
37. Richard N. Cote, *Strength and Honor: The Life of Dolley Madison* (Mt. Pleasant, S.C.: Corinthian Books, 2005), 279, 330; James Madison to Edward Coles, July 7, 1816; Edward Coles to James Madison, July 11, 1816.
38. James Monroe to U.S. Consul at St. Petersburg, Aug. 6, 1816; Ketcham, *Madison*, 555–6; Edward Coles to John Coles, Oct. 4, 1816.
39. Edward Coles, "Interesting Views of the Russian Empire," *Richmond Enquirer*, Dec. 13, 16, 1817.
40. Edward Coles to James Monroe, Dec. 14, 1816; Harry Ammon, *James Monroe: The Quest for National Identity* (Charlottesville: University Press of Virginia, 1990), 350.
41. Edward Coles to William Barry, June 25, 1858.
42. Donald G. Mathews, *Religion in the Old South* (Chicago: University of Chicago, 1977), 51–2; 75–6; Finney cited in William H. McLoughlin, *The American Evangelicals, 1800-1900* (New York: Peter Smith Publisher, 1985), 12.
43. Lester S. Hyman, *United States Policy Towards Liberia, 1822-2003: Unintended Consequences?* (Cherry Hill, N.J.: Africana Homestead Legacy Publishers, 2003), 2.
44. Edward Coles to William Barry, June 25, 1858; Morris Birkbeck, *Notes on a Journey in America* (London: James Ridgway, 1818; reprint, 1966), 20.

Chapter 4

1. Richard Lee Mason, *Narrative of Richard Lee Mason in the Pioneer West* (New York: Charles F. Hartman, 1915), 40; cited in Solon J. Buck, *Illinois in 1818* (Urbana: University of Illinois, 1967), 124.
2. Washburne, *Sketch of Edward Coles*, 38; Edward Coles to Nicholas Biddle, April 8, 1815.
3. Tench Ringgold to Edward Coles, April 23, 1815.
4. Edward Coles to John Coles, June 1815; Edward Coles to Mrs. Sarah Stevenson, Sept. 11, 1815; Edward Coles to Isaac Coles, Sept. 11, 1815.
5. Ferdinand Ernst, "Travels in Illinois in 1818," *Transactions of the Illinois State Historical Society* 8 (1903); Coles' partnership in the 6,000 acres is outlined in "Ledger: Land Transactions 1819-1869," "Some Accounts of Hugh Roberts Estate" and "Account Book, 1819" in the Coles papers at the Historical Society of Pennsylvania, cited in Guasco, "Confronting Democracy," 130; Edward Coles to Nicholas Biddle, Nov. 15, 1816.
6. Edward Coles to Nicholas Biddle, Nov. 15, 1816; the Illinois Public Domain Land Tract Sales database reports Coles' purchase of two 69-acre tracts in Randolph County, recorded in August 1817.
7. Frederick G. Hollman, "The Autobiography of Frederick G. Hollman," n.d., Wisconsin Historical Society.
8. Mason, *Narrative*, cited in Buck, *Illinois in 1818*, 124, 126.
9. Arthur C. Boggess, *The Settlement of Illinois, 1778-1830* (Freeport, NY: Books for Libraries, 1970), 110.
10. Charles Chapman, ed., *History of Pike County* (Chicago: Chapman, 1880), 347–8; on Southern flavor to migration, see Boggess, *Settlement of Illinois*, 132–3; James E. Davis, *Frontier Illinois* (Bloomington: Indiana University Press, 1998), 127–34.
11. John Mason Peck, *A new guide for Emigrants to the west, containing sketches of Michigan, Ohio, Indiana, Illinois, Missouri, Arkansas with the territory of Wisconsin and the adjacent parts* (Boston: Gould, Kendall & Lincoln, 1837), 83; John Bradbury, "Remarks on Illinois and the western Territories," in Reuben G. Thwaites, *Early Western Travels, 1748-1846*, vol. 5 (Cleveland: Arthur H. Clark, 1905), 275.
12. John G. Henderson, *Early History of the "Sangamon Country": being notes on the first settlements in the territory now comprised within the limits of Morgan, Scott and Cass counties* (Davenport, Iowa: Day, Egbert & Fidlar, 1873), 13.
13. Braxton Parrish, "Pioneer Life in Egypt," *Golden Era* 36 (Sept. 4, 1874).

14. Birckbeck, *Notes on a Journey*, 121.
15. *Illinois Intelligencer*, May 14, 1817.
16. Gershom Flagg to Azariah Flagg, Dec. 7, 1817.
17. Ford, *History of Illinois*, 23.
18. Peter Cartwright, *Autobiography of Peter Cartwright, the backwoods preacher* (Cincinnati: Cranston and Curts, 1856), 244.
19. Hedrick quoted in Dumond, *Antislavery*, 88.
20. Parrish, op cit. On the large presence of antislavery Southerners in Illinois, see Carrie P. Korfoid, "Puritan Influences in the Formative Years of Illinois History," *Transactions of the Illinois State Historical Society* 10 (1905): 308–10.
21. Flint, in Thwaites, *Early Western Travels*, vol. 9, 233–6.
22. Elias Pym Fordham, *Personal Narrative of Travels in Virginia, Maryland, Pennsylvania, Ohio, Indiana, Kentucky; and of a residence in the Illinois Territory: 1817-1818*, ed. Frederic Ogg (Cleveland: Arthur H. Clark, 1906; reprint, Kentuckiana Digital Library), 126.
23. Ninian W. Edwards, *History of Illinois, from 1778 to 1833: And Life and Times of Ninian Edwards* (Springfield: Illinois State Journal Co., 1870), 23, 184; Clerk's Register, Randolph County, recordations June 8, July 14, 1810 and June 17, 1811, cited in Harris, *History of Negro Servitude*, 11–2.
24. Edward Coles, "History of the Ordinance of 1787," reprinted in Alvord, "Gov. Edward Coles," 382; 378 summarizes Jefferson's view. For the status of slavery in the Northwest Territory generally, see Eugene H. Berwanger, *The Frontier Against Slavery* (Urbana: University of Illinois Press, 1967), 8–9; Jacob P. Dunne, ed., "Slavery Petitions and Papers," *Indiana Historical Society Publications* 2 (1894): 429–529; Finkelman, *Slavery and the Founders*, 48–55.
25. Ford, *History of Illinois*, 19; Philip Pittman, "The Present State of the European Settlements on the Mississippi," 19970, cited in Harris, *The History of Negro Servitude*, 4; for population estimates, Harris, *History of Negro Servitude*, 5.
26. Coles, "History of the Ordinance of 1787," reprinted in Alvord, "Gov. Edward Coles," 382–3, 385.
27. U.S. Census, 1800; Coles, "History of the Ordinance," 386.
28. U.S. Census, 1810.
29. Harris, *History of Negro Servitude*, 7–12; B. E. Hoffmann, ed., *History of Madison County, Illinois* (Edwardsville, Ill.: W. R. Brink, 1882), 117–8.
30. Harris, *History of Negro Servitude*, 8–9; Ford, *History of Illinois*, 17.
31. U.S. Census, 1820; Coles, "Autobiography."
32. Edward Coles to Nicholas Biddle, May 15, 1816; Tench Ringgold to Edward Coles, April 15, 1815; Edward Coles to Payne Todd, Jan. 3, 1815.
33. Isaac Coles to Joseph Cabell, Aug. 1, 1819, cited in Langhorne, Lay, and Rieley, *A Virginia Family*, 108; "Notes on Edward Coles" tells us only that Walter bought Rockfish.
34. Birkbeck, *Notes on a Journey*, 123, 126; George Flower, *History of the English Settlement in Edwards County, Illinois, Founded in 1817 and 1818 by Morris Birkbeck and George Flower* (Chicago: Fergus Printing Co., 1882), 60.
35. Coles, "Autobiography"; Illinois' rush to statehood is outlined in Buck, *Illinois in 1818*, 200–231; Davis, *Frontier Illinois*, 155–66.
36. Daniel Cook to Ninian Edwards, Oct. 2, 1817, cited in Edwards, *History of Illinois*, 271.
37. Edwards, *History of Illinois*, 253–4, has details of Cook's early life; the quote is from Ford, *History of Illinois*, 46.
38. *Illinois Intelligencer*, Nov. 20, 1817.
39. *Illinois Intelligencer*, Nov. 27, 1817.
40. *Illinois Intelligencer*, Dec. 11, 1817.
41. The rush to statehood, and the initial indifference of most people outside of a small political class, are discussed in Buck, *Illinois in 1818*, 232; see also Robert P. Howard, *Illinois*, 97–105.
42. The scale and processes of the salt works are outlined in George W. Smith, "The Salines of Southern Illinois," *Transactions of the Illinois State Historical Society* 9 (1904): 245–58, and John Moses, *Illinois Historical and Statistical*, vol. 1 (Chicago: Fergus Printing, 1889), 265–6; for a sense of the critical importance of the salt works to the state economy, see Evarts B. Greene and Clarence W. Alvord, eds., *The Governors' Letter-Books, 1818-1834* (Springfield: Illinois State Historical Society, 1909), 3; Howard, *Illinois*, 132; for the important to eastern Illinois politics, see Buck, *Illinois in 1818*, 200.
43. *Illinois Intelligencer*, April 11, 1818.
44. Buck, *Illinois in 1818*, 216.
45. *Illinois Intelligencer*, Jan. 1 and Jan. 13, 1818.
46. *Illinois Intelligencer*, April 18, 1818.
47. For Southern character of Illinois and Southern resentment of the new arrivals from the North, see Boggess, *Settlement of Illinois*, 145, 186; Simeone, *Democracy and Slavery*, 62, 145, 149; Davis, *Frontier Illinois*, 160; the Gillespie quote is from Joseph Gillespie, "Recollections of Early Illinois and her noted men," *Fergus Historical Series* 13 (Chicago, 1880): 6; Tillson's is from Christina H. Tillson, *A Woman's Story of Pioneer Illinois* (Carbondale, Ill., SIU Press, 1995), 24–5.

48. Fordham, *Narrative*, 221.
49. Coles enumerated his western Illinois land purchases in a memorandum dated Aug. 15, 1818, as well as in "Ledger, Land Transactions, 1818-1839" and "Some Accounts of Hugh Roberts Estate, 1836-66," both in the Coles Collection, Historical Society of Pennsylvania. The November 1818 Pike County purchase, for $3,500, and six arpents in St. Louis, purchased for $3,000 that September, are also noted in the "Ledger."
50. Warren, "Replication," *Free West*, May 3 1855, cited in Alvord, "Gov. Edward Coles," 339; unnamed correspondent to Thomas Sloo, Jr., cited in Simeone, *Democracy and Slavery*, 224 (interestingly, Simeone cites this letter in questioning whether Coles really freed his slaves, although it predates the 1819 emancipation).
51. Flower, *History of the English Settlement*, 275; John F. Snyder, *Adam W. Snyder and his period in Illinois History 1817-1842* (Springfield, Ill.: H. W. Rokker, 1903), p. 6.
52. Ford, *History of Illinois*, 15; for Thomas's story, see Buck, *Illinois in 1818*, 187-192; Howard, *Illinois*, 72; Simeone, *Democracy and Slavery*, 99-100.
53. Pease, *The Frontier State*, 94; Clarence Alvord, *The Illinois Country* (Urbana: University of Illinois, 1987), 416-26, discusses the formation of Thomas' faction, as do Buck, *Illinois in 1818*, 200-1, and Simeone, *Democracy and Slavery*, 99-104.
54. John Reynolds, *My Own Times Embracing Also the History of My Life* (Chicago: Fergus Printing, 1879), Fordham, *Narrative*, 210.
55. Kane, quoted in Buck, *Illinois in 1818*, 257; Kane's role is also discussed in Pease, *Frontier State*, 96, and Simeone, *Democracy and Slavery*, 108.
56. Buck, *Illinois in 1818*, 257; *Illinois Intelligencer*, June 24, 1818.
57. *Illinois Intelligencer*, May 6, June 17, 1818.
58. *Illinois Intelligencer*, July 1, 1818.
59. Buck, *Illinois in 1818*, 266; *Illinois Intelligencer*, Aug. 5, 1818.
60. Ford, *History of Illinois*, 11.
61. Buck, *Illinois in 1818*, 268, 273-4, 283; the Breese comment is from John F. Snyder, "Forgotten Statesmen of Illinois: Hon. Conrad Will," *Transactions of the Illinois State Historical Society* 10 (1905): 360.
62. Howard, *Illinois*, 114-6; Buck, *Illinois in 1818*, 274-5, discusses the governor's power and 280-1 the indenture question; *Illinois Intelligencer*, Aug, 19 1818.
63. *Illinois Intelligencer*, Aug. 19, 1818.
64. Buck, *Illinois in 1818*, 280-1.
65. Ford, *History of Illinois*, 23-4.
66. Buck, *Illinois in 1818*, 280-1.

Chapter 5

1. Edward Coles to Henry Dodge, Secretary of the Agricultural Society of Illinois, Feb. 22, 1821, printed in the *Illinois Gazette*, May 5, 1821.
2. Ninian Edwards to Edward Coles, Jan. 18, 1818; Edward Coles to James Monroe, Oct. 11, 1818; Washburne, *Sketch of Edward Coles*, 54.
3. Edward Coles to James Madison, July 20, 1819; the Prairieland purchase is recorded in "Ledger, Land Transactions, 1818-1839"; Coles paid $1,800 for the farm. Malcolm J. Rohrbough, *The Land Office Business: The Settlement and Administration of American Public Lands, 1789-1837* (New York: Oxford University Press, 1968), 31, discusses registrars' functions and pay.
4. Coles' Account Book 1819-1839, and Edward Coles to John Mason Peck, April 30, 1855, cited in Alvord, "Gov. Edward Coles," 353-4, discusses the freed slaves' employment, wages and other recompense as well as Ralph's death. His Feb. 22, 1821 letter to Henry Dodge also discusses the freedmen's work.
5. "Deed of Emancipation," in *Madison County Court Records 1813-1818* and *Indenture Records 1805-1826* (Springfield, Ill.: Folk Works Research, 1993), 101-104. For the toast see *Edwardsville Spectator* July 10, 1819.
6. Guasco, "Confronting Democracy," 137-8, tallies Coles' expenses and income; Simeone, *Democracy and Slavery*, 46, 228-9, demonstrates how long it could take most farmers to clear their debts in this period.
7. Edward Coles to Henry Dodge, Feb 22, 1821.
8. "The Land Office at Edwardsville in Account with Edward Coles"; D.W. Meinig, *The Shaping of America: A Geographical Perspective on 500 Years of History*, vol. 2 (New Haven: Yale University Press, 1993), 236-45, and Rorhbough, *Land Office Business*, 75-6, describe the auction process and registrar's role; the details about Edwardsville are from W.T. Norton, *Centennial History of Madison County, Illinois and its People, 1812-1912* (Chicago: Lewis Publishing, 1912), 497-502; Stephenson and the bank are discussed in Pease, *Frontier State*, 55.
9. Coles, "Account Book, 1818-1839"; Boggess, *Settlement of Illinois*, 105, 137.
10. Edward Coles to William Crawford, Secretary of the Treasury, Nov. 10, 1820, American State Papers, Public Lands, vol. 3, 478.
11. Edward Coles, "Report," American State Papers, Public Lands, vol. 3, 480, 485.
12. Edward Coles to Daniel Cook, Nov. 15, 1820.

13. Coles, "Report," 485.
14. Moore, *Missouri Controversy*, 34.
15. Moore, *Missouri Controversy*, 35, 39.
16. Annals of Congress, 15th Congress, 2nd Session. 1195.
17. Annals of Congress, 16th Congress, 1st Session, 239.
18. *St. Louis Enquirer*, Oct. 27, 1819.
19. Edwards, *History of Illinois*, 184.
20. Warren, "Replication," *Free West*, May 3, 1855, cited in Alvord, "Gov. Edward Coles," 341–2.
21. Edwards, *History of Illinois*, 185. Warren's animus to Coles (worth remembering, given the degree to which he has been relied upon in assessing Coles) reflected in his 35-years-later recollections in the 1855 "Replication," in which he remembers Coles trying to cover up that there had been an effort to set up a proslavery press; *Free West*, May 3, 1855.
22. Reynolds, *My Own Times*, 234; Pease, *Frontier State*, 103.
23. Edward Coles to Daniel Cook, Nov. 15, 1820.
24. Washburne, *Sketch of Edward Coles*, 55–6.
25. Edward Coles to Josiah Meigs, Aug. 5, 1819.
26. Gershom Flagg to Artemas Flagg, March 31, 1821, "Pioneer Letters of Gershom Flagg," *Transactions of the Illinois State Historical Society* (1910): http://www.iltrails.org/madison/moreflaggletters.htm#5; for Menard see Ford, *History of Illinois*, 26.
27. Annals of Congress, 16th Congress, 2nd Session, Jan 11, 1821, 160. Although Coles' investment in land was smaller than many of his opponents, and although Illinoisans saw those opponents' involvement in state banking as an abuse of power and source of riches, James Simeone, in *Democracy and Slavery*, 26, declares Coles "was ... an easy target on the wealth and status issue ... he owned more than 6,000 acres, much of it granted to him as a consequence of his appointed positions." The problem with this assertion (unbacked by any citation of land or financial records) is that Coles' holdings in Illinois were not that large and that he paid for them as well as his Missouri properties, which few in Illinois knew anything about, even those most eager to discredit him (see, e.g., Hooper Warren, "Replication," *Free West*, May 10, 1855, recycling a false charge that Coles sent slaves to his brother's Missouri farm). All in all, Coles' records show he owned about 4,400 acres in Illinois, 4,900 in Missouri; none was granted. The newspaper letter Simeone cites as evidence that Coles was a "whipping boy" because of his wealth does not in fact say anything about that subject but focuses on the national government and people from outside Illinois trying to dictate to the state (see *Illinois Intelligencer*, Dec. 14, 1822). Simeone's view of Coles as a wealthy, arrogant man, disconnected from the mass of people, informs much of his analysis of the anti-slavery struggle, without really coming to terms with the mix of resentment, resignation and support settlers felt towards other even wealthier politicians—the wealthiest of whom succeeded Coles as governor. At a time when most farmers scraped by on eighty- or 160-acre farms, Coles had a lot of land (though many of his "republican" opponents had more). And if land rich, he was cash poor. Without his land office income, after all, he risked going bust.
28. Roy Robbins, *Our Landed Heritage: The Public Domain, 1776-1990* (Lincoln: University of Nebraska Press, 1976), chapter 3, discusses the 1820 and 1821 act; Edward Coles to Mary Carter, April 18, 1821, mentions his decision to stay in Illinois because of his relief act obligations, as does the *Edwardsville Spectator*, Nov. 7, 1821; the notice to land-owners is from the *Edwardsville Spectator*, Sept. 17, 1821.
29. Ford, *History of Illinois*, 14.
30. *Edwardsville Spectator*, April 21, May 22, 1821.
31. *Edwardsville Spectator*, June 5, 1821; *Illinois Intelligencer*, July 3, 1821; John Reynolds, *My Own Times*, 144.
32. Edward Coles to Mary Carter, April 18, 1821; *Edwardsville Spectator*, Oct. 30, 1821.
33. *Edwardsville Spectator*, Nov. 27, Dec. 4, 1821.
34. Edwards, *History of Illinois*, 133; Pease, *Frontier State*, 76.
35. Warren, "Replication," *Free West*, May 10, 1855, cited in Alvord, "Gov Edward Coles," 346–7.
36. *Illinois Intelligencer*, May 11, 1822; *Edwardsville Spectator*, Feb. 19, March 5, 1822.
37. *Illinois Intelligencer*, June 29, July 6, 1822.
38. Warren, "Replication," *Free West*, May 10, 1855, cited in Alvord, "Gov. Edward Coles," 346, for his decision to reprint the Jefferson letters; the remarks on emancipation as a ploy for Methodist and Yankee votes is from *Edwardsville Spectator*, April 2, 1822, while the accusation Coles had only freed worthless slaves is from the *Edwardsville Spectator*, April 17, 1822; Coles' reply is in the edition of July 6, 1822; for Warren's continued assertion that Coles really held slaves, see Warren, "Replication," *Free West*, May 10, 1855, 349.
39. *Edwardsville Spectator*, April 13, 1822.
40. Warren, "Replication," *Free West*, May 10, 1855; cited in Alvord, "Gov. Edward Coles," 346.

41. *Edwardsville Spectator*, July 13, 1822.
42. Nathaniel Buckmeister to John Buckmeister, April 14, 1822; Horatio Newhall to his family, May 11, 1822; Reynolds, *My Own Times*, 248.
43. Theodore C. Pease, "Illinois Election Returns, 1818–1848," *Collections of the Illinois State Historical Library* 18 (1923): 14–18.
44. *Edwardsville Spectator*, Aug. 17, 31, 1822; *Illinois Intelligencer*, Sept. 7, 1822.
45. James Madison to Edward Coles, Oct. 19, 1822.
46. Paul E. Stroble, Jr., *High on the Okaw's Western Bank, Vandalia, Illinois, 1819–39* (Urbana: University of Illinois Press, 1992), 16.
47. *Illinois Intelligencer*, Dec. 7, 1822.
48. Ibid.
49. Ibid.
50. Ibid.
51. Ibid.

Chapter 6

1. *Illinois Intelligencer*, Dec. 21, 1822; Washburne, *Sketch of Coles*, 72; Simeone, *Democracy and Slavery*, 123–4.
2. Recollections of T.W. Smith by Judge Joseph Gillespie, cited in Washburne, *Sketch of Coles*, 121, and Stroble, *High on the Okaw's*, 72. Smith's ill-dealing with Crawford and Cobb is detailed in Edward Coles, "Sketch of Emancipation," though he is not named there; but Smith was the one who signed the advertisement for brickyard jobs in the *Edwardsville Spectator*, June 26, 1821.
3. *Journal of the Senate*, 1823, 163.
4. Moore is described in Washburne, *Sketch of Coles*, 104–5; Will's background from Simeone, *Democracy and Slavery*, 20, 223, and Stroble, *High on the Okaw's*, 71; Emmitt is a mystery—a southern county man who, it will be seen, plays a critically important role in the weeks to come, with an act of conscience; his actions, perhaps, will suggest Southern or "White Folks" attitudes towards slavery were not as predictable as many have thought. For Coles' rejection of Will's proposal to take over the U.S. (or Muddy) Saline, see Edward Coles to Conrad Will, April 10, 1823.
5. Gillespie, cited in Washburne, *Sketch of Coles*, 123, 124.
6. Ibid, 98; for Churchill's petition see *Edwardsville Spectator*, May 31, 1823.
7. *Edwardsville Spectator*, May 31, 1823.
8. *Illinois Intelligencer*, Dec. 21, 1822.
9. Ibid.
10. Richard S. Newman, *The Transformation of American Abolitionism: Fighting Slavery in the Early Republic* (Chapel Hill, N.C.: University of North Carolina Press, 2002) summarizes the Pennsylvania Abolition Society's focus on legal work and genteel political agitation, especially in 21–9. He argues that free blacks' frustration with the lack of progress in ending American slavery and the need to protect their own rights as free men and women led first to the formation of their own associations with more forceful calls for freedom, as in Walker's work, which in turn inspired the Massachusetts men and women, like William Lloyd Garrison, who would give abolitionism a new life in the 1830s. Lundy's cautionary remarks are to be found in the *Genius of Universal Emancipation*, April 29, 1827. The *Antelope* case is reported in 10 Wheaton 66 and in John T. Noonan, *The Antelope: The Ordeal of the Recaptured Africans in the Administrations of James Monroe and John Quincy Adams* (Berkeley: University of California Press, 1977).
11. Flower, *History of the English Settlement*, 206.
12. *Edwardsville Spectator*, March 8, 1823.
13. Coles quoted in the *Illinois Intelligencer*, May 14, 1824; Sloo's remarks from "Selections from the Torrence Papers," *Quarterly Publication of the Historical and Philosophical Society of Ohio* (1911): 56, cited in Simeone, *Democracy and Slavery*, 116–7.
14. John Hallway, *Western Illinois Heritage* (Macomb, Ill.: Illinois Heritage Press, 1983), 22–5; Washburne, *Sketch of Coles*, 75.
15. Shaw in the *Edwardsville Spectator*, Dec. 13, 1823.
16. Ibid.
17. William P. McKee to Edward Coles, Aug. 17, 1822; *Edwardsville Spectator*, July 10, 1819.
18. *Illinois Intelligencer*, Feb. 15, 1823.
19. Washburne, *Sketch of Coles*, 73, 78–81, 85–89; Ford, *History of Illinois*, 31–2; Pease, *Frontier State*, 78–80; Simeone, *Democracy and Slavery*, 121–2.
20. *Illinois Intelligencer*, May 14, 1824; Simeone, *Democracy and Slavery*, 123.
21. *Illinois Intelligencer*, May 14, 1824.
22. *Illinois Republican*, June 1, 1824.
23. *Illinois Intelligencer*, Feb. 1, 1823; Stroble, *High on the Okaw's*, 92.
24. Quoted by Gillespie in Washburne, *Sketch of Coles*, 70–1.
25. *Edwardsville Spectator*, Feb. 22, 1823.
26. *Edwardsville Spectator*, April 19, 1823; Washburne, *Sketch of Coles*, 84–5.
27. *Edwardsville Spectator*, Feb. 15, 1823; see also *Illinois Intelligencer*, Feb. 21, 1823.
28. *Edwardsville Spectator*, Feb. 15, 1823; *Illinois Intelligencer*, Feb 21, 1823.
29. *Edwardsville Spectator*, Feb. 15, 1823.

30. *Edwardsville Spectator*, Feb. 15, 1823; Stroble, *High on the Okaw's*, 49.
31. *Edward,ville Spectator*, Feb. 15, 1823.
32. Ibid.
33. *Edwardsville Spectator*, Feb. 15, 22, 1823.
34. *Edwardsville Spectator*, Feb. 22, 1823; *Illinois Intelligencer*, Feb. 21, 1823.
35. *Edwardsville Spectator*, Feb. 22, 1823.
36. *Edwardsville Spectator*, Feb. 15, 1823; Edward Coles to James Madison, April 25, 1823.
37. Ford, *History of Illinois*, 32. Ford here gives Kinney the title he won in the 1826 election; he was a state senator at this time.
38. Horatio Newhall to J. Newhall, March 22, 1823; *Edwardsville Spectator*, Sept. 27, 1823; Reynolds, *My Own Times*, 241.
39. Gillespie, in Washburne, *Sketch of Coles*, 122; William Kinney, letter in the *Edwardsville Spectator*, May 3, 1823.
40. *Illinois Intelligencer*, Feb. 21, 1823.
41. Ibid; Merton L. Dillon, "Antislavery Movement in Illinois, 1800-1844" (Ph.D. diss., University of Illinois, 1951), 85-6, and Leichtle, "Coles: An Agrarian," 176, discuss Coles' role in writing the memorial; Leichtle believes he wrote it, as indeed the language suggests.

Chapter 7

1. Coles to the Senate, Feb. 14, 1823, cited in Washburne, *Sketch of Coles*, 138-9.
2. Ibid.
3. Edward Coles to John Lofton, Feb. 16, 1823.
4. *Illinois Intelligencer*, Feb. 15, 1823.
5. *Illinois Intelligencer*, Feb. 22, 1823.
6. *Illinois Intelligencer*, March 15, 1823; *Illinois Gazette* March 15, 1823.
7. *Edwardsville Spectator*, March 8, 1823; Edward Coles to Nicholas Biddle, April 22, 1823.
8. *Edwardsville Spectator*, March 15, 1823.
9. *Edwardsville Spectator*, July 12, 1823.
10. Edward Coles to Nicholas Biddle, April 22, 1823; Edward Coles to Eliza Carter, March 15, 1823, describes his difficult journey to Edwardsville.
11. *Edwardsville Spectator*, March 8, 1823.
12. Edward Coles to Eliza Carter, March 15, 1823.
13. *Edwardsville Spectator*, April 12, 1823; for the Bond County meeting see *Edwardsville Spectator*, March 15, 1823.
14. Thomas Lippincott, "Early Days in Madison County, No. 42"; McKee, Lippincott and the others were reported at the Monroe County meeting in the *Edwardsville Spectator*, July 12, 1823.
15. Edward Coles to Roberts Vaux, June 27, 1823; Coles' donation of his salary is reported in John Mason Peck to Hooper Warren, March 27, 1855, cited in Alvord, "Gov. Edward Coles," 335.
16. Thomas Lippincott, "Early Days in Madison County, No. 10."
17. Edward Coles to Nicholas Biddle, April 22, 1823.
18. Edward Coles to Richard Flower, April 12 1823.
19. Crocker is quoted in the *Edwardsville Spectator*, April 19, 1823; John Mason Peck to Hooper Warren, March 27, 1855, cited in Alvord, "Gov. Edward Coles," 334.
20. *Edwardsville Spectator*, April 19, 1823; Horatio Newhall to J. Newhall, May 21, 1823.
21. Greene County reported in the *Edwardsville Spectator*, Aug. 9, 1823; Sangoman County, *Edwardsville Spectator*, July 12, 1823; Fulton County, *Edwardsville Spectator*, Aug. 30, 1823. For Monroe and Morgan Counties, see the *Edwardsville Spectator* of July 12, 1823 and the *Illinois Intelligencer* of July 26, 1823. For other western counties, see the *Edwardsville Spectator* of Sept. 20, 1823. The *Edwardsville Spectator*, on March 1 and 22 and on April 22, 1823, outlines organizing efforts in St. Clair and the eastern counties.
22. *Illinois Republican*, April 19, 1823; *Illinois Intelligencer*, July 15, 1823.
23. *Illinois Intelligencer*, Nov. 15, 1823.
24. *Illinois Intelligencer*, March 29, 1823.
25. *Illinois Intelligencer*, May 3, 1823; Reynolds' position is characterized some months later in the *Edwardsville Spectator*, July 6, 1824.
26. *Illinois Intelligencer*, March 29, 1823; *Illinois Intelligencer*, May 14, 1824; Coles is quoted some months later, after he took control of the *Intelligencer*.
27. *Illinois Intelligencer*, May 3, 1823.
28. Morris Birkbeck, as Jonathan Freeman, in the *Illinois Gazette*, June 14, 1823; Birkbeck's pamphlet is reprinted in *Transactions of the Illinois State Historical Society* 10 (1905): 147-60.
29. *Illinois Intelligencer*, May 24, 31, 1823. Coles claimed to be Aristides, as well as "One of Many," "The Voice of Virtue" and "Wisdom and Experience on the Subject of Negro Slavery" in an exchange with Thomas Lippincott, printed in "Edward Coles, Second Governor of Illinois—Correspondence with Rev. Thomas Lippincott," *Journal of the Illinois State Historical Society* 3 (1911): 61.
30. "Martus" in *Republican Advocate*, July 3, 1823; Lawrence County address, *Edwardsville Spectator*, Sept. 16, 1823.
31. *Illinois Intelligencer*, May 31, 1823.
32. Birkbeck, "An Appeal."

33. *Illinois Intelligencer*, May 17, 1823; *Edwardsville Spectator*, May 18, 1823.
34. *Illinois Republican*, Feb. 2, 1824; *Illinois Intelligencer*, June 7, 1823.
35. *Illinois Intelligencer*, May 3, 1823; *Illinois Intelligencer*, Nov. 22, 1823.
36. *Edwardsville Spectator*, June 7, 1823.
37. *Edwardsville Spectator*, July 19, 1823.
38. *Illinois Intelligencer*, July 23, 1823; *Illinois Intelligencer*, May 24, 1823.
39. *Edwardsville Spectator*, Aug. 30, 1823; the pamphlets are described in Roberts Vaux to Edward Coles May 2, 1823; Coles' request for pamphlets with an economic focus is in Edward Coles to Roberts Vaux, June 27, 1823.
40. *Edwardsville Spectator*, April 19, 1824; Reynolds, *My Own Times*, 240; Joseph Gillespie, "Recollections of Early Illinois and her noted men," *Fergus Historical Series* 13 (Chicago, 1880): 8; *Edwardsville Spectator*, Aug. 30, 1823.
41. *Illinois Intelligencer*, June 7, 1823; *Illinois Gazette*, July 26, 1823.
42. Pease, *Frontier State*, 55–6.
43. *Edwardsville Spectator*, April 13, 1824.
44. *Illinois Intelligencer*, May 24, 1823.
45. *Edwardsville Spectator*, July 19, 1823.
46. Edward Coles to Nicholas Biddle, Sept. 18, 1823; John Mason Peck to Hooper Warren, March 27, 1855, cited in Alvord, "Gov. Edward Coles," 334.
47. Reynolds, *My Own Times*, 241; *Illinois Intelligencer*, Nov. 8, 1823.
48. Edward Coles to Rebecca Coles, Sept. 6, 1823; Edward Coles to Roberts Vaux, Dec. 11, 1823.
49. *Illinois Intelligencer*, Feb. 20, 1824.
50. Edward Coles to Roberts Vaux, Dec. 11, 1823; Edward Coles to Morris Birkbeck, Jan. 29, 1824.
51. Edward Coles to Roberts Vaux, Dec. 11, 1823; Stroble, *High on the Okaw's*, 78.
52. Edward Coles to Morris Birkbeck, Jan. 29, 1824.
53. *Edwardsville Spectator*, Dec. 13, 1823.

Chapter 8

1. Edward Coles to Morris Birkbeck, Jan. 29, 1824; Mary Carter to Rebecca Coles, Feb. 18, 1824.
2. For Coles' spending, see Coles, Account Book 1818–1839; his comments about the lawsuit in his letter, Edward Coles to Morris Birkbeck, Jan. 29, 1824.
3. Edward Coles, "Sketch of Emancipation."
4. Edward Coles to Morris Birkbeck, Jan. 29, 1824; Edward Coles to Sarah Carter, Feb. 13, 1824.
5. *Edwardsville Spectator*, Feb. 17, 1824.
6. *Illinois Intelligencer*, Feb. 27, 1824.
7. Reynolds, *My Own Times*, 241.
8. William Brown, *The Early Movement in Illinois for the Legalization of Slavery* (Chicago: Chicago Historical Society, 1864); *Illinois Republican*, March 16, 1824.
9. *Republican Advocate*, Jan. 8, 1824; *Illinois Intelligencer*, Feb. 13, 1824; *Illinois Intelligencer*, Jan. 30, 1824.
10. *Illinois Republican*, April 20, 1824.
11. *Edwardsville Spectator*, April 13, 1824.
12. Edward Coles to Andrew Stevenson, April 7, 1824.
13. Ford, *History of Illinois*, 38.
14. Edward Coles to Andrew Stevenson, April 7, 1824.
15. *Edwardsville Spectator*, Feb. 17, 1824; Edward Coles to Nicholas Biddle, Sept. 18, 1823.
16. *Illinois Intelligencer*, May 3, 1823.
17. John Mason Peck to Hooper Warren, March 27, 1855, cited in Alvord, "Gov. Edward Coles," 335–6; Reynolds, *My Own Times*, 242.
18. *Illinois Intelligencer*, May 14, 1824.
19. *Illinois Intelligencer*, May 28, 1824.
20. *Illinois Intelligencer*, June 4, 1824.
21. *Illinois Intelligencer*, July 2, 1824.
22. *Illinois Intelligencer*, June 25, 1824.
23. *Illinois Intelligencer*, Jan. 30, 1824.
24. *Illinois Intelligencer*, June 25, 1824.
25. *Illinois Republican*, June 15, 1824.
26. Washburne, *Sketch of Coles*, 192.
27. See, e.g., "One of Many" in *Illinois Intelligencer* June 13, July 2, 1824.
28. Edwards, *History of Illinois*, 260.
29. *Illinois Gazette*, April 10, 1824.
30. *Illinois Intelligencer*, May 14, 1824.
31. *Edwardsville Spectator*, July 17, 1824.
32. *Illinois Intelligencer*, July 30, 1824.
33. William W. Sweet, *Religion on the American Frontier: The Baptists* (New York: Henry Holt, 1931), 587.
34. "Edward Coles Correspondence with Rev. Thomas Lippincott," *Journal of the Illinois State Historical Society* 3 (1911): 61; John Kingston, "Early Western Days," *Report and Collections of the State Historical Society of Wisconsin* 7 (1876): 315–6.
35. Pease, *Illinois Election Returns*, 24–9.
36. Pease, ibid. Here is how the Cook-Bond vote compares to the convention vote:

County	Congressional vote		Convention Vote	
	Cook	Bond	No	Yes
Northern frontier counties				
Bond	267	40	240	63
Clark	96	54	116	31
Crawford	257	142	262	134
Edgar	237	0	234	3

County	Congressional vote		Convention Vote	
	Cook	Bond	No	Yes
Fayette	158	89	121	125
Fulton	70	3	60	5
Greene	392	163	379	164
Montgomery	111	55	90	74
Morgan	455	21	432	42
Pike	176	12	165	19
Sangamon	789	90	722	153
American Bottom				
Madison	644	285	563	351
Monroe	200	143	196	141
St. Clair	575	402	506	408
Eastern Illinois				
Edwards	487	103	391	189
Hamilton	48	226	85	173
Lawrence	281	144	261	158
Wayne	134	168	111	189
Southern Illinois				
Alexander	84	57	51	75
Franklin	126	177	113	170
Gallatin	286	462	133	597
Jackson	77	197	63	180
Jefferson	31	111	43	99
Johnson	94	59	74	74
Marion	53	46	52	45
Pope	319	328	124	273
Randolph	319	328	284	357
Union	289	174	240	213
Washington	201	94	173	112
White	336	357	326	355
Total	**7592**	**4530**	**6610**	**4972**

37. Horatio Newhall to J. Newhall, undated.

38. Roberts Vaux to Edward Coles, Sept. 1, 1824.

Chapter 9

1. "Coles Correspondence," 61; *Edwardsville Spectator*, Aug. 10, 1824.

2. *Edwardsville Spectator*, Aug. 10, 1824.

3. For the legal argument, see "Plea of Edward Coles against the Declaration of the County Commissioners," by Starr and Lockwood, attorneys, filed with the Circuit Court of Madison County and reprinted in Alvord, "Gov. Edward Coles," 207–8; Coles, "Sketch of Emancipation," also outlines his legal position and notes the Crawfords' tax-paying status; the Crawford's tenancy at Prairieland is outlined in Coles, Account Book 1818–1839.

4. Coles, "Sketch of Emancipation"; Edward Coles to Morris Birkbeck, Sept. 22, 1824.

5. "Reasons for New Trial Advanced by Edward Coles," Sept. 22, 1824, Circuit Court of Madison County; certificates of emancipation, July 4, 1819, Circuit Court of Madison County, cited in Alvord, "Gov. Edward Coles," 209; the language in the emancipation deeds is quoted, among other places, in Washburne, *Sketch of Edward Coles*, 53.

6. Coles, "Sketch of Emancipation"; the Illinois Supreme Court ruling is in *Edward Coles v. County of Madison*, 1 Breese 154–161.

7. Washburne, *Sketch of Edward Coles*, 231–2, discusses the special session and Coles' request for the repeal of the Black Code; Edward Coles to William Barry, June 25, 1858, discusses Birkbeck's nomination; Leichtle, "Coles: An Agrarian," 204–5, discusses the emergence of parties in Illinois.

8. Coles, "Sketch of the Emancipation"; Edward Coles to William Barry, June 25, 1858.

9. Edward Coles to Roberts Vaux, Feb. 8, 1826; Ford, *History of Illinois*, 38.

10. Pease, *The Frontier State*, 109–111; Howard, *Illinois*, 139–140; Ford, *History of Illinois*, 40–41.

11. Pease, *The Frontier State*, 107; Ford, *History of Illinois*, 48.

12. Ford, *History of Illinois*, 40.

13. Pease, *The Frontier State*, 130–4.

14. For the speech, see *Illinois Intelligencer*, Dec. 9, 1826.

15. Ibid.

16. Ibid.

17. Illinois Session Laws, 1826: "An Act Concerning Apprentices"; Illinois Session Laws, 1827: "An Act Concerning Practice"; Illinois Session Laws, 1829: "An Act on Negroes"; *Nance v. Howard*, 1 Breese 242; *Phoebe v Jay*, 1 Breese 270–1; Jon Musgrove, "Black Kidnappings on the Wabash and Ohio Valleys of Illinois," http://www.illinoishistory.com/black kidnappings.html.

18. Testimony of Nathaniel Niles of Belleville and James Hood of Sparta, cited in Harris, *History of Negro Servitude*, 58–9.

19. *Western Citizen*, Oct. 26, 1843, details the Lovejoy case; the Jarrott case is reported in 2 Gilmore 1.

20. Lincoln and allies cited in Howard, *Illinois*, 185; the riot and death of Lovejoy are recounted in "Memoir of Lovejoy by his brothers," *Alton Telegraph*, Nov. 15, 1837, and in the *Alton Observer*, Dec. 28, 1837.

21. *Illinois Intelligencer*, July 28, 1827; Nicholas Hansen to Edward Coles, Dec. 23, 1826; Ford, *History of Illinois*, 45; William Archer to Jacob Harlan, Dec. 8, 1826, cited in Leichtle, "Coles: An Agrarian," 216; *Illinois Intelligencer*, June 30, 1827.

22. Edward Coles to James Madison, June 12, 1832.

23. *Kaskaskia Republican*, May 20, 1831.

24. Pease, *Illinois Election Returns*, 70–3; the

quote from Coles is from his announcement in the *Republican,* May 20, 1831.

25. Illinois Public Domain Land Tract Sales Database, Illinois State Archives, show Crawford bought forty acres in Madison County on Oct. 6, 1832, and another forty on Aug. 16, 1836. Coles bought his two tracts on June 18, 1832. In comparison to the $1.25 an acre the Crawfords paid, the going rate for improved land ranged between $2.50 to $3.50 an acre; see, e.g., David Schob, *Hired Hands and Plowboys: Farm Labor in the Midwest, 1815-1860* (Urbana: University of Illinois Press, 1975), 263.

26. Coles, "Sketch of Emancipation"; Edward Coles to Robert and Kate Crawford, Feb. 7, 1837; William Prickett to Mellie Armstrong, Aug. 16, 1919.

27. Edward Coles to Thomas Randolph, Dec. 29, 1831.

28. Washburne, *Sketch of Edward Coles,* 246; Guasco, "Confronting Democracy," 279-80, 286.

29. Edward Coles to James Madison, Oct. 31, 1834.

30. Langhorne, Lay, and Rieley, *A Virginia Family,* 141; Guasco, "Confronting Democracy," 289.

31. Howard, *Illinois,* 195.

32. Coles, "Ledger, Land Transactions 1818-1869"; Edward Coles to Dolley Madison, Jan. 11, 1837.

33. Edward Coles to Robert and Kate Crawford, Feb. 7, 1837; Coles, "Sketch of Emancipation."

34. Coles, "Autobiography."

35. For the *Richmond Enquirer* article, see "Letter to James Monroe." Coles wrote on colonization in Edward Coles to Thomas Randolph, Dec. 29, 1831; urged Madison to revise his will in Edward Coles to James Madison, Jan. 8, 1832, and described the slave traders at Montpelier in Edward Coles to Sally Stevenson, Nov. 12, 1836. As Coles after his return from Illinois grew both strongly opposed to Andrew Jackson and more and more insistent that Madison free his slaves, he was in the view of at least one historian badly misunderstanding the ex-president's principles and political inclinations; see Drew McCoy, *The Last of the Fathers: James Madison and the Republican Legacy* (Cambridge: Cambridge University Press, 1989), 310-29.

36. Edward Coles to Robert and Kate Crawford, Feb. 7, 1837.

37. Edward Coles to Isaac Prickett, Nov. 5, 1839, Chicago Historical Society; Edward Coles to Isaac Prickett, Dec. 20, 1842.

38. Edward Coles to Winfield Scott, April 29, 1842.

39. Winfield Scott to Edward Coles, April 30, 1842.

40. Winfield Scott to John Tyler, April 30, 1842.

41. Edward Coles to Winfield Scott, May 3, 1842.

42. Edward Coles to Martin Van Buren, July 25, 1842; Martin Van Buren to Edward Coles, Aug. 4, 1842.

43. U.S. Census, 1850, Population Schedule, cited in Leichtle, "Coles: An Agrarian," 234.

44. Edward Coles to B. W. Richards, Sept. 9, 1848.

45. Edward Coles to Henry Clay, March 15, 1850; Henry Clay to Edward Coles, March 21, 1850.

46. Edward Coles, "Who was the Author of the Ordinance of 1787," *National Intelligencer,* Jan. 4, 1853.

47. Coles, "History of the Northwest Ordinance," 1856.

48. Ibid.

49. "Explanation" by Nicholas Trist, cited by Guasco, "Confronting Democracy," 340.

50. For Missouri, see Moore, *The Missouri Controversy,* 258-73, and Litwack, *North of Slavery,* 34-9; for Ohio and Indiana see Walter Havighurst, *Ohio: A History* (Urbana: University of Illinois Press, 2001), 6, 57; Howard H. Peckham, *Indiana: A History* (Urbana: University of Illinois Press, 2003), 43-7; Litwack, *North of Slavery,* 3, 67-9; see also Henry Farnum, *Chapters in the History of Social Legislation in the United States to 1860* (Washington: Carnegie Institution, 1938), 219-20; for Vermont, see Vermont Constitution of 1777, chapter 1, and John Duffy and Vincent Feeney, *Vermont: An Illustrated History* (Sun Valley, Ca.: American Historical Press, 2000), 57, 63; "Letters and Documents Relating to Slavery in Massachusetts," *Massachusetts Historical Society Collections, Fifth Series* 3 (1877): 401-2.

51. Edward Coles to John Rutherford, Oct. 15, 1861.

52. Roberts Coles to unidentified friend, Oct 13, 1861; Roberts Coles to Jenny Cary Fairfax, Feb. 7, 1862.

Bibliography

Books

Adams, Alice Dana. *The Neglected Period of Anti-Slavery in America, 1808-1831.* Boston: Ginn & Co, 1908.

Alvord, Clarence W., ed. "Governor Edward Coles." *Collections of the Illinois State Historical Library* 15 (1920).

———. *The Illinois Country.* Urbana: University of Illinois, 1987.

Ammon, Harry. *James Monroe: The Quest for National Identity.* Charlottesville: University Press of Virginia, 1990.

Anthony, Katherine S. *Dolley Madison, Her Life and Times.* Garden City, NY: Doubleday, 1949.

Barnhart, John D. "Sources of Southern Migration in the Old North-West." *Mississippi Valley Historical Review* 22 (1935).

———. "The Southern Influence in the Formation of Illinois." *Journal of the Illinois State Historical Society* 32 (1939).

Berwanger, Eugene. *The Frontier Against Slavery.* Urbana: University of Illinois Press, 1967.

Birkbeck, Morris. *Notes on a Journey in America.* London: James Ridgway, 1818.

Boggess, Arthur C. *The Settlement of Illinois, 1778-1830.* Freeport, NY: Books for Libraries, 1970.

Bradbury, John. "Remarks on Illinois and the western Territories." In Vol. 5 of *Early Western Travels*, edited by Reuben G. Thwaites. Cleveland: Arthur H. Clark Co., 1905.

Brant, Irving. *James Madison, Commander in Chief, 1812-1836.* Indianapolis: Bobbs-Merrill, 1961.

Breen, T.H. *Tobacco Culture: The Mentality of the Great Tidewater Planters on the Eve of Revolution.* Princeton: Princeton University Press, 1985.

Brown, William H. *Early History of Illinois.* Chicago: Fergus Printing, 1881.

———. *The Early Movement in Illinois for the Legalization of Slavery.* Chicago: Chicago Historical Society, 1864.

Buck, Solon J. *Illinois in 1818.* Urbana: University of Illinois, 1967.

Carlson, Theodore L. *The Illinois Military Tract:* Urbana: University of Illinois Press, 1951.

Cartwright, Peter. *Autobiography of Peter Cartwright, the backwoods preacher.* Cincinnati: Cranston and Curts, 1856.

Cassidy, John T. "The Issue of Freedom under Governor Coles." *Journal of the Illinois State Historical Society* 57 (1964).

Chapman, Charles C., ed. *History of Pike County, Illinois.* Chicago: Chapman, 1880.

Coles, Edward. "Edward Coles, Second Governor of Illinois—Correspondence with Rev. Thomas Lippincott." *Journal of the Illinois State Historical Society* 3 (1911).

———. "Gov. Coles; Autobiography Letter to W.C. Flagg, March 28, 1861." *Journal of the Illinois State Histocial Society* 2 (1910).
———. "History of the Northwest Ordinance." *Historical Society of Pennsylvania Press* (1856).
———. "Interesting Views of the Russian Empire." Richmond *Enquirer*, Dec. 13, 16, 1817.
———. "Letters of Gov. Edward Coles bearing on the Struggle of Freedom and Slavery in Illinois." *Journal of Negro History* 3 (1918).
———. "Letters of Edward Coles." *William & Mary Quarterly*, 2nd series, 7 (1927).
Coles, William B. *The Coles Family of Virginia and its Numerous Connections, From the Emigration to America to the Year 1915*. New York: privately printed, 1931.
Cote, Richard N. *Strength and Honor: The Life of Dolley Madison*. Mt. Pleasant, S.C.: Corinthian Books, 2005.
Cox, Isaac J. "Thomas Sloo Jr : A Typical Politician of Early Illinois." *Transactions of the Illinois State Historical Society* 16 (1911).
Crothers, A. Glenn. "Quaker Merchants and Slavery in Early National Alexandria, Virginia, the Ordeal of William Hartshorne. *Journal of the Early Republic* 25 (2005).
Dabney, Virginius. *Virginia: The New Dominion*. Charlottesville: University Press of Virginia, 1983.
Davis, David Brion. *The Problem of Slavery in the Age of Revolution 1770-1823*. New York: Oxford University Press, 1999.
Davis, James E. *Frontier Illinois*. Bloomington: Indiana University Press, 1998.
Davis, Richard B. *The Intellectual Life of the South in Jefferson's Virginia, 1790-1830*. Knoxville: University of Tennessee Press, 1972.
Degler, Carl. *The Other South: Southern Dissenters in the Nineteenth Century*. New York: Harper and Row, 1974.
Dictionary of National Biography. New York: Charles Scribner's Sons, 1933.
Dillon, Merton L. "Antislavery Movement in Illinois, 1800–1844." Ph.D. diss., University of Illinois, 1951.
———. "John Mason Peck, A Study of Historical Rationalization." *Journal of the Illinois State Historical Society* 50 (1957).
———. "Sources of Early Antislavery Thought in Illinois." *Journal of the Illinois State Historical Society* 50 (1957).
Dowrie, George W. *The Development of Banking in Illinois*. Urbana: University of Illinois Press, 1913.
Duberman, Martin, ed. *The Antislavery Vanguard: New Essays on the Abolitionists*. Princeton: Princeton University Press, 1965.
Duffy, John, and Vincent Feeney. *Vermont: An Illustrated History*. Sun Valley, Ca.: American Historical Press, 2000.
Dumond, Dwight Lowell. *Antislavery: The Crusade for Freedom in America*. Ann Arbor: University of Michigan Press, 1961.
Dunne, Jacob P., ed. "Slavery Petitions and Papers." *Indiana Historical Society Publications* 2 (1894).
Edwards, Ninian W. *History of Illinois, from 1778 to 1833: And Life and Times of Ninian Edwards*. Springfield: Illinois State Journal Co., 1870.
Egerton, Douglas R. *Gabriel's Rebellion: The Virginia Slave Conspiracies of 1800 and 1802*. Chapel Hill: University of North Carolina Press, 1993.
Ely, Melvin P. *Israel on the Appomattox*. New York: Knopf, 2004.
Ernst, Ferdinand. "Travels in Illinois in 1818." *Transactions of the Illinois State Historical Society* 8 (1903).
Farnum, Henry. *Chapters in the History of Social Legislation in the United States to 1860*. Washington: Carnegie Institution, 1938.
Faux, William. "Memorable Days in America, 1823." In Vol. 11 of *Early Western Travels*, edited by Reuben G. Thwaites. Cleveland: Arthur H. Clark Co., 1907.

Finkelman, Paul. *Slavery and the Founders: Race and Liberty in the Age of Jefferson*. Armonk, NY: M.E. Sharpe, 1996.
Flagg, Gershom. "Pioneer Letters of Gershom Flagg." *Transactions of the Illinois State Historical Society* (1910).
Flower, George. *History of the English Settlement in Edwards County, Illinois, Founded in 1817 and 1818 by Morris Birkbeck and George Flower*. Chicago: Fergus Printing Co., 1882.
Ford, Thomas. *A History of Illinois From Its Commencement as a State in 1818 to 1847*. Urbana: University of Illinois, 1995.
Fordham, Elias Pym. *Personal Narrative of Travels in Virginia, Maryland, Pennsylvania, Ohio, Indiana, Kentucky; and of a residence in the Illinois Territory: 1817-1818*. Edited by Frederic Austin Ogg. Cleveland: Arthur H. Clark Co, 1906.
Fremont, Lewis D. *The Philadelphia Years of Governor Edward Coles*. Alton, Ill.: privately printed, 1955.
Gillespie, Joseph. "Recollections of Early Illinois and her noted men." *Fergus Historical Series* 13 (Chicago, 1880).
Gitz, Nina C. "Coles and Slavery, a Reevaluation of the Role of Political Factions in the Convention Contest of 1824 in Illinois." Master's thesis, Sangomon State University, 1978.
Greene, Evarts B., and Clarence W. Alvord, eds. *The Governors' Letter-Books, 1818-1834*. Springfield: Illinois State Historical Society, 1909.
Guasco, Suzanne C. "Confronting Democracy: Edward Coles and the Cultivation of Authority in the Young Nation." Ph.D. diss., College of William and Mary, 2004.
Gwalthney, John. *Twelve Virginia Counties: Where the Western Migration Began*. Richmond, Va.: Deitz Press, 1937.
Hallway, John. *Western Illinois Heritage*. Macomb, Ill.: Illinois Heritage Press, 1983.
Harris, N. Dwight. *The History of Negro Servitude in Illinois and of the Slavery Agitation in That State, 1719-1864*. New York: Haskell House, 1969.
Havighurst, Walter; *Ohio: A History*. Urbana: University of Illinois Press, 2001.
Henderson, John G. *Early History of the "Sangamon Country": being notes on the first settlements in the territory now comprised within the limits of Morgan, Scott and Cass counties*. Davenport, Iowa: Day, Egbert & Fidlar, 1873.
Hoffmann, B.E., ed. *History of Madison County, Illinois*. Edwardsville, Ill.: W.R. Brink, 1882.
Hollman, Frederick G. "The Autobiography of Frederick G. Hollman." Wisconsin Historical Society, n.d.
Howard, Robert P. *Illinois: A History of the Prairie State*. Grand Rapids, Mich.: William B. Eerdmans Publishing Co., 1972.
_____. *Mostly Good and Competent Men*. Springfield: Institute for Public Affairs, 1999.
Hyman, Lester S. *United States Policy Towards Liberia, 1822-2003: Unintended Consequences?* Cherry Hill, N.J.: Africana Homestead Legacy Publishers, 2003.
Isaac, Rhys. *The Transformation of Virginia, 1740-1790*. Chapel Hill: University of North Carolina Press, 1999.
Jefferson, Thomas. *Notes on Virginia*. Chapel Hill: University of North Carolina Press, 1982.
Jordan, Winthrop D. *White over Black: American Attitudes Toward the Negro, 1550-1812*. Chapel Hill: University of North Carolina Press, 1968.
Ketcham, Ralph. *James Madison: A Biography*. Charlottesville: University Press of Virginia, 1990.
_____. "The Dictates of Conscience: Edward Coles and Slavery." *Virginia Quarterly Review* 36 (1960).
Kingston, John. "Early Western Days." *Report and Collections of the State Historical Society of Wisconsin* 7 (1876).

Korfoid, Carrie P. "Puritan Influences in the Formative Years of Illinois History." *Transactions of the Illinois State Historical Society* 10 (1905).
Langhorne, Elizabeth. "Edward Coles, Thomas Jefferson and the Rights of Man." *Virginia Cavalcade* 23 (1973): 30–36.
Langhorne, Elizabeth, K. Edward Lay, and William D. Rieley. *A Virginia Family and Its Plantation Houses*. Charlottesville: University Press of Virginia, 1987.
Leichtle, Kurt. "Edward Coles: An Agrarian on the Frontier." Ph.D. diss., University of Illinois at Chicago Circle, 1982.
"Letters and Documents Relating to Slavery in Massachusetts." *Massachusetts Historical Society Collections, Fifth Series* 3 (1877).
Lippincott, Thomas. "Early Days in Madison County." *Alton (Illinois) Telegraph*, Sept. 2, 1864—Aug. 11, 1865.
Litwack, Leon F. *North of Slavery: The Negro in the Free States 1790–1860*. Chicago: University of Chicago Press, 1965.
Madison, James. "An Address to the Members of the Protestant Episcopal Church in Virginia, 1799." Worcester, Mass.: American Antiquarian Society, 1964.
Mancell, Peter C., and Joshua L. Rosenblum. "Slave Prices and the Economy of the Lower South." http://www.eh.net/Clio/Conferences/ASSA/Jan_00/rosenbloom.shtml.
Mason, R.L. *Narrative of Richard Lee Mason in the Pioneer West*. New York: Charles F. Hartman, 1915.
Mathews, Donald G. *Religion in the Old South*. Chicago: University of Chicago, 1977.
McColley, Robert. *Slavery and Jeffersonian Virginia*. Urbana: University of Illinois Press, 1964.
McCoy, Drew. *The Last of the Fathers: James Madison and the Republican Legacy*. Cambridge: Cambridge University Press, 1989.
McLoughlin, William H. *The American Evangelicals, 1800–1900*. New York: Peter Smith Publisher, 1985.
Meinig, D.W. *The Shaping of America: A Geographical Perspective on 500 Years of History*. Vol. 2. New Haven: Yale University Press, 1993.
Miller, Howard. *The Revolutionary College: American Presbyterian Higher Education, 1707–1837*. New York: New York University Press, 1976.
Moore, Glover. *The Missouri Controversy 1819–1821*. Lexington: University of Kentucky Press, 1953.
Moses, John. *Illinois Historical and Statistical*. Vol. 1. Chicago: Fergus Printing, 1889.
Musgrove, Jon. "Black Kidnappings on the Wabash and Ohio Valleys of Illinois." http://www.illinoishistory.com/blackkidnappings.html.
Newman, Richard S. *The Transformation of American Abolitionism: Fighting Slavery in the Early Republic*. Chapel Hill, N.C.: University of North Carolina Press, 2002.
Noonan, John T. *The Antelope: The Ordeal of the Recaptured Africans in the Administrations of James Monroe and John Quincy Adams*. Berkeley: University of California Press, 1977.
Norton, Margaret. *Illinois Census Returns, 1820*. Springfield: Illinois State Historical Library, 1934.
Norton, Wilbur T. *Centennial History of Madison County, Illinois and its People, 1812–1912*. Chicago: Lewis Publishing, 1912.
_____. *Edward Coles, Second Governor of Illinois*. Philadelphia: J.B. Lippincott and Co., 1911.
Office of the Chief of Military History. *American Military History*. Washington: U.S. Army, 1988.
Onuf, Peter S. *Statehood and Union: A History of the Northwest Ordinance*. Bloomington, Ind.: Indiana University Press, 1987.

Park, Siyoung. "Land Speculation in Western Illinois: Pike County 1821–1835." *Journal of the Illinois State Historical Society* 77 (1984).
Parrish, Braxton. "Pioneer Life in Egypt." *Golden Era* 36 (Sept. 4, 1874).
Pease, Theodore C. *The Frontier State 1818–1848.* Urbana: University of Illinois Press, 1987.
———. "Illinois Election Returns." *Collections of the Illinois State Historical Library* 18 (1923).
Peck, John Mason. *Memoirs of John Mason Peck:* Carbondale, Ill.: SIU Press, 1965.
———. *A new guide for Emigrants to the West.* Boston: Gould, Kendall & Lincoln, 1836.
Peckham, Howard H. *Indiana: A History.* Urbana: University of Illinois Press, 2003.
Perrin, William H., ed. *History of Alexander, Union and Pulaski Counties, Illinois.* Chicago: O.L. Baskin Co., 1883.
Reynolds, John. *My Own Times Embracing Also the History of My Life.* Chicago: Fergus Printing, 1879.
———. *Pioneer History of Illinois.* Chicago: Fergus Printing, 1887.
Richardson, Eudora. "The Virginian who made Illinois a Free State." *Journal of the Illinois Historical Society* 45 (1952).
Robbins, Roy. *Our Landed Heritage: The Public Domain, 1776–1990.* Lincoln, Neb.: University of Nebraska Press, 1976.
Rohrbough, Maxwell. *The Land Office Business: The Settlement and Administration of American Public Lands, 1789–1837.* New York: Oxford University Press, 1968.
Rose, Willie Lee. *A Documentary History of Slavery in North America.* Athens, Ga.: University of Georgia Press, 1999.
Russell, John H. *The Free Negro in Virginia.* Baltimore: Johns Hopkins University Press, 1913.
Sapp, Peggy L., ed. *Madison County Court Records 1813–1818 and Indenture Records 1805–1826.* Springfield: Folk Works, 1993.
Schob, David. *Hired Hands and Plowboys: Farm Labor in the Midwest, 1815–1860.* Urbana: University of Illinois Press, 1975.
Sidbury, James. *Ploughshares into Swords: Race, Rebellion, and Identity in Gabriel's Virginia, 1730–1810.* Cambridge: Cambridge University Press, 1997.
Simeone, James. *Democracy and Slavery in Frontier Illinois: The Bottomland Republic.* DeKalb, Ill.: Northern Illinois University Press, 2000.
Smith, George W. "The Salines of Southern Illinois." *Transactions of the Illinois State Historical Society* 9 (1904).
Snyder, John F. *Adam W. Snyder and his period in Illinois History 1817–1842.* Springfield: H.W. Rokker, 1903.
———. "Forgotten Statesmen of Illinois: Hon. Conrad Will." *Transactions of the Illinois State Historical Society* 10 (1905).
Spencer, Donald S. "Edward Coles: Virginia Gentleman in Frontier Politics." *Journal of the Illinois State Historical Society* 61 (1961).
Starobin, Robert S. *Industrial Slavery in the Old South.* New York: Oxford University Press, 1979.
Stevens, Wayne E. "The Shaw-Hansen Election Contest." *Journal of the Illinois State Historical Society* 7 (1914–15).
Stroble, Paul E., Jr. *High on the Okaw's Western Bank, Vandalia, Illinois, 1819–39.* Urbana: University of Illinois Press, 1992.
Sutton, Robert M. "Edward Coles and the Constitutional Crisis in Illinois, 1822–1824." *Illinois Historical Journal* 82 (1989).
Sweet, William W. *Religion on the American Frontier: The Baptists.* New York: Henry Holt, 1931.
Thwaites, Reuben G., ed. *Early Western Travels, 1748–1846.* Vol. 5. Cleveland: Arthur H. Clark, 1905.

Tillson, Christina H. *A Woman's Story of Pioneer Illinois*. Carbondale, Ill.: SIU Press, 1995.
Tise, Larry E. *Proslavery: A History of the Defense of Slavery in America, 1701-1840*. Athens: University of Georgia Press, 1974.
Washburne, Elihu. *Sketch of Edward Coles*. Chicago: Jansen, McClurg & Co., 1881.
Wheeler, S.P. (Mrs.). "Edward Coles, Second Governor of Illinois." *Transactions of the Illinois State Historical Society* (1903).
Williams, Frederick D. *The Northwest Ordinance: Essays on Its Formation, Provision and Legacy*. E. Lansing, Mich.: Michigan State University Press, 1987.

Other Sources

Edward Coles Papers, Chicago Historical Society
Coles Collections, Historical Society of Pennsylvania
Edward Coles Papers, Princeton University Library
Carter-Smith Family Papers, University of Virginia
George Churchill collection, Illinois State Historical Library
John Coles Account Books, University of Virginia
Roberts Coles letters, Virginia Historical Society
Horatio Newhall papers, Illinois State Historical Library
Albemarle County, Will Book, vol. 4
Alton Observer
Alton Telegraph
American Convention of Abolition Societies, Minutes and Proceedings
American State Papers, Public Lands, vol. 31
Annals of Congress, 11th Congress, 2nd Session
Annals of Congress, 15th Congress, 2nd Session
Annals of Congress, 16th Congress, 1st Session
Breese, Decisions of the Illinois Supreme Court
Clerk's Register, Randolph County
Edwardsville Spectator
Gilmore, Illinois Supreme Court reports
Illinois Gazette, Shawneetown
Illinois Intelligencer, Vandalia
Illinois Public Domain Land Tract Sales database, Illinois State Archive
Illinois Session Laws, 1823, 1824, 1826, 1829
Legislative Petitions, Virginia State Archives, Library of Virginia
Madison County Circuit Court Records
Republican, Kaskaskia
Republican Advocate, Kaskaskia
St. Louis Enquirer
Western Citizen, Chicago

Index

"AB" 121
Abolitionists 17, 31, 47, 80, 105–106, 124, 163–164
Adams, John 44
Adams, John Quincy 158, 159, 165
Alabama 89
Albemarle County, Va. 22, 23, 24, 75
Albion, Ill. 125
Alexander, Archibald 25
Alexander, Samuel 115
Alexander, William 102, 104, 113, 115, 116, 134, 142
Alexander County, Ill. 96n, 151, 151n
Alexandria, Va. 31
Alton, Ill. 128, 135, 149, 164
American Bottom 50, 53–54, 59
American Colonization Society 47, 106
Antelope 106
Anti-convention party 118, 121, 122, 123, 125, 126, 128–129, 130, 131–132, 135, 136, 137, 143, 149, 151–153, 160, 174; appeals to resentment of privilege 128–129, 136; and clergy 127, 153; dissolves 161; economic arguments 133, 135; racism in 132; views on slavery 120, 123, 127, 130, 131–132
Appeal to the Colored Citizens of the World 106
Archer, William 164
"Aristides" 129, 132
Arkansas 108
Armisted, Will 28
Armstrong, John 39
Atlas, Ill. 109

Bank of Edwardsville 78, 135
Bank of Illinois 135
Bank of the United States 84
Belleville, Ill. 123, 145
Bernard, Etienne 79
Berry, William 120, 144
Biddle, Nicholas 23, 38, 50, 59, 121, 124, 125, 135, 166, 174
Birkbeck, Morris 46–47, 48, 52, 60, 91, 125, 128–129, 134, 135, 139, 140, 147, 149, 157,
174; dies 158; ejected as Secretary of State 158
"Black Codes" 16, 20; in Illinois 57–59, 74, 102, 104, 105, 106, 158, 161, 162, 163, 168
Blackwell, David 123, 145, 147, 174
Blackwell, Robert 120
Blondeau, Dreezy 79
Bonaparte, Jack 58
Bond, Shadrach 88, 148
Bond County, Ill. 94, 96, 96n, 125, 151n
Boston 106
Bradsby, William 63, 64
Breese, Sidney 72
Briggs, "Daddy" 64
Bristol, England 22
Brown, William 98, 120–121, 141, 144, 147, 174
Browne, Thomas 90, 91, 92, 93, 94, 96
Brownsville, Pa. 12
"Brutus" 132
Buckmeister, Nathaniel 94
Bureau County, Ill. 163
Burgess, Thomas 133

Cahokia, Ill. 67
Calhoun, John 167
California 171
Camp Ridge revival 47
Canada 41
Carlyle, Ill. 149
Carmi, Ill. 128, 149
Carrollton, Ill. 126
Carter, Sarah 141
Cartwright, Peter 54
Casey, Zadock 115
Caton, J.D. 163
Cedar Creek Meeting 23
Charivari 116, 117
Church of England 23, 27–28
Churchill, George 70n, 104, 114, 115, 121, 123
"Citizen of Madison County" 122
Clark County, Ill. 96, 96n, 102, 151n, 164
Clay, Henry 47, 171
Cobb, Tom 14, 20, 32, 59, 76, 78, 102, 157

197

Cobbett, William 48
Coles, Edward 1, 2–6, 9–10, 11–14, 15–17, 18–19, 20, 21, 22, 24, 30, 31, 34–35, 36, 38, 43, 49, 51, 54, 59–60, 72, 73, 75, 86, 88, 89, 91, 101, 102, 106, 107, 110, 111, 116, 118, 119, 121, 122, 123, 128, 130, 132, 139, 142, 149, 152, 155, 163, 173, 174, 175–176; absentee landowner 21, 167; accuses opponents of vote-rigging 129; as "Agis" 69–71; anachronistic 5; argues against diffusion 146; as "Aristides" 129, 132, 134; attempt to depose 158–159; believes Madison intended to free his slaves 172; born 22; calls for end of Black Code 161, 162; campaigns against convention 126, 132–133; campaigns to limit expansion of slavery 171; childhood 25, 36; concerns about national union 171–172; confused with Cowles 89; considers moving west 34, 36, 41, 47–48, 49–50, 59–60; conventionists offer U.S. Senate seat 143; convinces legislation to back canal financing 167; corresponds with Jefferson about slavery 13, 43; criticizes State Bank of Illinois 159, 160–161; dancing 26; decides to free his slaves 2, 30, 32, 33; declines to contribute to statehouse rebuilding fund 137–138; dies 175; and Dolley Madison 317, 41, 45; economic arguments against slavery 133, 134, 135, 146, 152; education 25, 26, 28, 27, 29, 31; elected Governor 94, 98; emancipation misrepresented 92–93, 178n, 183n; European tour 46, 61, 91; expects to lose election 97–98; failed politician 5, 164–165; family relations 9, 10, 13, 24, 32, 34–35, 43, 49, 87, 166; farewell address 160–161; as farmer 40, 76, 77, 140; finances 18, 40, 76, 77 140, 167, 169–170; fire at farm 137; flirtations 26, 39–40; forbids whipping slaves 12–13; and former slaves 6, 12–13, 14, 15–17, 18–19, 20–21, 32, 57, 59, 76, 78, 80, 137, 140, 157, 165–166, 167–168, 169; former slaves ill-treated by neighbors 20, 59; fractures leg 26, 31, 48; frees slaves 11–14, 76, 92–93, 140, 156, 167; gives lands to former slaves 18–19; governor of Illinois 1, 2, 94, 98, 99–100, 104, 105, 119, 124, 138, 141, 153, 158–159, 160–161, 165; hard-money view 84–85, 92, 135; health 9, 41, 42, 135, 177n; hires former slaves 19; historians' views 4, 4n, 5, 7n, 137n, 154n; "the improbable" 12; inaugural speech 99–100, 104, 105, 124, 173; inheritance 18, 32, 33; and Jefferson 13, 92; Land Office registrar 76, 77, 78, 79, 80, 83–84, 86, 87, 96, 97, 165; land purchases 18, 50, 60, 65–66, 86, 108, 140; land sales 167; leads anti-convention party 123, 143, 173; links conventionists to slavery 149; links slavery to "anti-republicanism" 130, 146, 148, 150; lobbies bankers for canal financing 167; marries Sally Logan Roberts 166; mission to Russia 9, 45–46, 60; misunderstands ex-slaves' status in Illinois 59, 139; moves to Illinois 75, 89, 90; nominates Blackwell as Secretary of State 144–145; nominates Birkbeck as Secretary of State 158; observations on serfs 46; observes 1818 Illinois constitutional convention 66; as "One of Many" 146, 148, 149; oppositiion to slavery 29–30, 32, 42–43, 47, 80, 92, 93, 96, 97n, 98, 100, 130, 132, 135, 157, 161, 166, 175; organizes anti-convention party 123, 124–125, 143, 171; pledges salary to anti-convention campaign 123, 140, 144; political ambition 5, 36, 89, 165, 175; political opponents 101, 102, 119, 122, 126–127, 157; praised 164, 172; President of the Board of Canal Commissioners 166, 167; purchases Illinois Intelligencer 144–146; quarrels with Van Buren 170; referendum victory 151–155; religious views 30; returns to Enniscorthy 31–32; runs for Governor 89, 91–93, 94, 97–98; in Russia 46; secretary to Madison 3, 9, 12, 35–36, 37–39, 41, 42–43, 44–45, 46, 66, 91, 165; sees emancipation tied to emigration to Liberia 167; seeks federal post 169–170; seeks seat in Congress 165; seeks U.S. Senate seat 164–165; seen as non-Illinoisian 89–90; settles in Illinois 57, 75, 76, 77; settles in Philadelphia 166, 171, 172; and slaves 2, 9 12, 13, 14, 25, 32, 39, 47–48; sued for freeing his slaves 59, 139, 140, 141, 156, 157–159, 161; supports gradual emancipation 168; supports national road 99; supposed arrogance 4n, 18; supposed elitism 4n, 5, 6, 86, 97, 97n, 137n, 155, 175, 177n, 184n; tactics in anti-convention campaign 124, 126, 132–133, 145–146, 149; victor in convention campaign 4, 5, 6; views on democracy 130, 161; views on Illinois 46, 66, 75; views on Lake Michigan canal 92, 99; views on liberty 30, 98; views on Northwest Ordinance 56, 57, 99–100, 172; views on partisan politics 160, 165; views on public lands 85, 86, 87, 88; views on public schools 99; views on racial equality 16–17, 18, 76, 124, 130, 132, 146, 148, 168, 175; visits east coast 158, 166, 166; Washington social life 37, 29; wealth 18; western journeys 9, 12, 49, 50, 59, 60, 65; Whiggish views 161, 166; youth 9, 22, 25, 26, 27, 29–30, 31–33, 34–36
Coles, Isaac (brother) 27, 35, 36, 40, 49–50, 60
Coles, John (brother) 13, 35, 39, 40, 41
Coles, John (father) 22, 23, 24, 31–32, 33, 34, 36, 39
Coles, John (grandfather) 22–23

Coles, Mary (aunt) 28
Coles, Mary Eliza (sister) 26, 139
Coles, Rebecca (mother) 12, 13, 21, 24, 166
Coles, Roberts (son) 176
Coles, Sally (sister) 49
Coles, Sally Logan Roberts (wife) 166–167, 168
Coles, Tucker (brother) 31
Coles, Walter (brother) 18, 40
Coles, Walter (uncle) 23
Coles County, Ill. 164
Coles Grove, Ill. 109, 110
Coles Hill, Va. 28
Coles Rolling Road 24
College of William and Mary 25, 26, 27–28, 29, 31
Congress 37, 38, 39, 40, 41, 42, 56, 57, 98, 162
Constellation dance 39
Constitution, Illinois 19, 83, 88, 101
Constitution, U.S. 10, 34, 105
Constitutional Convention of 1818 70, 71, 72–73, 74, 83, 90, 102, 104
Constitutional Convention proposed to establish slavery 101, 106, 111, 112, 116; rejected 151, 156–157
Convention campaign of 1823–1824 4–5, 101, 110, 116, 117, 120, 121–123, 124, 125–6, 127–128, 133, 134, 135–136, 141–142, 144, 145–146, 147, 148, 156, 160
"Conventionist" 130
Conventionists (pro-convention party) 101, 110, 111, 116, 117, 121, 122, 125, 127, 128, 129, 130–131, 135, 137, 140, 141, 142, 147, 148, 149, 152, 156, 157, 161; appeal to sectionalism 128–129; claim to be democrats 130–131, 143, 148–149; economic arguments 133–134; racial attitudes 147–148; reorganize 137; views on slavery 101, 117, 128, 131, 133–134, 142
Cook, Daniel 61, 62, 63, 79, 82, 83, 84, 88, 90, 98, 125, 126, 148, 151, 157, 159–160
Copeland, John 69
Council of Revision 72, 128, 142
County Wexford, Ireland 22
Covenanters 71–72
Covington, Ill. 149
Crawford, Betsey 14, 17
Crawford, Kate 6, 14, 17, 20, 21, 32, 59, 76, 137, 140, 157, 165–166, 167, 169
Crawford, Mary 14, 17
Crawford, Polly 14, 17, 32, 59
Crawford, Ralph 12, 13, 14, 19, 20, 32, 59, 76
Crawford, Robert 6, 14, 20, 21, 32, 59, 76, 78, 102, 137, 140, 157, 165–166, 167, 169
Crawford, Thomas 14, 17
Crawford, William (freed slave) 14, 17
Crawford, William (Secretary of the Treasury) 38, 79, 86, 87, 90, 98, 148, 158

Crawford County, Ill. 96n, 102, 151n
Crocker, Seth 125

Dabney, H.Y. 29
Daimwood, J.G. 113
Dallas (revenue cutter) 106
Daschkoff, J.M. 45, 46
Davenport, James 115
Dearborn County, Ind. 67
Delaware 103
Deschamps, Antoine 79
Detroit 41
Diffusion theory 146
Dilsey 58
Duane, William 39
Duncan, Joseph 165, 166
DuVal, Benjamin 29
Dwyer's Store, Va. 25

Edgar County, Ill. 102, 126, 151n, 153, 164
Edwards, Ninian 55–56, 58, 61, 62, 64, 65, 67, 68, 70, 75, 78, 81, 82, 83, 86, 87, 88, 89, 90, 97, 135, 143, 148, 158, 160; faction 56, 82, 90, 93, 96, 102, 110, 117
Edwards County, Ill. 48, 96n, 125, 151n
Edwardsville, Ill. 44, 75, 76, 77, 84, 93, 94, 98, 110, 122, 123, 135, 143, 158, 164, 165
Edwardsville Land Office 17, 38, 75, 77–78, 84, 90, 110, 123, 145
Edwardsville Spectator 78, 82, 88, 124, 164
Election of 1822 88, 90, 91, 92–95, 96–100, 101, 107, 109, 150, 173
Election of 1824 148, 151, 158, 159–160, 187–188n
Election of 1826 159, 160
Election of 1828 164
Election of 1860 4
Emancipation 14–15
Emmitt, John 102, 104, 105, 106, 111, 116
English Settlement 91, 125
Enniscorthy 22, 23, 24, 35, 176
Ensinger, Emanuel 162
Ernst, Ferdinand 50
Ewing, L.D. 158

"Farmer" 122, 134, 143
Fayette County, Ill. 96, 96n, 120, 151n
Field, Alexander 103, 104, 106, 107, 110, 112, 113, 117
Finley, Robert 47
Finney, Charles Grandison 47
Fisher, George 63, 67
Flagg, Gershsom 54, 85
Flint, James 55
Flower, George 48, 60, 91
Flower, Richard 124
Fontaine, Felix 79
Ford, R.C. 110, 114, 115
Ford, Thomas 3, 5, 17, 54, 59, 67, 160
Fordham, Elias Pym 55, 65, 68

Index

Forquer, George 158
Frank 58
Franklin County, Ill. 96n, 151n
Free Soil Party 171
Freedmen 15, 20, 59, 97, 104, 105, 106, 162; bonds 139, 140, 156, 157
French settlers 2, 10, 56–57, 63, 67, 73, 96, 100, 112
Fulton, Robert 39
Fulton County, Ill. 110, 114, 119, 120, 126, 151n, 152

Gabriel's Rebellion 33
Gaines, Nancy 14, 20, 59
Gallatin County, Ill. 73, 74, 82, 96n, 148, 151n, 152
Garrison, William Lloyd 167
Genius of Universal Emancipation 105
Gilham, William 121
Gillespie, Joseph 6, 17, 64, 102, 134
Gilmore, Walter 139
Goldsborough, Howard 38
Good, James 133
Grammar, John 101, 112, 150
Graveline, Joseph 79
Green Mountain 13, 22, 34–35, 37, 41, 59
Greene County, Ill. 96, 96n, 110, 111, 126, 151n
Gulf Coast 106

Haiti 33
Hamilton County, Ill. 68, 96n, 115, 151, 151n
Hampden-Sidney College 25–26
Hanover County, Va. 22
Hansen, Nicholas 107, 108–109, 110, 111, 114, 115, 116, 120, 121, 126, 164; ousted from legislature 115, 117, 146; switches vote to oppose convention 113
Hargrave, Willis 137
Harrison, William Henry 67
Hartshorne, William 31
Hawkins, Joseph 34–35, 38
Hedrick, Benjamin 54
Henrico County, Va 23
Henry, Patrick 36
Hollman, Frederick 50
Hubbard, Adolphus 98, 143, 158–159
Hutt, William 33–34

Illinois 1–2, 3, 6, 10, 17, 19, 47, 48, 49, 50, 51, 52–53, 59, 60–61, 68, 74, 76, 80, 88, 89, 98, 104, 109, 112, 124, 133, 141, 156, 162, 163, 166, 171, 174, 175, 176; Attorney General 72; Auditor of Public Accounts 72, 112; becomes a state 61–62, 63, 65, 80; campaign for statehood 61, 62, 63, 64, 65, 67, 80; courts 62, 117, 128; frontier conditions 49, 51–52, 54, 55, 61–62, 84; General Assembly 72, 98, 103, 104, 117, 119, 157; hard-currency shortages 23, 38, 52, 84–85, 96, 97, 99, 134, 135, 156; land prices 19, 52, 78, 86, 87, 167; Paymaster General 158; population 1; powers of the Governor 72; proposals to move capital 128, 137, 149; schools 99; Secretary of State 112, 145; settlement 52, 54, 55, 76–77, 87, 88, 125, 134; slavery plot of 1820 82–83; slaves 2, 54, 55, 56–58, 59, 62–63, 64, 67, 72, 73, 74, 89, 96–97, 98, 100, 102, 103, 112, 120, 139–140, 156–157, 161–162, 163, 172; state bank 85, 94, 111–112, 134, 159; Statehouse 99, 111, 128, 137, 140; taxes 108, 110, 111
Illinois Gazette 92
Illinois House of Representatives 102, 104, 106, 107, 110, 111, 112, 113, 115
Illinois Intelligencer 61, 72, 98, 124, 126,
Illinois-Michigan canal 92, 94, 97, 97n, 99, 107, 116, 159
Illinois Republican 142
Illinois River 51, 107
Illinois State Senate 101, 104, 109, 112, 119, 124
Illinoisans: anti-slavery sentiment 64, 71, 93, 103, 105, 106, 118, 129; pro-slavery views 82, 83, 88–89, 91, 92, 93, 94, 96, 98, 101, 107; racial attitudes 104, 123–124, 132, 147–148, 152; resentment of outsiders 128; resentment of wealth 4, 4n, 129, 132; views on currency 84–85; views on democracy 150, 153; views on religion 128; views on slavery 62, 68, 69, 72, 74, 76, 82, 88, 94, 96–97, 150
Indentures 2, 56, 58, 63, 64, 67, 72, 74, 97, 102, 104, 106, 162; as defacto slavery 58; repeal attempted 63–64
Indiana 10, 40, 59, 67, 68, 72, 126, 174
"Instructions" 111
Invasion of Canada 41

Jackson, Andrew 47, 158, 159, 165
Jackson County, Ill. 96n, 102, 151n
James 28
Jarrot, Joseph 163
Jay, Joseph 162
Jefferson, Thomas 3, 4, 11, 13, 22, 28, 29, 34, 35, 37, 40, 43, 44, 56, 92, 98, 124, 167, 168, 171, 172
Jefferson County, Ill. 96n, 115, 151n
Joe 34
Johnson County, Ill. 69, 96n, 113, 151–152, 151n
"Jonathan Freeman" 128, 134, 147, 149
Jones, Michael 135
Jones, William 141

Kane, Elias Kent 67, 68, 69, 70, 71, 72, 82, 83, 85, 88, 148, 166
Kansas-Nebraska Act 172
Kansas slavery referenda 3, 174
Kaskaskia, Ill. 19, 50, 61, 65, 66, 67, 71, 75, 90, 93

Kelly, James 112
Kentucky 1, 21, 52, 55, 59, 72, 82, 151, 171
kidnapping 102, 104, 156
Kinkade, William 112, 118
Kinney, William 86, 116, 117, 123, 134, 160, 162–163
Kostoff, Russian Consul 45, 46

Lafayette, Marquis de 28
Land speculation 84, 86, 87, 89, 99, 109, 133
Lavassier, Pierre,
Lawrence County, Ill 96n, 126, 129, 151, 151n
Lemen, James 73, 74, 123, 153
Liberia 21, 106, 167
Lincoln, Abraham 164, 172, 174
Lincoln County, Mo. 50
Lippincott, Thomas 123, 150, 159
Locke, John 27, 29
Lockwood, Samuel 123, 145, 162, 174
Lofton, John 119–120
Louisiana 39
Louisiana Purchase 80, 81
Louisville, Ky. 21
Lovejoy, Elijah 164, 167
Lovejoy, Owen 163
Lowery, William 110
Lucy 58
Lundy, Benjamin 105
Lusk, A.J. 169
Lusk, J.T. 169

Madison, Dolley 36, 37, 39, 41, 42, 44, 45, 169, 172
Madison, James (bishop) 26, 27, 28, 29, 30, 31, 70, 76
Madison, James (president) 3, 22, 29, 35, 37, 38, 39, 42–43, 44, 45, 69, 98, 116, 124, 160, 164–165, 166, 169, 171, 172
Madison County, Ill. 18, 19, 57, 59, 72, 74, 83, 94, 96n, 103, 104, 109, 110, 122, 126, 128, 130, 132, 137, 141, 151n, 152, 153, 157, 158
Madison County Circuit Court 139
Madison County Commissioners Court 141
Maillet, Hypolite 79
Maine 81
Manuel 14, 20, 93
manumission 14, 15; bonds 59, 139–140; in Illinois 59, 139–140, 156–157, 161–162, 163; in Virginia 15, 28
Marion County, Ill. 115, 151, 151n
Marshall, John 106
Mason, Hail 140
Mason, Richard Lee 49, 51
Massachusetts 3, 16, 174
Massachusetts General Colored Association 106
Matheny, Charles 63, 64
Mather, Thomas 111, 115
McFatridge, William 113, 116, 134

McFerron, John 69, 115, 116
McKee, William 77, 110, 123
McLean, John 68, 135
McRoberts, Samuel 137, 157, 158, 160, 161
"Mechanic" 149
Meigs, Josiah 85
Memphis 153
Menard, Pierre 67, 86
Messinger, John 123
Mexican War 171
Military Tract 18, 53, 76, 99, 107, 109
"Miss A" 40
"Miss Swann" 39
Mississippi 63, 89
Mississippi River 50, 65
Missouri 56, 59, 65, 80–81, 82, 89, 98, 109, 110, 115, 124, 130, 133, 134, 147, 148, 151, 162, 171, 174
Missouri Compromise 2, 10, 81, 82
Mr. White's Academy 25
Mobs: at Alton 164; negative reaction to 121, 126; in Vandalia 114, 116, 117, 121, 122, 137, 149
Monongahela River 12
Monroe, James 36, 38, 46, 47, 49, 61, 75, 76, 124, 168, 171
Monroe County, Ill. 96n, 115, 123, 125, 126, 142, 151, 151n
Montgomery County, Ill. 96n, 120, 151n
Montpelier 22, 169
Moore, James 93, 94
Moore, Risdon 102, 104, 105, 106, 107, 111, 118, 123
Morgan County, Ill. 111, 119, 126, 151n, 153
Moulton, Charles 65

Nance vs. Howard 162
Nancy 163
Nelson County, Va. 12, 22
New England 129
New Orleans 50, 163
New York 27, 129, 174
Newhall, Horatio 94, 116
Nichols, Cary 25
Norfolk, Va. 24
Northwest Ordinance 2, 10, 56, 57, 59, 69, 80, 104, 105, 172, 174
"Not a Methodist" 128

Ogle, Benjamin 150
Ogle, Jacob 104, 123, 150
Ohio 2, 3, 9, 15, 16, 51, 55, 55, 59, 72, 174
Ohio River 9, 10, 50, 54, 56, 167
"One of Many" 146, 148, 149
Orleans Territory 39
Ottwell, William 122–123

Paine, Thomas 27, 29
Pamlico Sound 176
Panic of 1819 77, 84

Index

Parker, Daniel 102, 164, 174
Parrish, Braxton 52, 54
Party politics 160
Payne, John 28
Peck, John Mason 51, 52, 123, 125, 126, 135–136, 144–145, 146, 164, 174
Pelagie 163
Pennsylvania 37, 105, 166
Peoria 78–80, 83
Peter 58
Philadelphia 10, 28, 39, 41, 43, 45, 105, 106, 135, 166, 167, 172
Phillips, Alexander 115
Phillips, Joseph 88, 89, 91, 92, 93, 94, 96, 116
Phoebe 162
Phoebe vs. Jay 162
Pike County, Ill. 96, 96n, 107, 108, 109, 110, 111, 115, 116, 119, 126, 151n
Pike County, Mo. 66
Pilette, Louis 79
Pin Oak Township, Ill. 59, 78, 80, 156, 166
Pinckney, William 38, 45
Pittman, Capt. Philip 57
Pittsburgh 12, 15
"Plain Citizen" 121, 128, 144–145
Pleasants, Robert 15
Pogue, Joseph 121
Pope, John 61
Pope, Nathaniel 88, 90, 91, 93, 94
Pope County, Ill. 96n, 115, 151, 151n
Poydras, Julian 39
Prairieland 76, 78, 86, 140, 157
Prairies 50, 51, 60, 75, 76
Preston, William 37
Prickett, David 123
Prickett, Isaac 169
Prickett, William 166
Pritchet, Abraham 74
Prometheus 45
Prosser, Gabriel 28
Public Lands Act 86, 123
Public lands sales 77–78, 84, 86, 87, 89

Quakers 22, 23, 31, 47, 166
Queenston Heights Battle 41
"Quock Walker" cases 3, 174

Randolph, John 37
Randolph, Richard 31
Randolph, Thomas Jefferson 166, 168
Randolph County, Ill 71, 73, 96n, 111, 151, 151n
Rattan, Thomas 110, 113, 115
Referendum of 1824 1, 2, 4, 121, 148, 150–151, 156, 173
Relief Act of 1821 87, 97
Replevin law 85–86, 160–161
"Republican" 142
"Republicanism" 5, 27, 30, 118, 130

Reuben 58
Reynolds, John 68, 83, 90, 94, 110, 117, 128, 130, 134, 136, 141, 146, 160
Reynolds, Thomas 90, 116
Richards, B.W. 171
Richmond, Va. 10, 23, 28, 31, 48
Ringgold, Tench 59
Riots, 114, 116, 117, 138, 139, 149
Roanoke Island, N.C. 176
Roberts, Levi 115
Roberts, Sally Logan (Coles) 166, 167, 168
"Rockfish" 12, 13, 18, 32, 34, 40, 60, 74, 77
"Roger" 130
Roi, Simon 79
Ross, Leonard 109
Ross, O.M. 109
Rousseau, Jean-Jacques 27
Rush, Richard 38

St. Clair County, Ill. 73, 96, 96n, 102, 117, 123, 125, 130
St. Louis 20, 50, 51, 60, 66, 167
St. Petersburg, Russia 45
Salines and saltworks 62, 71, 72, 73, 74, 82, 94, 96, 102, 103, 113, 152
Sam 58
Sangamon County, Ill. 96n, 126, 151n, 153
Sarah 58
Scott, James 81
Scott, Winfield 169, 170
Scottsville, Va. 24
Second Great Awakening 47, 106
Sectional tensions 55, 63, 146, 167, 171–172; in Illinois 64–65, 70, 97, 127–129, 130, 149, 153
Shaw, John 108–110, 111, 115, 116
Shawnee Prophet 40
Shawneetown, Ill. 52, 68, 94, 162
"Shoal Creek Farmer" 132
Silvey 58
Slave trade 34, 106, 162–163, 169
Slaves, hiring 62, 74
Slavery 3, 5, 6, 10, 14–15, 22, 29–30, 34, 47, 80, 89, 106, 131–132, 162–163, 167, 171–172; abolished 3, 16; expansion to west 3, 171; in Illinois 2, 54, 55, 56–58, 59, 62–63, 64, 67, 72, 73, 74, 89, 96–97, 98, 100, 102, 103, 112, 120, 139–140, 156–157, 161–162, 163, 172; in Missouri 82; in the Northwest Territory 10; in the southwest 3, 89; in Virginia 13–14, 16, 25, 28, 29, 30, 32, 33–34, 48; voted on 4, 151, 156–157
Sloo, Thomas 68, 107, 158, 159
Smith, Daniel 108, 135
Smith, Samuel 39
Smith, Theophilus 101, 102, 112, 117, 127, 159
Soulard, Tousant 79
South Carolina 162
Southern immigrants to Illinois 1, 46, 51,

52, 54, 64, 89, 96, 129, 147, 151, 152, 154; attitudes to slavery 6, 54, 96, 152, 154
Sparta, Ill. 163
"Spartacus" 147
Spoon River, Ill. 109
Starr, Henry 122
State Bank of Illinois 85, 94, 111–112, 134, 159
Stephenson, Benjamin 78, 84, 135
Storey, Joseph 38
Street, Joseph 82, 83
Sukey 14, 20, 32, 93
Synge, Philip (Dr. Physick) 41, 42

Tallmadge, James 11, 80, 81
Tecumseh 40
Templeman, Samuel 33–34
Tennessee 1
Texas 171
Thames River, Ont. 42
Thomas, Jesse B. 62, 67–68, 70, 81, 86, 87, 88, 89, 91, 110, 130, 158, 159, 160; political faction 68, 91, 92, 96, 109, 110, 148
Tillson, Christina Holmes 64
Tobacco 24, 40
Todd, Payne 41, 45
Turney, James 113, 116
Twist, Mose 163
Tyler, John 27, 169, 170

Union County, Ill. 69, 96, 96n, 101, 103, 112, 151, 151n, 152

Van Buren, Martin 170
Vandalia, Ill. 98, 109, 111–112, 114, 116, 117, 121, 135, 136, 137, 139, 142
Vaux, Roberts 123, 132, 133, 136, 137, 137n, 149, 159, 166
Venezuela 106
Venus 162
Vermont 16, 174
Vincennes, Ind. 51
Virginia 1, 9, 13–14, 15, 22, 23, 25, 28, 29–30, 32, 33–34, 40, 47, 49, 97, 166, 168, 169, 171

Wabash River 49, 50
Walker, David 106
Walker, John 163
Wanborough 46, 147
War of 1812 18, 40–41, 42, 45, 46, 56, 90, 107
Warren, Hooper 17, 44–45, 66, 67, 69, 74, 78, 81, 82, 83, 88, 89–90, 91, 92, 93, 97, 98, 124, 126, 136, 141, 144, 156, 164; animus to Coles 17, 44–45, 66, 184n
Washburne, Elihu 5
Washington, George 10, 15, 30–31
Washington County, Ill. 96n, 151, 151n
Washington, D.C. 37, 38, 41, 42, 43, 78, 135
Waterloo, Ill. 65
Wayne County, Ill. 96n, 151n
West, Emmanuel 103, 104, 106, 107, 110, 112, 113, 115, 117, 157
West Indies 106
Whigs 161, 166
White, Leonard 74
White County, Ill. 96, 96n, 102, 111, 125, 128, 130, 142, 151n, 152
Whiteside, S. 121
Widen, Raphael 115
Wilette, Angelica 79
Wilette, Francis 79
Will, Conrad 102–103, 104, 106
Williamsburg, Va. 23, 28
Winston, Isaac 23
Winston, Lucy 23
Winston, Mary 23
Wisconsin slavery referendum 3
Wistar, Caspar 166
Woodward, Charles 126
Wright, Josias 132
Wythe, George 31

"Yankee" 127–128, 130

www.ingramcontent.com/pod-product-compliance
Ingram Content Group UK Ltd.
Pitfield, Milton Keynes, MK11 3LW, UK
UKHW042005140426
5217IPUK00015B/997